BURN
BEFORE
READING

ADMIRAL
STANSFIELD TURNER

BURN
BEFORE
READING

PRESIDENTS, CIA DIRECTORS,
AND SECRET INTELLIGENCE

NEW YORK

Library of Congress Cataloging-in-Publication Data

Turner, Stansfield
  Burn before reading : presidents, CIA directors, and secret intelligence / Stansfield Turner.—1st ed.
    p. cm.
  Includes bibliographical references and index.
  ISBN: 0-7868-6782-5
  1. Intelligence service—United States—History.   2. United States. Central Intelligence Agency—History. [1. United States—Foreign relations—20th century.]   I.Title

JK468.I6T868 2005
327.1273'09—dc22

2005046264

FIRST EDITION

10 9 8 7 6 5 4 3 2 1

To Marion

Whose perceptive advice and constant encouragement made this book possible

CONTENTS

ACKNOWLEDGMENTS

This book was inspired by a suggestion from my good friend and literary agent Bill Adler. Ironically, though, the book is nothing like Bill's original concept. That was for a compendium of true spy stories. With the advent of the events of 9/11, Bill, Hyperion, and I decided that a more substantial look at the state of American intelligence was in order, and that is what this is.

Gretchen Young of Hyperion offered invaluable advice along the way. Jim Wade was a most useful editor as we came down the home stretch.

My close friends and longtime associates in the Navy and the CIA, George Thibault and Charles Battaglia, provided absolutely invaluable advice on the substance of the book and on editing it.

Because the book deals so much in the personalities of presidents and chiefs of intelligence, it was most important for me to be able to view those people through the eyes of others who knew them well. I am intensely grateful to many individuals for granting me the interviews that enabled me to do that. These were:

Former presidents Gerald Ford and Jimmy Carter in person; George H. W. Bush by correspondence; and Dwight Eisenhower in the person of his son John.

Former Directors of Central Intelligence James Schlesinger, William Webster, Robert Gates, James Woolsey, John Deutch, and Deputy Director of Central Intelligence Bobby Inman.

Former Secretary of Defense Harold Brown.

Former Assistants to the President for National Security Brent Scowcroft and Zbigniew Brzezinski.

Former members of the OSS Fisher Howe and Ned Putzell.

Former CIA historian J. Kenneth McDonald.

Executive Director of the International Spy Museum and former member of the CIA Peter Earnest.

Experts and writers on intelligence David Kahn and Robert Dallek.

Finally, the support, advice and encouragement of my executive assistant, Pat Moynihan, was both unstinting and essential.

All statements of fact, opinion, or analysis expressed are mine and do not reflect the official positions or views of the CIA or any other U.S. government agency. Nothing in the contents should be construed as asserting or implying U.S. government authentication of information or Central Intelligence Agency endorsement of the author's views. This material has been reviewed by the CIA only to prevent the disclosure of classified information.

INTRODUCTION

The fact that the events of 9/11 occurred without warning was a failure of our system of collecting and evaluating intelligence. It was a failure that ranks even higher than Pearl Harbor. The fact that we invaded Iraq in 2003 on the assumption that there were weapons of mass destruction there was another serious failure of intelligence. Consequently, the public's attention is focused today on our nation's intelligence apparatus as never before.

It should be obvious to the public that the intelligence organization we established in 1947 is not serving us adequately. It consisted of a director of central intelligence (DCI) to coordinate all intelligence activities, a single Central Intelligence Agency (CIA) to serve the country's overall needs for intelligence, and a series of intelligence bureaus within various departments of government to serve both national and departmental needs. Over the fifty-eight years since this organizational arrangement was established, numerous commissions have studied how well or poorly it has been working. The majority of these—and they go back some fifty years—have come to the conclusion that stronger central direction of the intelligence apparatus is needed. For one reason or another, we were not able to move very far in such a direction until December 2004, when Congress passed legislation restructuring our intelligence organization. The ink was hardly dry on that, however, before there were calls to redo it because there were too many ambiguities in the new law.

We, the public, need to understand whether that truly is the case, because today a great deal hinges on the effectiveness of our intelligence apparatus. The primary threat to the country has shifted from one of military attacks to one of terrorist acts. In combating terrorism, intelligence must be our first line of defense. If we cannot stop terrorists from committing heinous deeds, but can only respond after the fact, we will lose much of what our country stands for. Already our society is considerably different as a result of the actions we have found it necessary to take to ward off terrorists. The more such actions we feel compelled to take, the more we lose.

Our public, then, deserves to understand why it took so long to correct the flaws in our intelligence system, even though they have been pointed out repeatedly, and whether the changes that were finally made are the best we can do. This book seeks those answers through studying how each president from Franklin D. Roosevelt to George W. Bush has interacted with his DCI and how those relationships have shaped the position of DCI into what it is today. Hopefully, understanding how we got to where we are will help us understand where we should go next. Making the right move could be vital to our future as a nation.

CHAPTER ONE

FRANKLIN D. ROOSEVELT AND "WILD BILL"

America's First Central Intelligence Apparatus

The teams of OSS officers and enlisted men on the ground were trained to expect and anticipate almost anything. They were trained to operate well behind enemy lines, in this instance in Burma during World War II. But no one had prepared them for a visit by their own commander, William "Wild Bill" Donovan, brigadier general and head of the Office of Strategic Services (OSS). He held an incredible storehouse of American military secrets in his head; he really shouldn't have exposed himself to the risk of being captured.

But Donovan was, in the words of his assistant, Ned Putzell (who was also on this trip), the sort of leader who "couldn't ask somebody to do something he himself wouldn't do."[1] He would appear unexpectedly in dangerous locations just to pay a visit to the operatives he'd sent there. In this case, Donovan arrived with Colonel Carl Eifler, head of OSS operations in Burma, in a "damn little biplane," landing on an improvised airstrip at an OSS base well behind Japanese lines. After Donovan had completed his tour of inspection and was talking with both OSS personnel and the Kachin guerrillas they were training and supplying, someone came running. The enemy was closing in. Donovan had to leave. Donovan's men pulled the camouflage off the very short airstrip, which ended in a river. On the other side was the face of a cliff. The men on the ground held the tail of the biplane until the pilot had the prop up to full speed. The plane carrying America's only spymaster then shot down the runway, barely getting off the ground before reaching the river, and just gaining sufficient altitude to make the turn before crashing into the cliff. Donovan was thrilled. Putzell was "sure as the Lord made little apples" that Donovan had escaped certain death.[2]

Never since Donovan has one of America's spymasters been so deeply involved in operations. None of his successors would have dreamed of making a clandestine visit behind enemy lines. To be honest, when I was director of central intelligence, I considered myself a manager, nothing more. But "Wild Bill" Donovan, who got the ball rolling, couldn't shake the romance of the profession. He had to live it.

Now, Donovan didn't come to the job with any intelligence experience to speak of. He was a lawyer. He was not a close friend of Franklin D. Roosevelt. In fact, he was a Republican. So how did such an unlikely character end up crafting America's first centralized intelligence service?

Preparing for war, a war that would propel America permanently onto the world stage, President Franklin Roosevelt made some changes at home. With incredible political dexterity, he threw the Republican National Convention of 1940 into disarray by appointing two Republicans, Frank Knox and Henry Stimson, to his cabinet. Knox would become secretary of the navy and Stimson, who had served under President Hoover just a few years before, would be secretary of war. Both believed, as did the president, that the war that had broken out in Europe in 1939 would inevitably, and soon, involve the United States. Roosevelt did not know at the time that he had just paved the way for Donovan to enter his inner circle of advisors, and that doing so would lead to the creation of America's first full-fledged intelligence service.

What Roosevelt did know was that the intelligence apparatus he had was quite inadequate. What the president had available to him were offices dedicated to intelligence in the Army, the Navy, and the State Department, plus some foreign intelligence gathering by the FBI. None of it, however, was very aggressively oriented. Today, with Pearl Harbor, the Cold War, and 9/11 behind us, it is difficult to appreciate how naïve we Americans were about collecting intelligence clandestinely prior to World War II. Spying simply did not fit with our notions of "fair play." For instance, the president felt it necessary to emphasize in a press conference in 1938 that he would never "sanction espionage by American agents abroad."[3]

The one exception, where our intelligence was reasonably aggressive, was in intercepting and deciphering radio and cable messages of other nations. Back in 1929, Secretary of State Henry Stimson had closed down Army code-breaking operations. Fortunately, the Army pursued code breaking nonetheless. By August 1940, we had broken the code known as PURPLE, in which the Japanese government communicated with its embassies around the world. Roosevelt, then, did have available to him deciphered Japanese diplomatic messages. These were of inestimable value as Pearl Harbor approached. Fewer than forty people—including the president; the secretaries of war, navy, and state and the top military brass; and those who worked on the codes—knew of this operation and had access to the decrypted messages. This system of intercepting and deciphering was named MAGIC, and it was the most productive intelligence operation we had as we headed for World War II.

Through all this, the way MAGIC was processed for delivery to the president was almost a comedy. While the Army had broken the Japanese code, the Navy had the best translators of Japanese. Processing the sheer volume of messages required both their efforts, and they worked together smoothly. But a certain amount of friction developed over the question of which military service would deliver the transcripts to the president. As will be seen throughout this book, intelligence services get their light and air from the chief executive. How much a president brings them into his plans and thinking determines how well they can target their efforts to serve him. How much a president, in turn, supports them in bureaucratic disputes is vital to their ability to function. How strongly a president backs their secret activities before Congress and the public can determine their long-term viability. So a fight that developed between the Army's and Navy's intelligence services over who would deliver MAGIC to the Oval Office was over more than just bragging rights.

The compromise arrangement was that the Army would deliver messages during odd-numbered months and the Navy during even ones. This was not so bad in itself, until July 1941, when there was a breach of security with MAGIC. It came from FDR's Army aide. This led the Army's chief of intelligence to begin sending summaries only, rather than complete messages, to the president. Thus, if there were another breach, it would not be so obvious that we had the actual texts of Japanese messages. The Navy, however, continued providing the complete texts. It took some time for Roosevelt to deal with this ridiculous anomaly. As diplomatic relations with Japan deteriorated, he demanded the actual transcripts from the Army, rather than summaries. It had to be crystal clear to Roosevelt that there was a serious lack of coordination and cooperation between at least two of his three key intelligence services: Army, Navy, and State. The fourth, the FBI, was collecting a certain amount of intelligence in Latin America and elsewhere through its personnel stationed at various American embassies. He could only guess how much his lack of adequate intelligence was due to such rivalry.

Roosevelt went about filling his intelligence gap in his own inimitable manner. Not only in intelligence, but also in almost every area of concern to the executive branch, he liked to have several sources of information. In the case of intelligence he simply deputized a number of individuals and groups to be unofficial intelligence services reporting to him directly. One was Joseph Grew, U.S. ambassador to Japan. Grew had graduated from Groton and from Harvard two years ahead of Roosevelt. They knew each other from days on the *Harvard Crimson*. Grew, whose view of Secretary of State Cordell Hull was less than flattering, visited FDR as well as Hull every time he came to Washington. He also felt free to write to the president directly from time to time. On December 14, 1940, he wrote: "It seems to me increasingly clear that we are bound to have a showdown [with the Japanese] some day, and the principal question at issue is whether it is to our advantage to have that showdown sooner or have it later."[4] Interestingly, because Army intelligence had so few observers, let alone spies, in Japan, the chief of Army intelligence considered Grew his best source on what was going on there.

There were also some private citizens FDR used for intelligence gathering. One of them was the wealthy and well-connected Vincent Astor. Astor organized a secret club called "the Room" that met in New York to discuss gossip in the guise of foreign intelligence, aided by heavy drinking. In 1938 the president sent Astor and Kermit Roosevelt, a cousin of his and a son of Theodore Roosevelt, into the Pacific on Astor's yacht to collect information about Japanese installations. It appears that Astor had a thrilling adventure but did not return with any groundbreaking intelligence. Astor, though, was a director of the Western Union Telegraph Company, which allowed him to provide FDR with the text of sensitive telegrams and cables. And he had a number of bankers in his "Room" who allowed him to gather intelligence on transfers of funds. Roosevelt's directions to Astor are not on record, but Astor's messages to Roosevelt suggest that FDR fully approved of these questionable activities.

Still another unofficial intelligence operative was John Franklin Carter, a friend of the president's, who obtained FDR's approval for "a small special intelligence and fact-finding unit" that would get its funding from the State Department. Assistant Secretary of State Adolf Berle, a skeptic about centralized intelligence, grumbled, "I am not, of course, familiar with what the President has asked him to do, nor do I wish to be."[5] Carter himself later evaluated his contribution as minimal: "It was a picturesque and wildly funny affair at times. Very fantastically amusing things happened as they always do in off-beat operations and I think we all had fun."[6] One of Roosevelt's first directives to Carter was to spy on and report about Vincent Astor's operation.

Much more effective and even more mysterious was Wallace Banta Phillips, a rather quiet and colorless businessman with a London-based rubber company. With Roosevelt's approval, Phillips entered the espionage field through the Office of Naval Intelligence in May 1940. The fact that Phillips's rubber company already had an industrial espionage ring in place meant that the Navy could spy without having to endanger its own attachés. Astor quickly learned of this newcomer and complained to FDR that the businessman was just a dangerous "social climber."

In each of these failed experiments, we see a president hungry for information direct from the source, delivered by people untainted by politics. In some cases, we see Roosevelt using a shroud of secrecy to bypass Congress. In spring 1938, he wanted to support the Spanish Loyalists, then fighting Francisco Franco's Nationalist forces, but the 1936 Neutrality Act tied his hands. Roosevelt, though, was able to route supplies to the Loyalists in the Spanish Civil War in direct violation of the neutrality legislation. He built a tiny spy ring for this operation, consisting of his wife, Eleanor Roosevelt, who cabled messages to Ambassador William Bullitt in Paris; a journalist; and his brother-in-law G. Hall Roosevelt. A scheme to supply 150 airplanes to the Loyalists fell apart when France began to seal its porous border with Spain.[7] Much later, when Roosevelt again felt tied down by the neutrality law, he was able to turn to Bill Donovan.

Donovan was a second-generation Irish Catholic born in Buffalo, New York, in 1883. His family, which had fought for labor rights, was decidedly not Republican. Donovan showed early promise in college (while also working in factories and on construction sites) and obtained a scholarship to attend Columbia University Law School. Athletic, articulate, and handsome (those who knew Donovan, male or female, always remarked specifically on his dazzling blue eyes), Bill Donovan came into his own at the law school where FDR was a student contemporary, though Roosevelt barely knew Donovan there. After graduating, Roosevelt would soon be involved in politics and public service, while Donovan would return to Buffalo to start a law firm.

During the First World War, the defining event of their generation, each served in a way appropriate to his station in life. Roosevelt was an assistant secretary of the navy, while Donovan was a lieutenant colonel serving in the army in France. Roosevelt cultivated the image of a rule-breaker, a rebel inside a staid bureaucracy who got things done for the good of the men and women in uniform. Donovan already had earned the nickname "Wild Bill" while chasing after Pancho Villa along the Mexican border in 1916. Then, serving in the "Fighting 69th" regiment in France in 1918, he personally led an assault on an extremely well fortified German position and remained engaged and exposed even after being shot by an enemy machine gun. He received medals from several foreign governments for this action, and eventually the U.S. Congressional Medal of Honor, the Distinguished Service Medal, and many other medals, becoming one of the most decorated men in American military history. But he often broke down crying when he spoke of the men who "died out of loyalty to me" and requested that his Medal of Honor be deposited with his regiment.[8]

After the war, Donovan's law practice flourished, but he was also drawn into state politics on the Republican side as U.S. attorney for the western district of New York. He made an unsuccessful bid for lieutenant governor of New York. When one of his law school mentors, Harlan Fiske Stone, became U.S. attorney general in 1924, Donovan joined him as an assistant attorney general. Now Donovan started to get a glimpse of where his unbridled ambition might take him. Within a year, he thought of being in the president's cabinet, maybe not as secretary of state right away, but eventually. By 1928, there was muted talk of a Hoover-Donovan ticket.

Donovan's labors on behalf of the Hoover campaign of 1928 did not go unnoticed; it seemed almost certain that the administration would reward him with an appointment to a significant position in the government. He was offered the job of governor-general of the Philippines. He refused, citing family reasons, but the real reason was that he felt it meant being exiled from Washington. Donovan tried to reenter public life by running for governor of New York in 1932, the same year Governor Franklin Roosevelt first ran for president. The gubernatorial election was a disaster for Donovan. His defeat—he received only a third of the votes— by a banker in the midst of the Great Depression seemed to put a final cap on his political ambitions.

Still, he traveled to Europe frequently in the early 1930s, and each time he came back he was more convinced that it was time for America to take a more active role in the world. Because of his distinguished war record, Donovan had entrée to important people all over Europe. He met with Mussolini in Italy and a number of top officials in London. He saw impressive demonstrations of German military hardware. After these experiences, he told a group of American veterans: "In an age of bullies, we cannot afford to be a sissy."[9] By the end of the 1930s, more people were coming around to this view, but a majority of the American public (not to mention the Republican party) were isolationist, so Donovan was going against the grain. His attempts to draw the nation's attention to the dangers posed by the rise of two aggressive powers, Germany in Europe and Japan in East Asia, brought him closer to Roosevelt.

Donovan had no experience in intelligence—either spying or analysis. He had limited experience in government, and practically none in managing large bureaucracies. So why did Roosevelt give him the job—initially with the intriguing title of Director of the Office of the Coordinator of Information (COI)—of creating and heading a new intelligence operation? Donovan had a wide and diverse network of connections that enabled him to recruit talented people ranging from businessmen and Wall Street lawyers to academics from Yale and other elite institutions. He essentially was in the right place at the right time. He also had enormous charm and charisma. "He could charm anybody," recalled Ned Putzell. "He experienced idolatry everywhere. And people admired him so damn much."[10] Another former Donovan subordinate in the OSS, Fisher Howe, remembered, "When you were with him, you were the only person that counted, and that is a tremendous talent."[11]

In 1940, Donovan's daughter was tragically killed in an auto accident. Donovan was not yet involved in White House discussions and there was no indication that he would ever be a person of consequence in government, but Roosevelt wrote a personal note of condolence that meant a great deal to Donovan. (I have some insight into how he might have felt. When I was in an accident myself in early 2000, President Clinton, whose charm and empathetic power has often been compared to Roosevelt's, took time to call my family and spent about a half hour on the phone with them. I had retired from government service, and I barely knew the president. The fact that he took this time out of his day made me believe it was much more than a gesture.) The letter from FDR to Donovan was their first contact in a number of years, a personal touch that helped create a bond between the two men.

Just a few months later, on June 5, 1940, German troops crossed the Somme and the Battle of France began. On the fourteenth, the Germans entered Paris. On the sixteenth, Marshal Henri-Philippe Petain became head of the French government, and the next day asked for an armistice. On July 9, Secretary of the Navy Frank Knox and Roosevelt discussed the fall of France. They had already come to the conclusion that such a rapid fall could never have been achieved by regular military operations alone. Very quickly, rumors of a German "fifth column" provided a convenient answer. Knox suggested to Roosevelt that the non-isolationist Republican Bill Donovan be sent to Europe on a fact-finding mission. If such a fifth column existed and had played a role in the amazingly rapid collapse of French forces, Donovan was tasked to find out how this operation of internal subversion had succeeded. Second, he was asked to address an even more important question: Could Britain survive? The British had such a vested interest in convincing Donovan they would survive that they unveiled their war plans to him. They claimed they would win not through "traditional" warfare but through strategic bombing, economic pressure, the creation of widespread revolt in Germany's occupied territories, and the "making of chaos and revolution."[12] They were vastly outnumbered and alone. Initially at least, fighting such a non-traditional war with limited resources was their only hope. Donovan reported this to Knox on August 5. A meeting with Roosevelt followed on August 9 at Roosevelt's home in Hyde Park.

Roosevelt needed a spymaster, since his intelligence resources consisted of uncoordinated agencies, each going its own way to meet the perceived needs of its parent organization and not necessarily cooperating with the others. Donovan was a candidate for heading an entirely new intelligence operation, someone who would, because of the evolving personal relationship, have a direct line to FDR. The president had, at least in the early days, a high opinion of Donovan because of his open interventionist streak, his unconventional thinking, and his enthusiasm and verve. He must have seen Donovan as an ideal coconspirator. "Wild Bill's" scattershot enthusiasm fitted neatly with FDR's willingness to try almost anything if it had a reasonable chance of working (and if the Supreme Court or Congress didn't stop him). Donovan was a bull in a china shop and an empire builder who was quite naïve when it came to what other, more powerful players thought of him. The same qualities and behavior that would have caused other presidents to double-bolt their Oval Office doors caused Roosevelt to swing them wide open when Donovan came knocking. Both men have been described as the sort who believed in not letting the right hand know what the left hand was doing. Both enjoyed being the one holding the invisible strings. For instance, when Donovan later needed to forge some German passports, he went to FDR to obtain the services of seventeen counterfeiters in federal prisons. FDR agreed, with the condition that if the Secret Service ever found out, Donovan would be out of business. They never did.[13]

Neither FDR nor Donovan concerned himself with details. Both were idea men. Donovan spent so much time focusing on the big picture that he proved to be a disastrous administrator. Both ran with ideas long before they had the details or framework even barely sketched out. Remembering Donovan, Fisher Howe recalled something that Dean Acheson used to say. "Ah, but a man's reach should exceed his grasp (except for diplomats and trapeze artists)."[14] For domestic policy, Roosevelt had the "brain trust," an exciting group of eager, young go-getters. On the other hand, he had a cautious and traditionalist secretary of state, Cordell Hull, a man FDR found "exceedingly vague."[15] With such a diverse mix of personalities and temperaments, FDR knew how to play each one, telling Hull one thing one day, and cabinet secretaries Harold Ickes or Henry Morgenthau something quite different on another day. By masking his intentions and playing one man off the other, FDR got where he wanted to go. But this method could work only to a limited degree. In the military, he was dealing with men like General George C. Marshall, the army chief of staff, and Admiral Harold R. Stark, the chief of naval operations, neither of whom were inclined to try out wildly innovative ideas. Nor were their civilian bosses, old-line Republicans Stimson and Knox. Donovan was quite another matter. He embarked on many a bold and innovative scheme but would find himself, over the next five years, dealing with and outmaneuvered by consummate political and bureaucratic operators, men like J. Edgar Hoover of the FBI.

But Donovan was a breath of fresh air for FDR, and an innovator. To an insightful OSS historian, Donovan was FDR's "Oval Office playmate," someone with whom he could bounce around ideas, someone who shared his enthusiasm.[16] "The relationship," recalled Donovan's assistant, "was such an easy one"[17]—at first.

One CIA legend suggests that their relationship was so easy that Donovan could get away with firing a gun in the Oval Office. In order to demonstrate to FDR a new super-silent .22-caliber pistol, Donovan emptied the magazine, ten shots, into a bag of sand. Roosevelt was on the phone and never heard a thing. Donovan put the smoking gun on the president's desk and told him what had just happened. We can presume that they never informed the Secret Service that Donovan had entered the Oval Office with a loaded weapon.[18]

In April 1941, Roosevelt expressed concern about a "twilight zone" between several of his departments. He had asked at least twice before that the FBI, Army, Navy, and State get together and "coordinate" intelligence. Now, with the help of the British, in particular Rear Admiral John H. Godfrey and the future creator of James Bond, Ian Fleming, Donovan had drafted a sweeping plan to take over intelligence by becoming the "Coordinator of Information" (COI). He submitted this directly to the president. It was written to please Roosevelt's interventionist leanings and to send the message that Donovan was ready to take charge. Donovan promised to build an agency that would "constitute a means by which the President, as Commander-in-Chief, and his Strategic Board would have available accurate and complete enemy intelligence reports upon which military operational decisions could be based."[19] Roosevelt, quite tired of mediating Army-Navy disputes, approved everything in Donovan's memo.

As could be expected, Donovan's proposal invited attacks by the military services, presaging a struggle between centralized intelligence and the military that continues to this day. The last thing the military wanted was some civilian interloper telling them how to conduct intelligence operations. And, alarmingly to them, the directive stated that the COI was to provide the president and his "Strategic Board" with information "upon which *military* [emphasis added] operational decisions could be based." Putting this out in front of military commanders at a time like that was like waving a red flag in front of a bull. The military and State opened fire on the plan, particularly the part Donovan valued the most—his direct access to the president.

General Marshall, already a towering presence, diagrammed a scheme whereby intelligence developed by the COI would be routed through the Army and Navy before going to the president. Donovan consented to this plan in principle, but in practice seldom filtered his information and evaluations through the Army and Navy while he was Coordinator of Information. Roosevelt did not object.

Next, the people in the president's own budget office fretted over the fact that no one really knew what this emerging office with the evasive name of Coordinator of Information was actually going to do and cost. And there were any number of specific decisions on whether COI would encroach on other entities in order to do coordination. In a number of these cases Roosevelt did not give COI all the authority Donovan sought. The most glaring of these was that COI was not given access to MAGIC and was forbidden to set up its own code-breaking operation. Access to MAGIC was so restricted that it appears that no one, including Roosevelt, even considered that Donovan should ever have it. How useful, though, could a "coordinator of information" be if the best information on the increasing tensions in East Asia and the Pacific remained out of his reach? And what does that say about how Roosevelt viewed the role Donovan and this new agency should play? Such limits on our central authority for intelligence have persisted ever since.

Still another issue was how far COI's writ carried into the field of propaganda, or "psychological warfare," something about which Donovan felt strongly. New York mayor Fiorello LaGuardia had been appointed director of civilian defense and was assuming a role in domestic propaganda. FDR assured LaGuardia that COI would conduct psychological attacks only on foreign populations, whereas LaGuardia's responsibility was to "sustain the morale of our people within the national boundaries."[20] Donovan, nonetheless, developed domestic propaganda plans, but this placed him in direct conflict with a powerful opponent.

Donovan also found himself in an internecine struggle with the wealthy and well-connected Nelson Rockefeller, who was serving as coordinator of inter-American affairs, a presidential appointment. Rockefeller saw himself as responsible for managing the propaganda message in South America and viewed Donovan as an amateur and interloper. Donovan overplayed his hand when he told Rockefeller that he would not "enter into a compromise" and insulted his adversary with a condescending conclusion to an uncompromising letter: "I think I don't need to assure you, Nelson, that this is no mere jurisdictional question. It is a matter of major policy."[21] Rockefeller responded by going directly to FDR, bringing with him a draft executive order prohibiting COI from doing propaganda work in South America. Roosevelt made a few changes and sent the order out on the same day. Donovan made a feeble attempt to regain control of radio broadcasts in South America, to no avail.

Thus, the first presidential effort to give central direction to American intelligence still left the country with a mélange of virtually autonomous intelligence agencies and uncertainty as to just what the role of the new coordinator would be. It was less than five months before the country was jolted by what, until 9/11, was the greatest intelligence failure in our history—Pearl Harbor. This failure was, at least in some measure, the result of both a lack of exchange of data among intelligence agencies and a failure to coordinate and focus their efforts. Alarmingly, both issues still plague our intelligence today.

Since Donovan's agency was quite new, and since he did not have access to MAGIC, hardly anyone has placed any blame on Donovan for failing to predict Pearl Harbor. But Donovan was part of the problem. As Coordinator of Information, he did very little coordinating. Instead, he added to the pile on FDR's desk—more than 260 memos and phone calls during his first six months as COI.[22] Very little in this blizzard could be considered either evaluated intelligence or the "accurate and complete enemy intelligence reports" that Donovan's original proposal had promised. Instead, Roosevelt got volumes and volumes of unprocessed material.

When it came to Japan, Donovan failed to offer an evaluated estimate. Instead, he offered two contradictory statements.

On November 13, 1941, Donovan relayed "the substance of statements" made by Hans Thomsen, German chargé d'affaires, to one of Donovan's "assets." According to Mr. Thomsen, Japan was going to attack: "If Japan waits, it will be comparatively easy for the United States to strangle Japan." Time was not on Japan's side. "Japan is therefore forced to strike now, whether she wants to or not."[23] Of course, this was just one man's opinion. And it was buried in the transcript—neither highlighted nor analyzed.

This statement of Japan's intentions, as useless as it was, was soon contradicted by another COI report. A journalist traveling in China on a COI mission asserted that as long as Russia was still a force, "Japan would do nothing to provoke a major war." He concluded that "time is really on our side."[24] On the twenty-eighth of November, Donovan discussed the issue over breakfast with Roosevelt, and the president lamented that "it was difficult now to find a formula in dealing with Japan."[25]

The stunning thing about this conversation is that Roosevelt had already concluded, based on what he had read in intercepted Japanese messages, that war with Japan was inevitable. But he continued to keep Donovan, his own intelligence chief, in the dark about MAGIC, as well as the conclusions he had drawn from reading it. To the military chiefs, who knew about MAGIC and what it foretold, Donovan must have looked like a rank amateur who did not, in fact, enjoy presidential support.

On November 25, 1941, days before that breakfast with Donovan, Roosevelt had met with the secretaries of war, navy, and state, as well as the chief of naval operations and the chief of staff of the army. The subject was budgets. Roosevelt, though, told them in no uncertain terms that the Japanese were planning a surprise attack, perhaps as soon as December 1. In short, rather than these officials informing the president of what their intelligence agencies told them, the president was drawing his own conclusions and warning his subordinates.[26]

As a result of the president's warning, the military leaders transmitted an alert to the Pacific commanders with no ambiguity whatsoever: "This dispatch is to be considered a war warning. Negotiations with Japan looking toward stabilization of conditions in the Pacific have ceased and an aggressive move by Japan is expected within the next few days."[27] What was missing, of course, was where our commanders should expect the action. Tokyo was apparently being very close-mouthed with its diplomats on this. Concurrently, though, there had to be Japanese military message traffic that was more specific. It probably lay in Japanese naval transmissions, which were not being deciphered.

When the Japanese attack struck Pearl Harbor at dawn on December 7, it was about 1:00 P.M. on the East Coast of the United States. Donovan was surprised when loudspeakers called him out of a football game in New York. He reached Washington and was in the Oval Office late that evening after the president's meetings with the cabinet, congressmen, and military advisors were over. Roosevelt still had a long-standing appointment with newscaster Edward R. Murrow, which he elected to keep, even though it was around midnight. It was the last meeting of the worst day of Roosevelt's presidency. They—FDR, Murrow, and Donovan—ate sandwiches, and Roosevelt continued to lament the losses. "They caught our ships like lame ducks! Lame ducks, Bill," and "They caught our planes on the ground, by God, on the ground!" Then he remarked to Donovan (as Donovan remembered it), "It's a good thing you got me started on this . . . ," meaning Donovan's having pushed for centralization of intelligence in COI.[28]

When Donovan left the Oval Office very late that evening, he must have thought that he was in a uniquely promising position. Here he was, one of a handful of advisors the president had summoned when the news of Pearl Harbor broke. He was the last of them to be with the president that night, and his meeting closed with Roosevelt's acknowledgment that Donovan's ambitious plan for coordinating intelligence had merit. Beyond that, Donovan *was* the Coordinator of Information. That meant he had direct access to the president, even if he were required to coordinate some of his reporting with other agencies and departments. Donovan must have assumed he might well become the leader of U.S. intelligence.

It did not work out that way for three reasons: The first was that Donovan overplayed his hand; second, the Joint Chiefs of Staff, who became a very powerful force in wartime, chose to cut him down to size; and third, the president did not protect Donovan. In retrospect it is easy to suggest that Donovan was an ill-suited personality to be Coordinator of Information if that meant that providing information was his principal responsibility. He was a man of considerable ambition, likely aspiring to be president of the United States, certainly governor of New York. He was a man of action, as is any winner of the Congressional Medal of Honor. Simply providing information upon which others would make decisions was far too passive a role for someone with a nickname of "Wild Bill."

Still, Donovan's activist image was a big plus for COI. It helped attract highly qualified people who wanted to make a contribution to our role in a war that so many saw inevitably coming. Even college presidents, such as James Phinney Baxter of Williams, signed up for the Research and Analysis (R&A) branch of COI. R&A under Donovan played a very important role in the war and at the same time laid the foundation for the worldwide analytic ability the United States would need after World War II.

Donovan also started spying with people—gathering "human intelligence"—at a time when no one in the military or State Department would do it. During World War II, this was accomplished primarily by placing agents in neutral countries—the prime example being Allen Dulles, who served in Switzerland and later would become Eisenhower's DCI. But Donovan's heart lay in what we now call covert action. Covert action is making things happen without it being known the United States is the instigator; whereas intelligence is providing information. Donovan thought COI should focus not just on gathering intelligence but also on covert actions like propaganda, sabotage, assassination, political manipulation, psychological warfare, and guerrilla actions. His passion for action, as well as his attempts to influence policy-making and military strategy, carried him past where Roosevelt could support or even respect him.

One such instance concerned Baja California. Immediately following Pearl Harbor, rumors of Japanese infiltration into the West Coast flew to Washington on wings of near panic. Talk of five thousand Japanese moving from Central America and mainland Mexico to Baja California was among the rumors. Donovan's R&A branch looked at these rumors and concluded that Mexico did not have the trains, boats, or roads to support such a large-scale move and that the barren desert of the region could not conceal a secret base. Furthermore, the Mexicans had been steadily pushing the few Japanese on the peninsula out of the fishing business, leaving any potential fifth column force landlocked.[29] This was an early example of how work between geographers, sociologists, and area scholars could create a useful strategic evaluation. Donovan sent Roosevelt the report on December 15.

However, Donovan's political objectives soon had him contradicting the conclusions of his own organization's report, giving us one of the earliest examples of a chief of intelligence "cooking the books." On December 21, Donovan wrote Roosevelt that there was a "strong possibility" that the Japanese had "hidden bases" for submarines and airplanes in Baja. The infiltrators perhaps numbered no more than one thousand, he averred, but he felt there were enough "to do considerable damage." He asked the president for permission to recruit the local fishing unions "to ferret them out."[30] Why the change of tune? Donovan's desire to undertake operations and get a piece of the action trumped the logic of the cooler heads who had written, just a week before, that there was not, and could not be, a Japanese threat from Baja. The very next day, Donovan sent his plans to create his own guerrilla warfare unit to the Oval Office. Then another memo from Donovan to FDR followed, recommending a no-holds-barred covert "intervention" in Baja.[31]

Luckily, the president did not approve Donovan's plan. In fact, he was already moving in an entirely different direction—away from Donovan. The same day he received the recommendation to flood Baja with operatives, he met with J. Edgar Hoover to discuss wartime espionage operations in South and Central America. Hoover felt that Donovan was getting in his way. After meeting with Hoover, FDR sent out an unambiguous directive: All other organizations had to seek approval for any "intelligence work" north and south of the U.S. borders with Hoover's FBI. Donovan supposedly didn't learn of the order for over a week,[32] but that didn't stop him from sending the president a report a month later boasting that he had "arranged with the United Fruit Company officials to have all of their division heads cover the territory through Central America. . . ."[33] Was Donovan assuming the president's directive didn't apply to him? Others in the government saw a man who had gone off the reservation. As Adolf Berle told the president, "Bill Donovan wants to take over the FBI work in South America. At least he does not say so, but he wants to put his own man in. He does not even say that, but you can never pin him down to saying what he really wants to do."[34]

Hoover and Donovan were locked in combat for the entire war, with Hoover remaining on the offensive and Donovan meekly trying to chip away at the limits set by FDR. Hoover even went to the length of planting a woman in COI's communications center. She supplied Hoover with verbatim communications regarding Donovan that could be embarrassing. Hoover, in turn, supplied these to the columnist Drew Pearson. Eventually the woman was caught and fired. Everyone, including FDR, knew who was behind this scheme.

A flurry of memos from Donovan—sometimes several in a day—were crossing FDR's desk. Many of them contained questionable intelligence and recommendations. For example, Donovan advised the president to conduct a direct attack on Japan from the sea with ten to fifteen thousand troops. He passed on rumors that the Germans were preparing to invade Spain. In response to such advice, Roosevelt was always polite to Donovan on paper and in person, but within six months of Pearl Harbor, FDR's enthusiasm for "Wild Bill's" "innovative thinking" had evaporated. According to Adolf Berle, Roosevelt was considering making Donovan a brigadier general, "after which he was thinking of putting him on some nice, quiet, isolated island, where he could have a scrap with some Japs every morning before breakfast. That, he thought, would keep Donovan happy and out of trouble."[35] By this time, then, any possibility that a strong, centralized intelligence authority would evolve from COI was dead. In brief, it was a personal relationship with the president that brought Donovan onto the scene, but it was the deterioration of that relationship that severely limited Donovan's effectiveness. As we will see, this relationship between presidents and their chiefs of intelligence can bear importantly on the effectiveness of our intelligence operations.

It is remarkable that COI survived in any form. J. Edgar Hoover, in addition to keeping COI out of Central and South America, had defeated Donovan on a number of other fronts. Moreover, the Joint Chiefs of Staff were ready to recommend doing away with COI as an intelligence agency when it was saved by one man, Lieutenant General Walter Bedell Smith (aka "Beetle" Smith). Smith, secretary of the JCS, persuaded the Joint Chiefs to absorb COI instead of dismembering it. His reasoning was that it would be better to have it under their control. Smith himself later became one of five of us who have served as director of central intelligence while on active military duty.

Donovan acceded to Smith's proposal to operate under the Joint Chiefs because it was his only chance to survive. Fisher Howe says, "Self-defense—it was the least bad of the choices that he had available."[36] Shortly after Smith proposed this, FDR signed two executive orders. One changed the name of Donovan's organization from COI to Office of Strategic Services (OSS). The other had OSS report to the Joint Chiefs of Staff. In addition, and much to Donovan's discomfort, one of the orders stripped OSS of the propaganda, or "psychological warfare," function. When told of this, according to one of his deputies, Donovan flew into "a state of fury such as I had never seen before, and was never to see again. It was controlled fury, but it was real fury, for he felt that the President had betrayed him."[37]

Far more debilitating to the basic function of OSS was a decision by the president to continue excluding Donovan from the intelligence yielded by Allied code-breaking operations. Donovan complained, quite rightly, that exclusion would impair the ability of OSS to discharge its mission. His pleas fell on deaf ears. What was probably the best raw intelligence of the war remained out of his hands and thus eliminated any possibility of Donovan's becoming a true coordinator of intelligence. Donovan personally, though, was probably much happier under the Joint Chiefs than under Roosevelt. Roosevelt's directives were often ambiguous and vague, reflecting the push and pull of various subordinates. The military operated with tight definitions of who did what. That was good for Donovan, the mediocre manager, and good for his organization and the morale of his people. And Donovan rediscovered that he was at heart a military man.

It was in part because of this military ethos that Donovan managed to make his mark with OSS. His units in the field and behind enemy lines provided some real intelligence and, as the war wound down, some great war stories, which Donovan fed into the publicity machine. An army report concluded that the landing in Southern France was the "best briefed invasion in history" and "a single example of what can be done by an agency of this kind."[38] Operation Torch, the invasion of North Africa, began with OSS reconnaissance to facilitate the landing, and all manner of cloak-and-dagger derring-do involving insertions of agents carrying bars of gold from submarines via rubber rafts. The army, it should be noted, had no special forces of its own at the time.

The least storied part of OSS, and perhaps the most effective, was R&A. This branch was "so respectable and respectful, so conscientious and helpful," concluded one historian, "that it inevitably acquired the aura of virtue."[39] R&A was the department that Donovan had focused on first while setting up COI, and he had turned not to the military for staff, but to academia. "One of the basic ideas behind it," wrote Roger Hilsman, an OSS operative in Burma and later head of the State Department's Bureau of Intelligence and Research, "was the novel and almost impish idea that scholars could in some respects take the place of spies."[40]

During the war, however, Donovan paid much less attention to R&A, and it developed its own culture and mores. The analysts realized something Donovan did not: OSS did not have any real power or standing of its own. If R&A people went around making policy recommendations, inevitably someone would disagree with them. If that someone was in a position of power—say, a political appointee or, worse, a cabinet secretary—then that person would make it a personal mission to quash OSS. The only way to survive was to stay neutral. "There is . . . no future for R&A as a pressure group, no matter how strongly we believe we are 'right,'" wrote an R&A man, Richard Hartshorne, to his colleagues. "On the contrary, to the extent that we do special pleading, we will very soon lose our entrée to all policy-makers other than those already committed to the same special causes."[41] So R&A decided that it would "not suggest, recommend, or in any way determine the strategy or the tactical decisions of the war."[42] Its realm was the facts. This was the genesis of an ethic of American intelligence that has been official policy ever since.

As early as September 1943, Donovan began looking to the longer run and the postwar role for himself and the OSS. He first discussed this with Beetle Smith. Donovan proposed that the Coordinator of Intelligence be a full and equal member of the Joint Chiefs of Staff. This idea was a nonstarter. There was no way the four-star members of the Joint Chiefs were going to accept as an equal this now one-star officer and former lawyer whose writ was limited to intelligence. In addition, back then the chiefs of the army and navy reported to the president through the secretaries of the army and navy. A chief of intelligence would presumably report directly to the president and might well become the most influential of the group, especially in peacetime. It is not surprising that this plan was quickly shelved, never to resurface. But it was evidence that Donovan was a very ambitious man, and that he was very interested in enhancing his own position. He took winning the war seriously, he cared about the OSS and the men and women in it, but, as one of his former subordinates points out, OSS "was a justification also for personal ambition."[43]

Just under a year later, on August 4, 1944, Donovan made another attempt to ensure OSS would have a role after the war was over. He sent the JCS a very credible report developed by R&A on the looming difficulty of establishing spheres of influence between the Allies and the Soviets in postwar Europe. Against the advice of his analysts in R&A, he appended to it an appeal to the JCS to recognize the importance of having a permanent organization such as R&A to do long-range studies. In short, R&A

should become a permanent fixture within the JCS. One month after they received Donovan's suggestion, the Joint Chiefs slapped Donovan down, hard, with the following letter from General Marshall:

> Activities of the Office of Strategic Services in Europe after the collapse of Germany should remain under the control of the United States Theater Commander, who can best determine in what manner and to what extent such activities can be employed most usefully in furtherance of our national policies. It is, therefore, deemed unnecessary for the Joint Chiefs of Staff to give consideration at this time to your memorandum of 4 August.[44]

Life under theater commanders would spell an end to the strategic, big-picture aspirations of Donovan for R&A. He realized that there could be no future under the military and began to long for a revival of his former relationship with Roosevelt.

Donovan's next proposal for continuance came quickly, and it took him full circle—once again he wanted to be appointed by and report directly to the president of the United States. He developed a bold plan that removed the proposed intelligence organization from military constraints altogether and put it "on the policy or strategy level." As such, the director was to be "appointed by the President, and be administered under Presidential direction." The OSS was to be the foundation: "It is not necessary to create a new agency. The nucleus of such an organization already exists in the Office of Strategic Services."[45]

In stark contrast to his approach in 1941, Donovan did not march into Roosevelt's office with his plan. Instead, he engaged in weeks of quiet lobbying around the White House to win the approval of those close to the president. Donovan's marketing of his plan at the White House, however, failed to sufficiently impress anyone who had significant access to FDR. The keeper of the gate, Harry Hopkins, was not impressed. The one true champion of the plan was Dr. Isadore Lubin, an economist in the White House Map Room, who on October 25, 1944, wrote to Roosevelt about it and attached a copy of the report. No one who has written on this period of intelligence history can resist quoting from this memo of Lubin's to Roosevelt, because it starts with the line: "As you no doubt know, Bill Donovan's Office of Strategic Services has been doing some swell work."[46]

Lubin continued: "It occurred to me that there will be more room after the war for a service in the United States Government which would carry on some of the work now being done under Donovan's auspices." To think that Roosevelt was unaware of Donovan's efforts and would actually believe that this idea had simply "occurred" to Lubin is amusing. Lubin even "borrowed" Donovan's language verbatim in his letter to FDR: "The nucleus of such an organization already exists in the Office of Strategic Services. It has the trained personnel, the foreign contacts, the administrative organization and the operating experience."[47] Attached to the letter was Donovan's plan. Roosevelt's only recorded reaction was to send both Lubin's letter and Donovan's plan to Acting Secretary of State Edward Stettinius Jr.

By November 7, no action had been taken on the plan placed in Roosevelt's hands by Lubin on October 25, but Donovan's staff was hard at work on a new executive order for the president's signature (even though he hadn't asked for one). This arrived at the White House on November 18. Donovan now wanted to focus on "the problems of peace." This meant that "intelligence control should be returned to the supervision of the President," or, more specifically, it should be a "central authority reporting directly to you."[48] This proposal essentially preserved the functions of OSS, including espionage, but transferred them to the executive office of the president. In fact, the proposed agency was really just a much better defined version of COI, with spying and "subversive operations abroad" actually listed as functions in the executive order.[49] The COI had actually not been given any directive in writing regarding such subversive activities, which both Donovan and Roosevelt thought best. If Roosevelt had put his pen to Donovan's proposed executive order, he would have openly endorsed "subversive operations abroad" and made himself and future presidents more publicly accountable for the agency's activities. It's not surprising, then, that this forward-thinking president, with an uncanny sense of where the political minefields lay, did not sign this order.

Donovan simultaneously sent copies of his plan to General Marshall; Admiral Ernest J. King; the secretaries of state, war, and navy; and six other military and civilian leaders, consistently stating (falsely) that the president had asked for this plan.[50] But instead of gathering opinions from these people at the top, Roosevelt did exactly what Donovan had been trying to avoid—on November 22, he kicked it down to the Joint Chiefs of Staff. From there, the sky darkened considerably for Donovan. The plan was passed down the line until it reached the Joint Intelligence Staff for evaluation and comment. Here, it met a group of military and naval intelligence officers with their knives sharpened.

A group of men met on December 22, 1944, to determine the fate of U.S. secret intelligence. They didn't know it at the time, but these individuals, holding jobs several notches down from the real "decision-makers"— the cabinet secretaries and chiefs of staff—would provide the framework for the Central Intelligence Agency. They would also determine the organizational relationship between future presidents and future directors of central intelligence.

That relationship was the main point of contention. Donovan wanted a direct line, but by the time of the December 22 meeting, Donovan's proposal had been pushed aside entirely in favor of two counterproposals— one backed by the military agencies, the other by the civilian members of the Joint Intelligence Staff. Neither of these tied the DCI directly to the president. The military couldn't even accept the DCI's being appointed by the president, as was proposed by the civilian staff members. One military participant, Major General Clayton Bissell of Army Intelligence, suggested that if the DCI were appointed by the president, the DCI "could go any time to the President and give the Secretaries a run-around, so that their control over him would be next to nil." The result would be a man who could direct the intelligence sections of other agencies and departments. "Such power in one man is not in the best interest of a democratic government. I think it is in the best interests of a dictatorship. I think it would be excellent for Germany; but I don't think it fits in with the democratic set-up we have in this country where you run things by checks and balances."[51] The issue Bissell identified, that of a chief of intelligence directing the intelligence sections of other agencies and departments, is still a key one being debated today.

Donovan's representative on this group barely spoke to Bissell, who complained that an important man like himself shouldn't even be wasting time in meetings like this while there was a war going on. But Max Ways, a member of the Joint Intelligence Staff and a self-described "mere civilian timid bureaucrat,"[52] became the voice of moderation and reason. What he said is important because it was heard by three men who were silent during the meeting but who would, each in his own way, contribute to the shaping of the CIA—Captain Sidney Souers, USN, who would become Rear Admiral Souers and America's first DCI; Ludwell Montague, who served with Max Ways on the Joint Intelligence Staff, and who would later become a CIA analyst and legend; and finally, James Lay, who would become executive secretary of the National Security Council (NSC), which dominated the CIA during its early years.

What these pioneers heard during this meeting, and what they would later apply to the CIA, was that the DCI had to be politically weak. "I think this man [the DCI] is a pretty feeble animal," Max Ways argued. He compared the government to a jungle, "in which the smaller an animal is, in one sense, the more chance he has to survive. . . . We are trying to get [the DCI] down as far as we can get him, and give him as much protective coloration as we can."[53] The protection was to come in the form of presidential appointment and the director's consequent prerogative of going directly to the chief executive when his or her intelligence evaluations ran counter to those of the cabinet secretaries. This setup, however, presumed a president who was interested in and responsive to intelligence. Mr. Ways's message did not carry the day but deserves to be highlighted: The DCI is weak by design, and the only protection the DCI has comes from the president. And, yes, government is a jungle.

Donovan, discouraged and frustrated, wrote to Roosevelt, trying to put the decision back in his lap. He wistfully hoped for a return to 1941, when the president could create an intelligence agency with a stroke of the pen. The situation appeared to him to be lost unless the president intervened. In fact, the plans debated on December 22 were reconciled a few days later without presidential intervention. In the resulting compromise the DCI would report to a National Intelligence Authority (NIA)—a board made up of the secretaries of war, navy, and state plus a representative of the Joint Chiefs. Below the DCI, monitoring him on a working level, would be the heads of the military and civilian departmental intelligence agencies. So the DCI and his agency were to be stuck between policy-makers on the cabinet level and the heads of all the other intelligence agencies on the working level. This arrangement seemed designed to guarantee that the DCI would have his every move watched by a member of the military or the State Department.

What was even more abnormal was that the DCI would be hired and

fired by the president only on recommendation of the National Intelligence Authority.[54] The president couldn't do it without the approval of
the NIA. Just as he had to get the advice and consent of the Senate for his
political and judicial appointments, the president would have had to get
the permission of several of his own subordinates to hire and fire a DCI!
So not only was the DCI placed in a weak position, but the plan reflected
an attempt to weaken presidential power. Further, the idea of the NIA led
directly to a postwar attempt to significantly limit presidential power in
foreign affairs. This was how we got the National Security Council,
which was originally envisioned as a body that would be a check and balance on the president. That is, while only the president could make decisions, the existence of the NSC as an advisory body made it necessary for
presidents to tread cautiously if they decided to go contrary to the advice
of the NSC.

The compromise plan for intelligence organization was sent up to the
Joint Chiefs, where it gathered dust for months. Roosevelt, hearing about
it from a displeased Donovan, didn't express a strong preference for either
Donovan's plan or the compromise plan. He also didn't seem to be in a
hurry. He felt that "at the end of the war there simply must be a consoli-
dation of Foreign Intelligence between State and War and Navy."[55] Roosevelt did not say it had to be achieved through the creation of an agency
like the one proposed by Donovan. In fact, by saying that it had to happen
"between" the three national security departments, he seemed to be asking
for mere coordination between departments—effectively reverting back to
the way things were before Donovan and COI came on the scene. Further, he emphasized, "I think it should be limited to military and related
subjects."[56] Donovan didn't want to be limited to military subjects—his
aspirations were to have a hand in foreign policy, but he had failed to make
his case either for immediate action or for direct responsibility to the pres-

ident. Roosevelt left for the Yalta Conference without making a decision on Donovan's plans and pleas.

On February 9, 1945, the secret compromise plan that had been sent to the Joint Chiefs of Staff was printed in the *Chicago Tribune*, thanks to a leak to a reporter named Walter Trohan, who was hostile to Roosevelt. The article made it look like preparations for an American Gestapo. Two prominent congressmen denounced the plan. Donovan was furious and helpless. He started an investigation into the source of the leak, but the list of potential suspects was far too long. His own people determined that the reporter had connections to the Department of the Navy, but Donovan was inclined to believe that it had been J. Edgar Hoover, who wanted to see his own South American spy operations expand globally after the war.[57] Some later historians suggested that it could have come from the Map Room in the White House.[58] The *Tribune* reporter, interviewed years later, stated that the president's secretary contacted him, claiming that Roosevelt "wanted the story out."[59]

While the source of the leak remains uncertain, what became obvious was Donovan's isolation. No one in the executive branch stepped up to defend the compromise plan. Donovan's appeals to the president claimed that "the disclosure was no mere leak but a deliberate plan to sabotage any attempt at reorganization of this government's intelligence services." The sabotage was focused, he felt, on his relationship to the president: "You will note that the strong effort in the revised plan is to avoid the direct reporting of the Director of the Intelligence Agency to you."[60] On his return from Yalta on March 1, at a press conference Roosevelt dodged questions about the plan, failing to either condemn or endorse it. To some, he appeared to have given the plan only cursory consideration.

At this point, Lubin pleaded with Roosevelt to reopen the issue. He prepared a memo, from Roosevelt to Donovan, for Roosevelt's signature that authorized the OSS director to "call together the chiefs of the foreign intelligence and internal security units in the various executive agencies, so that a consensus of opinion can be reached." The memo mentioned that all ten executive departments had "a direct interest in the proposed venture."[61] When Roosevelt signed this, it was the last known word from him on the subject, and they weren't his words—they had been prepared for him by Lubin (who had already shown a willingness to feed FDR words written by Donovan).

On April 12, Secretary of the Navy James V. Forrestal, Attorney General Francis Biddle, and Undersecretary of War Robert P. Patterson met with Secretary of State Edward Stettinius in his office to decide what to do with Donovan's latest approach. Stettinius left the group to respond to an urgent summons to the White House next door. He returned with the news that Roosevelt had died at 3:35 P.M.[62]

Donovan was in Paris when a messenger arrived at his hotel room with the news. His surprised aides watched him rush out of the bathroom in his shorts and undershirt, shaving cream still on his face, demanding a line to Washington. It may have been an indication of how Donovan felt about FDR's failure to support him that Donovan did not return for the funeral. He said there was too much to do in Europe.

Donovan would soon begin to realize how much his relationship with FDR, in its better days, had mattered. He started putting in requests to meet with the new president, but they met in person only once, on May 14, 1945. Truman had his own very different plans for organizing intelligence, and Donovan was not part of them. Truman's jaundiced view of Donovan was reinforced by the negative opinion of Donovan held by Budget Director Harold Smith and a devastating report from an army officer citing a wide range of alleged OSS misbehavior.

When all is said and done, centralized intelligence was truly Roosevelt's creation. Only an extremely strong president could have overcome the passionate objections to any centralized intelligence agency, as did Roosevelt in creating the Coordinator of Information. At the same time, once COI existed, Roosevelt was, at best, halfhearted about supporting his creation and protecting it from its rivals and detractors. There are a number of possible explanations for Roosevelt's unwillingness to have a strong director of intelligence operations:

- Roosevelt's personal style was to rely on multiple sources, and to keep each source largely in the dark about what the others were doing (as he did with Donovan and the breaking of Japan's codes).

- Roosevelt saw the American public as being more isolationist than interventionist, and still not prepared to sanction espionage and shady dealings.

- Roosevelt did not foresee the need for an espionage service during peacetime (because he did not foresee the Cold War).

- Roosevelt may, indeed, have worried that a secret intelligence organization could become an American Gestapo, one that could even become a rival power base to the presidency.

- There was strong opposition from the military (something that has never abated).

- There was strong opposition from J. Edgar Hoover—a man who had real power over several presidents.

Or, finally, Roosevelt just didn't like the idea of giving up control. "There's no accounting for presidents," reflected James Dunn, assistant secretary of state under Roosevelt. "They all become a little mad and be-cause of the office's constraints and frustration, they tend to look on intel-ligence, or whatever, as their own private model railroad which they can run as they personally and petulantly see fit."[63] Whether he intended it or not, though, Roosevelt had started this train rolling and had given it enough momentum to ensure that some form of centralized intelligence would emerge.

Responsibility for deciding just what shape that would take had passed to Harry S Truman. Roosevelt had notoriously kept his vice presi-dent uninformed and uninvolved. It was logical to think that Truman would want some time to get up to speed before making major decisions on the structure of U.S. intelligence. That was not to be the case.

CHAPTER TWO

HARRY S TRUMAN, SOUERS, VANDENBERG, HILLENKOETTER, AND SMITH

The Founding of the CIA

"Wild Bill" Donovan had seen Churchill's wartime Map Room in London, what today we would call a situation room or a war room. (The Map Room was one of the many rooms in a complex known as the Cabinet War Rooms that had been constructed beneath a block of government buildings on Whitehall. In addition to the Map Room there was a room in which the cabinet met, Churchill's bedroom, and another small room that housed the phone Churchill used to talk directly with FDR. This facility was effectively the nerve center of the British government.) Donovan recommended the creation of something similar in the White House as a way for FDR to stay current on the war. Donovan likely surmised that it would also be useful to him in remaining close to the seat of power. That is, if the president was briefed and made all of his decisions in the Oval Office, Donovan would have a voice only when he was invited. It would be easier to infiltrate his ideas into the more open forum of a Map Room. Unfortunately for Donovan, it did not quite work out that way. When his fledgling OSS organization was absorbed into the military, the military took over the Map Room. The OSS analysts tried to get the attention of the key people in this power center by routinely sending reports and analyses to the Map Room, but the Map Room's military staff routinely discarded them. Ironically, one member of this military staff put the first nail in the coffin of Donovan's intelligence career shortly after Roosevelt's death.

He was one of a number of lower-level military officers assigned to the Map Room and who came into regular contact with the president. Colonel Richard Park was a politically astute Army man with close ties to one of Donovan's harshest critics—Major General George Strong of the Army's Military Intelligence Service, G2. According to Park, Roosevelt quietly asked him to do an informal, confidential survey of Donovan's organization. It may seem odd to have had a colonel investigating a major general, but it would not have been an unusual way for Roosevelt to operate.

Colonel Park's report would not be finished for several months, but Truman got a preview of the juicier tidbits shortly after Roosevelt died: Donovan was a mere amateur; he had been easily duped by scribblings of an Italian pornographer, which he passed to the president as groundbreaking intelligence; he had lost a briefcase full of secrets while out cavorting in Bucharest, and when the documents were recovered they were in the room of an exotic dancer; and many of the men in OSS ran up bar bills at a "training camp" in Virginia while pulling down salaries well above those of other government employees. "If the OSS is investigated after the war," he wrote, "it may easily prove to have been the most expensive and wasteful agency of the government."[1]

This last could not have been a more telling comment for the new president. Harry S Truman had shot from obscure senator from Missouri to national hero by prompting and leading the Senate Special Committee to Investigate the National Defense Program. The Truman Committee, as it was known, was dedicated to finding and rooting out wasteful spending and duplication in the war effort. Truman's investigators had been fearless in going after not only contractors but also the Army's top brass itself. One Army Air Corps general officer had gone to jail as a result of information Truman's committee developed. Senator Truman was featured on the cover of *Time* and listed as one of the ten men most important to the war effort in Washington.

Now, what would Truman do with Donovan? After meeting with him following Roosevelt's death, the new president recorded that "Donovan came in to tell how important the Secret Service is and how much he could do to run the government on an even basis."[2] Truman hated those who suffered from what he called Potomac Fever, a misplaced sense of self-importance. Donovan certainly appeared to have a serious case of this malady. Truman "was dissatisfied with how intelligence was handled by the OSS," recalled Sidney Souers, who served as the nation's first director of central intelligence. Souers felt that "Donovan wasn't doing much of anything except writing books and making speeches and propagandizing his own great achievements."[3] Given the burden of allegations of OSS wastefulness and the fact that many generals, admirals, and influential government officials disliked or even hated him, Donovan didn't stand a chance. When Truman dismissed him and dispensed with the OSS in September 1945, Richard Neustadt, then a White House staffer and later a presidential historian, recalled that Truman "acquiesced very cheerfully in the demise of OSS. My suspicion is he was the more cheerful because of his feelings, for whatever reason, about Colonel [sic] Donovan."[4]

Truman immediately commenced building a new intelligence system.

He explained that "he had in mind a different kind of intelligence service from what the country had in the past,"[5] though he never made clear what exactly he had in mind. It was clear, though, that a permanent peacetime intelligence agency was needed. The issue was to make it fit the needs of the new president and be led by men who suited his decision-making style.

Part of that style was a deep suspicion Truman held about the government departments that served him. He suspected that they withheld information from him for their own purposes. "There were a large number of people in the State Department when I took over," he told Wayne Morse in 1963, "who were certain I did not know what was going on in the world and they tried to keep me from finding out."[6] The same was true, he felt, of the Army and the Departments of Agriculture, Commerce, and Labor.

As far as intelligence was concerned, Truman's first director of central intelligence, Rear Admiral Sidney Souers, a great admirer of Truman, remarked that the president had an "extremely simple" concept of what he wanted from his intelligence apparatus: "It was to keep him personally well-informed of all that was going on in the outside world."[7] In his first few months as president, Truman found himself being awakened repeatedly by aides bringing what they thought were dire warnings from different intelligence sources to his bedside. He was polite, but often wondered if there were not a better way to get critical—and reliable—information. Perhaps if this was all centralized, the items could be prioritized and his desk might not be so crowded. "Instead of the President having to look through a bunch of papers two feet high," he wrote decades after the CIA was a reality, "the information was coordinated so that the President could arrive at the facts."[8] This was indeed an extremely simple idea of what an intelligence service could and should do, but was perfectly legitimate as far as it went. However, the leader of an intelligence organization designed to do no more than this would have to be a background figure willing to present the facts without opinions, emphatically not a Donovan.

The man Truman selected as his first DCI, Sidney Souers, was then serving as deputy chief of naval intelligence. With the war over, he was looking forward to getting out of uniform and returning to his home base of St. Louis. However, when the Joint Chiefs of Staff and the State Department deadlocked over what form a new intelligence service should take, Souers was called in to troubleshoot. Souers came from humble beginnings, having saved up for college working on a passenger boat on the Hudson River. He graduated from Miami University in 1914 after only three years. By 1920, at age twenty-eight, he became president of the Mortgage and Securities Company in New Orleans. In 1929, he was commissioned a lieutenant commander in the U.S. Naval Reserve and moved to St. Louis, where he was an officer in the General American Life Insurance Company and also served as an intelligence officer in the naval reserve. When he was called to active duty in 1940, his salary dropped from $30,000 a year to $3,000 a year.[9] Applying as much energy to his career in naval intelligence as he had to business, despite the drop in pay, he was promoted to rear admiral and assigned as deputy chief of naval intelligence in early 1945.

Souers had been present during the December 1944 meeting of the Joint Intelligence Staff that effectively killed Donovan's plan for a strong, centralized intelligence service. Instead the committee proposed the plan designed to keep the DCI weak. Souers emphasized in his endorsement of the committee's report, "I am not a candidate for the job of Director and couldn't accept even if it were offered me."[10] Truman then turned around and offered it—or rather ordered him to accept it.

On January 22, 1946, Truman issued a presidential executive order setting up the National Intelligence Authority (NIA), Central Intelligence Group (CIG), and director of central intelligence. It fell, though, to the

National Intelligence Authority, composed of a presidential representative and the secretaries of state, war, and the navy, to flesh out what was a bare-bones presidential directive. It is worth noting that these secretaries represented the departments that would have to give up any authorities that the DCI would acquire under the new arrangement. What President Truman expected the director of central intelligence to do when he issued this executive order was embodied in law when Congress passed the National Security Act in 1947, creating the National Security Council and the Central Intelligence Agency.

With the signing of the executive order, the president presented Souers and Fleet Admiral William D. Leahy, the president's personal military advisor, with rubber daggers and dime-store disguises, telling them that a new era of espionage was upon us: "By virtue of the authority vested in me as Top Dog . . . I charge each of you not only to seek to better our foreign relations through more intensive snooping, but to also keep me informed constantly of the movements and actions of the other, for without such coordination there can be no order and no aura of mutual trust."[11] However, the president's young daughter, Margaret, stole the show as far as the media were concerned. With childlike enthusiasm she attempted to wrest the dagger from the recipients. To reporters, the president explained that CIG simply "combined the intelligence services" of the departments and the president. When asked if this was "a revival of OSS in general," he replied emphatically, "No it is not. It isn't."[12]

Truman was absolutely right. In the beginning, this organization was nothing like OSS. Its main activities were to meet Truman's requirement for "a digest every day, a summary of the dispatches flowing to and from the various departments . . . wherever such messages might have some influence on our foreign policy."[13] And so he started getting the "Daily Summary," a precursor to the now-famous "President's Daily Brief."

The first "Daily Summary" was only a few short paragraphs on large

issues that were surely covered elsewhere. But the president declared himself satisfied. "Here, at last, a coordinated method had been worked out,
and a practical way had been found for keeping the President informed as
to what was known and what was going on."[14] Secretary of State James
Byrnes (who had narrowly missed being vice president under Franklin
Roosevelt instead of Truman) pointed out that since this summary was
purely factual, it wasn't really intelligence. Truman, however, decided that
"it was information which he needed and therefore it was intelligence to
him," as Souers recalled.[15]

Even this modest role of providing "facts" to the president fired up inter-
departmental jealousy. A typical strategy of Souers was to fend off attacks
by giving up power. At the very first meeting of the NIA, Souers actually
requested that a very important part of Truman's executive order be rescinded. This was to exclude the DCI from access to the "policies, actions,
capabilities, and intentions of [the] United States with reference to foreign countries."[16] In other words, CIG was to report on other countries
without knowledge of or reference to what the United States was doing,
planning to do, or capable of doing. All that was deemed to be the domain
of various departments. Intelligence analysts were to be in the position of
a chess player who tries to figure out his opponent's next move without
knowing how his own pieces are arranged.

The adverse effects of Souers's distancing the DCI from U.S. capabilities and intentions were definitely felt in my day. For instance, in the late
seventies a key military issue was whether the Soviets could conduct a dis-
abling surprise attack on our nuclear forces, a "first strike." The military
was concerned about this possibility and wanted to build a new missile of
our own that supposedly would be less vulnerable, the MX. I was persuaded that this was totally unnecessary and directed the CIA to calculate
how many of our retaliatory forces the Soviets could possibly knock out
with a first strike. The secretary of defense objected strongly because this

meant the CIA would have to hypothesize what the capabilities of our own forces were; that is, how they would be deployed, how many submarines would be at sea, and how our forces would react if we saw the attack coming—for example, launching our missiles before those of the Soviets arrived. In his view, since those were U.S. capabilities, the precedent Souers had set precluded the CIA from doing such a study. The secretary of defense and I argued over this procedural issue for more than a year. In exasperation I finally just issued a report showing that after a Soviet first strike that was optimally designed from their point of view, we would still retain an immense retaliatory capability. Unfortunately, the Carter administration was by then coming to an end, and what could have been a valuable addition to the debate on nuclear forces had no impact.

While the military insisted on keeping the DCI out of analyses involving our own forces, they were more than happy to foist covert action onto the DCI. On April 2, 1946, the National Intelligence Authority ordered Souers to absorb the former OSS units that had conducted covert actions such as sabotage, which had been tucked away in a corner of the War Department. "I always felt strongly that CIG and CIA had no business to get involved as a principal in covert operations of a para-military type," Souers later recalled. But in 1946, he did as he was told.[17]

Souers left the position of DCI after five months, the most he would commit to serving. Truman, however, drafted him again, this time to serve as executive secretary of the new National Security Council. Souers recalled, "I recommended, and all parties agreed to, Lieutenant General Hoyt Vandenberg, who was then Deputy Chief of Staff for Intelligence of the Army to be Director." As a military officer, Vandenberg seemed to Souers to "symbolize the nonpolitical angle" of the position of DCI, even though he was a nephew to the powerful Republican senator Arthur Vandenberg. Like Souers, Vandenberg did not want the job, but saw it as a convenient place to wait while the U.S. Air Force was being formed—at which point he hoped to become its chief of staff. Vandenberg had entered flight training straight out of the U.S. Military Academy in 1923. In World War II, Vandenberg's combat missions put him over Tunisia, Sardinia, Sicily, and Italy, and he eventually commanded both the Twelfth and Ninth Air Forces. In 1943, while on the Air Staff in Washington, he had been assigned to Averell Harriman on his mission to Moscow. He also had been chief of staff to the famous flyer General James H. Doolittle, who led the first bombing raid over Tokyo in World War II. At about the same time Souers took over as DCI, Vandenberg had become assistant chief of intelligence of the Army.[18]

Where Souers had stepped lightly, Vandenberg went boldly, or at least made the attempt. Arriving with a number of loyal air force colonels in tow (amusingly, thirty-two years later, when I arrived to be DCI, I brought half a dozen naval officers with me), Vandenberg went behind closed doors with his own people and in ten days offered a plan for CIG that shocked the departmental intelligence chiefs. He wanted power to initiate his own collection and analysis projects, not just to be a compiler of other people's work, and to serve as executive director of the NIA. In some ways, he was aiming to go further than Donovan. His ideas were shuffled off to the side, however. They were seen as distracting from Truman's major national security initiative, the legislation that was to create the Department of Defense, the U.S. Air Force, and the CIA.[19]

Although Truman had set up CIG to provide him with a "newspaper," early in the summer of 1946 CIG received tasking for an analysis, not just reporting. In July, the president, encouraged by his closest advisor, Clark Clifford, who in turn had been encouraged by George Elsey of the White House staff, asked for a study of the Soviet Union. He received two. Clifford asked Elsey to prepare one, but also asked Admiral Leahy to take it to the NIA to be handled by the DCI. Elsey wouldn't complete his report until September, but Truman wanted the report from CIG before he left for a key conference in Paris, which meant almost immediately.[20]

Vandenberg handed the job to Ludwell Montague on Friday, July 19, with a Tuesday deadline. Given the bare-bones staff of the time (about one hundred people working in all of CIG), Montague produced the report practically by himself. Working on Saturday until 9:00 P.M. and Sunday and Monday until 3:00 A.M., he submitted it to the Joint Chiefs and the departmental intelligence agencies on Monday at 2:00 P.M. He then worked until midnight incorporating their comments. He delivered the report, "ORE-1 Soviet Foreign and Military Policy," on Tuesday afternoon. The only way he could have managed this was by relying heavily on materials already available. His key source was a series of cables from one of our diplomats in Moscow, George Kennan.[21] Kennan astutely interpreted where the Soviet Union was going under communism and advocated a policy of containment. The report started with what Stalin had said on February 2: "The Soviet Government anticipates an inevitable conflict with the capitalist world."

The report continued, however, "the Soviet Union needs to avoid such a conflict for an indefinite period." Defining this "indefinite period" became the most important question of the early Cold War years: When would Soviet strength relative to U.S. strength reach a peak? For when it did, in Montague's opinion, there would very likely be a war that could not be stopped by rational arguments, for the Communist approach is "not the result of objective analysis." And, most ominous, the Soviets can wait, because "time is calculably on the side of the Soviet Union, since natural population growth and projected economic development should result in a gradual increase in relative strength."[22] Since the report was largely based on the Kennan cables and military projections, this was nothing Truman had not heard of or read before, but it had the force of a coherent, unified document drawing on the best available information, and the stamp of the Central Intelligence Group. All in all, it was extremely frightening.

As useful as it was to Truman to have someone bring the relevant data together for him, it did not lead to his allowing the DCI to provide original intelligence and analysis. Instead, he blocked the DCI from doing that. Even more disturbing, he did so with the single most important question on the table: When would the Soviets get the A-bomb? When CIG was created, the issue of who would monitor the progress of other nations in the development of nuclear weapons was left in a dangerous limbo. The Manhattan Project was the only body that had expertise in the area, but it was rapidly disbanding. (The Atomic Energy Commission [AEC] would eventually take over its functions and facilities.) The military intelligence services were focused on counting tanks, aircraft, and ships, but not on reporting on emerging weapons systems, especially one as unfamiliar as the A-bomb. It made a lot of sense, then, to transfer the Manhattan Project intelligence unit to CIG. The secretary of the navy, the secretary of war, and Admiral Leahy were all in favor. But the State Department, with Truman's backing, blocked the proposal with an argument against "hasty action." It came to light, however, that what a lot of people in the State Department wanted, including Secretary James Byrnes and his deputy, Dean Acheson (who took over the department in 1949), was to get State involved in collecting and evaluating scientific intelligence. It is difficult to think of an agency less suited for this job, but it happened to fit with overly optimistic plans Truman had for atomic energy.

Truman never doubted that dropping the bomb was the right thing to do, but in some of his utterances one can tell that he was affected by the suffering it had caused. "You have got to understand," Truman told David Lilienthal, his first chairman of the AEC, "that this [the atomic bomb] isn't a military weapon. It is used to wipe out women and children and un-

armed people, and not for military uses. So we have got to treat this differently from rifles and cannon and ordinary things like that."[23] He tried
to treat it very, very differently. Truman wanted to share atomic secrets
with other countries, even the USSR, provided that atomic energy was for
peaceful uses only and that those countries gave the right of inspection to
the United Nations. Under this plan, there would have been little need for
the United States to do any atomic snooping. The UN would handle it. If
we did have an atomic intelligence unit, it would have made sense to put it
in the State Department, which worked most closely with the UN. (Another interesting point about Truman's plan from a contemporary perspective is that it dealt with the possibility of launching a preemptive and
preventive war. Any nation that attempted to build atomic weapons would
have faced immediate attack by the United Nations.)

Truman's dream was an incredible bid for peace, but the Soviets had
other plans. Truman persisted until mid-1949, when he finally became
convinced that the Kremlin would never go for it. During that entire time,
scientific and atomic intelligence foundered in an intelligence vacuum. To
paraphrase Secretary of War Robert Patterson, who was livid about the
inaction and fearful of an atomic Pearl Harbor, the government went
along acting as if atomic power didn't exist—simply because it knew
nothing about it.[24]

Just after CIG was rebuffed in its attempt to fill this void, it did pub-
lish a fully coordinated report on Soviet weapons and capabilities that admitted, "Our real information on [the atomic bomb] is meager."[25] But the
DCI's uncle, Senator Arthur Vandenberg, made it clear that if Truman
wanted the support of Congress for the Truman Doctrine, which supported Greece and Turkey against Communist subversion, he would have
to "scare the hell out of the country."[26] DCI Vandenberg was comfortable
enough with scaring the hell out of the country, despite having no evidence that the Soviets were close to getting the A-bomb or close to build-

ing delivery systems for A-bombs. He evoked the "era of atomic warfare" in testimony before the Senate in 1947.[27]

CIG, then, was providing little in the way of hard intelligence on the A-bomb or Soviet intentions, but it was beginning to provide plenty of fear. A direct Soviet attack "cannot be disregarded," Vandenberg wrote to Truman in August 1946. Despite the lack of Soviet troop movements or any significant delay in Soviet demobilization from World War II force levels, Vandenberg refused to rule out the "possibility of near-term Soviet action."[28]

Still, it is difficult to blame Vandenberg and CIG for inciting panic or overstating the seriousness of the tensions with the USSR. The situation was serious, and CIG was perhaps the calmest voice in the choir. CIG did not, though, push out on its own, break new ground, or question assumptions. There was an opportunity to do this early on, before the new national security apparatus became institutionalized with a host of new competitive players on the scene. That window started closing rapidly in 1947, when a deeply worried Secretary of State George Marshall returned from Europe in late April. The situation in Europe was so untenable, as he saw it, that he pushed through the urgent creation of the Marshall Plan to rebuild Western Europe. He also called on George Kennan to establish the Policy Planning Staff within the State Department to, among other things, prepare studies and reports on "broad politico-military problems."[29] CIG should have been doing something quite similar, but the Policy Planning Staff got going first. Vandenberg's efforts to strengthen the position of DCI again fell flat. After only eleven months he returned to the Army Air Corps, in May 1947. On October 1, he became vice chief of staff of the brand-new U.S. Air Force, and in 1948, its chief of staff.

After having had two DCIs who did not want the job, Truman went for a third reluctant candidate. Rear Admiral Roscoe Hillenkoetter was called in from a post in Paris, which he really didn't want to leave. Hillenkoetter, often referred to as Hilly, seemed tailor-made for DCI—especially at a time when CIG was about to expand into espionage. He had first become involved in intelligence when stationed in Panama in 1923, where he started "something" of a spy network. He'd then gone to Moscow with Ambassador Bullitt, posing as a State Department courier, and next served as naval attaché with Bullitt in Paris. He led the evacuation of the American Embassy there when the Germans invaded. Continuing his service from Vichy, he became deeply involved with the French underground, arranging escapes to North Africa and making a few clandestine trips himself.

Fate then placed him at the next big event that would propel the development of the intelligence services. At Pearl Harbor, as executive officer of the USS *West Virginia*, he was wounded by Japanese bombs and watched his ship sink. During the war, he established an intelligence center for the Pacific Ocean area for Admiral Chester W. Nimitz, then commanding the USS *Dixie*. In 1946, Hillenkoetter was back in Paris. Many of the people he'd helped in the French underground were now in government and willing to supply him with secret information. He felt he was providing a valuable service and, he admitted, he enjoyed the intrigue.[30]

By choosing another former resident of St. Louis, Truman sparked some speculation that he was leaning back to his midwestern roots for people he could trust, but Hillenkoetter and Truman weren't exactly chummy. Of the four DCIs who served him, Truman singled out Hillenkoetter by not mentioning him by name in his memoirs,[31] even as he cited reports that Hillenkoetter helped produce and meetings where he was present. Although Hillenkoetter delivered the Daily Summary each morning, it appears he did little more than drop it off. When asked later about the amount of his contact with the president, he claimed he saw him only once or twice a week. He added that he could call up and get an appointment any time, "within reason," of course.[32] Extremely loyal and dutiful, he seemed to think that the best way to serve the president was to get the information down on paper and then let the president get on with his busy schedule.

Hillenkoetter believed the only reason he was in Washington was to serve the president, even if he didn't agree with the president's direction. One of the first things he noticed and disagreed with was the emphasis on the Daily Summary at the expense of long-term analytical evaluations. But Truman quickly made it clear that he liked the Daily Summary and had set up the CIG to get it. Hillenkoetter allowed the system to go in what he thought was the wrong direction.[33]

Like Souers before him, Hillenkoetter almost immediately undercut his own authority in order to smooth things over with the Army, Navy, and State Department. He entered the job with the authority to "issue orders and directives" for the purpose of coordinating intelligence in other agencies. Apparently with the aim of minimizing friction with the military, he asked that this very useful authority be taken away. Secretary of the Navy James Forrestal (soon to be the first secretary of defense) agreed with this move—vesting this authority in the DCI could make "CIG appear as a Gestapo and cause unnecessary friction."[34] Hillenkoetter made an assumption here that as DCI he could work well with the departments and that Truman would back him up if he couldn't. He was wrong on both counts.

Truman's massive reorganization of the national security apparatus in 1947 had created the National Security Council, but soon thereafter he began to worry that the NSC might usurp his authority. He took a paradoxical approach to maintaining control over it—he didn't go to the meetings. One of his advisors suggested that this "would assure the advisory nature of the Council's actions and guard against its becoming an operating body with the President pressed to resolve spot issues."[35]

Since he was rarely at the NSC meetings, the president was at one remove from the actual directives that governed the CIA through National Security Council Intelligence Directives (NSCIDs). These were the DCI's marching orders, formulated by committee and compromise. In June 1948, the NSC distributed a directive, NSC 10/2, that established the Office of Special Projects (OSP) within the CIA for the purpose of planning and performing covert operations to counter the "vicious" activities of the Soviet Union. The OSP, later renamed the Office of Policy Coordination (OPC), was to operate "independently of other components of the Central Intelligence Agency."[36] Its chief was to be nominated by the secretary of state, the first being a former OSS man, Frank Wisner. Wisner reported to a panel in the State Department chaired by George Kennan and was even housed in the State Department. The OPC, then, was "in" the CIA, but it was not under control of the DCI.

There had been nothing in Hillenkoetter's job description about overseeing covert operations, and he had been opposed to the CIA's taking them on at all. The responsibility came to the CIA through one of the vaguest statements ever written into law. The CIA was directed to "perform such other functions and duties related to intelligence affecting the national security as the President or the National Security Council may from time to time direct."[37] Clark Clifford claimed that the vagueness was intentional. Still, when this idea was on the table, Hillenkoetter objected strongly several times. If State wouldn't allow the DCI to take full control of "this political warfare thing," he wrote, then "let State run it and let it have no connection at all with us." To Souers, then executive secretary of the NSC, he pointed out, "The proposed directive, if enacted, will establish a staff function providing for AUTHORITY in a delicate field of operation—without the RESPONSIBILITY."[38] Hillenkoetter's general counsel told him that the way the directive was written meant that the DCI would be accountable for a portion of the CIA budget without being able to control it and that he would be "giving his personal certification" to unvouchered funds "without any right to control or approve the expenditures in advance or to ascertain the actual propriety."[39] To Hillenkoetter the reasons for this labyrinthine setup were clear: "The State Department representatives were perfectly willing to, and did, direct OPC until mishaps occurred. They then switched to the other side of the street and said that OPC was part of CIA."[40]

Truman wanted the CIA focused on the Daily Summary. The NSC had now mandated that the CIA also take on covert action. There is, though, a wide gap between reporting on current events and secretly supplementing foreign policy with covert actions. In that gap there is analysis of trends and estimates of future developments. Decision-makers in government are happy to know what has been happening, but they really want insight into what is likely to happen next. The Policy Planning Staff of the State Department was partially filling this gap. It was, though, such a natural role for the CIA that it was inevitable it would move into longer-range analysis also.

As mentioned, the most critical area for forecasting in Hillenkoetter's early days was the question of when the Soviet Union would acquire nuclear weapons. In August 1947, Hillenkoetter reported that there was *no* new information on this. This void, however, did not seem alarming. Most of those concerned with this in Washington—scientists, military men, politicians—believed that atomic power would be out of Stalin's reach until at least 1953–1954. Some thought it would take another twenty years. Truman himself "never lost the view that the Soviets weren't Americans and that, technologically, they couldn't keep up."[41] In actual fact, the Soviets were moving quickly toward completing their own bomb. At about the same time that Hillenkoetter said he had no new intelligence, the Soviets were selecting their test site.

As he watched the CIA analysts assemble estimates on the Soviet atomic project, AEC chairman David Lilienthal found that the process "rather chills one's blood." Lilienthal saw a complete "lack of integrity" as the "meager stuff" was written up in a way that covered up their uncertainty and lack of information. The reader, he claimed, "is given the impression, and deliberately, that behind the estimates lies specific knowledge, knowledge so important and delicate that its nature and sources cannot be disclosed or hinted at."[42] But in fact, they had little or nothing to show.

What haunted Lilienthal was that someday a president would have to consider serious actions, including "anticipatory retaliation," as a result of CIA reports and estimates that were based on little or no reliable information. Unless intelligence was improved or at least made more honest, then this president or future presidents might start a preventive war "that may have been utterly needless."[43]

By July 1949, there was new information and the CIA revised its estimate of the Soviet atomic program quite markedly. The Soviets were trying to produce a plutonium bomb rather than sticking with the simpler uranium-235 design. This was good news because the CIA analysts knew that the Manhattan Project had struggled with this problem. If Soviet scientists were on this track, then they would not have a device before mid-1953.

On September 3, 1949, though, an Air Force B-29 equipped with specialized detection equipment picked up unusually high levels of radiation while flying from Japan to Alaska. Other planes pinpointed and tracked the radioactive cloud as it drifted across the Pacific. By September 19, the evidence was deemed conclusive. The Soviets had tested a nuclear device. Even worse—they had tested a plutonium device. Their technology matched ours.

The analysis of the radiation data and the discussion about what to do with it remained walled off from the CIA, however. Truman knew, his top scientists knew, the AEC chairman knew, but Hillenkoetter did not know. And so, the day after Truman learned that the Soviets had the bomb, he received Intelligence Memorandum No. 225 from the CIA, which read, "The earliest possible date by which the USSR might be expected to produce an atomic bomb is mid-1950 and the most probable date is mid-1953."[44] He might well have wondered if the CIA he had created could prevent another Pearl Harbor. Would there ever be a mechanism for accurate long-range forecasting?

In this case, the estimate would not have been so far off the mark if the CIA had known the depths to which Soviet intelligence had penetrated the Manhattan Project. Soon after Truman announced the Soviet test, Klaus Fuchs was arrested in London. Fuchs was a refugee from Germany who had come to Great Britain in 1933 and become a naturalized British subject in 1942. He was a high-level atomic scientist sent over by the British to work on the Manhattan Project, and he had access to information about the separation of uranium isotopes. He had passed a paper on this topic to his Soviet handler in 1944. Fuchs had been under FBI suspicion since 1948, but no one had told the CIA. (The basic physics were not a problem for Soviet scientists, but technical details supplied by people like Fuchs and others saved the Soviets a great deal of time and trouble. Fuchs returned to East Germany after his release from prison in Britain in 1959 and continued to be active in research on nuclear weapons.)

In addition, just as before Pearl Harbor and throughout World War II, some of the best information was in signals intelligence, but the fact that we could break a particular code was a closely held secret. In the Fuchs case, the Army Security Agency (ASA) had the code-breaking function. It shared its decrypts with the FBI but not with the CIA, which was deemed to be infiltrated with Soviet spies. The bitter irony, however, was how readily the FBI and ASA shared information with the hopelessly compromised British intelligence services. Kim Philby, a British intelligence liaison officer and perhaps the USSR's most highly valued mole, learned of Fuchs's pending arrest and attempted to warn him. Meredith Gardner of ASA recalled later how Philby had watched admiringly over his shoulder as he decrypted a message.[45]

These lockouts of the CIA had weakened the agency's potential for predicting one of the most important events of the century—the Soviet Union's acquisition of atomic weapons. This required a strong response. Hillenkoetter drafted a strongly worded memo to FBI director J. Edgar Hoover, but then filed it away and instead went to see him in person. Hoover assured him that "the press reports concerning knowledge of the Fuchs case for several years are entirely erroneous."[46] This was simply not the case. At best, Hoover was being disingenuous. At worst, the director of the FBI was flat-out lying to the DCI. Despite a promise to Hillenkoetter to supply all relevant intelligence, Hoover continued to use devious bureaucratic tactics to keep much of it out of the CIA's hands. The CIA was still begging for information on Fuchs two years later. Unfortunately, even today we see too much of this type of parochialism between intelligence agencies.

In early 1948, there was a similar case of lack of cooperation, this time involving Secretary of State George Marshall personally. He was in Bogotá, Colombia, when a riot broke out. First reports made it look like it was a revolution. As Hillenkoetter heard the reports, he knew he was about to be blamed for an intelligence failure. Weeks before, a report had come in from Colombia speculating on a possible plot to harass Marshall when he arrived for a conference. Hillenkoetter was about to send the report over to the State Department when two of his deputies told him that the U.S. ambassador in Colombia had already seen the report and had vetoed having it sent to State. An ambassador could overrule a DCI because the NSC had set it up so that the senior U.S. representative in the country where the information was collected had control over how it was dissemi-nated. The DCI was completely hamstrung.

Hillenkoetter wanted to disregard this obstacle, but his deputies con-vinced him not to rock the boat. CIA officers in South America were hav-ing considerable difficulties with the U.S. embassies there. Perhaps, if they followed the ambassador's wishes, they could "build up some credit" and get better cooperation. They talked for hours, and Hillenkoetter finally agreed.[47]

Now, with Bogotá burning and Marshall fuming, someone in the State Department let it leak to Congress that the CIA had withheld in-formation about a possible Communist coup in Colombia. Republican representative Clarence J. Brown of Ohio lambasted the DCI and called for an investigation. Hillenkoetter was called to Capitol Hill. His defense was robust, unapologetic, and laid the blame where it belonged, with the ambassador and the NSC directives that prohibited him from overruling the ambassador. He convinced Congress that he was in the clear and Con-gress let the matter drop, but he had to do this on his own: The president had not risen to his defense. Here again, Hillenkoetter had responsibility without authority.

In attempting to find the balance between the Daily Summary and long-range estimating, the CIA undertook a two-year Defense Project. This effort to create an encyclopedic body of work on the Soviet Union largely failed to turn up anything new, surprising, or useful. It was also the sort of intelligence work that was not tailored for presidential consump-tion. More and more, the CIA was catering to the needs of the NSC staff instead of the real decision-makers. Even so, as long as the president re-quired reporting only on immediate issues, there was little chance for long-term analysis to flourish.

There were, though, occasional successes when the CIA did undertake longer-term analyses. In early 1948, General Lucius Clay, our military governor in Berlin, reported a vague personal impression that, he said, "I cannot define, but which now gives me a feeling that [an attack by the USSR] may come with dramatic suddenness."[48] Coincidentally, through a very unusual set of circumstances, I, then a very junior naval officer, had been in a small after-dinner conversational group in London with General Clay just a few weeks prior to his sending this cable. In that discussion Clay said that the Soviets had just brought a division of Mongolian soldiers to the outskirts of their side of Berlin. He was concerned that the Soviets often employed Mongolians as cannon fodder when they expected to go to war and have high initial losses. However, at nearly the same time, DCI Hillenkoetter reported from a more studied analysis at the CIA that there were not sufficient Soviet troop movements to support such an attack. There followed a series of reports that validated this position, and projected it out several months.[49] The tension Clay's telegram had raised was eased by this CIA analysis.

Another area of relatively successful long-range analysis was Korea. An estimate published in October 1948 read: "Withdrawal of U.S. forces from Korea in the spring of 1949 would probably in time be followed by an invasion."[50] This was exactly the sort of "underpinning for policy" that an intelligence organization can and should provide, but the warning was completely ignored. With full agreement of the NSC, Truman pulled the U.S. troops out anyway. CIA analyst and later deputy director for analysis Ray Cline has suggested that while the CIA's warnings about Korea were there, they were not "emphatic" enough.[51] Truman himself recalled that he received warnings and reports of capabilities, "but this did not apply alone to Korea. These same reports also told me repeatedly that there were any other number of spots in the world which Russians 'possessed the ability' to attack."[52] Thus, not only was all the necessary information there, it was conveyed to the right people. Yet it did not provoke the right response. What we can learn from Cline and Truman is that a DCI sometimes has to push the president; sometimes has to cross the line between simply providing information and making a clear and straightforward statement about policy. Hillenkoetter was not the sort of DCI who would do this, especially after being burned in the past.

With his mix of failures and successes, Hillenkoetter faced two investigations of the CIA. The first started only six months after the agency opened its doors. It brought OSS alumnus Allen Dulles into the picture. Dulles had been a harsh critic of the legislation establishing the CIA, so there was little question how his investigation would go. The other investigation was run by Wall Street banker Ferdinand Eberstadt as part of an investigation headed by former president Herbert Hoover. It was a review of the entire national security apparatus. Both investigations ended up being deeply critical of failings in the CIA's analysis, covert actions, and collection efforts. Neither took into account just how much the NSC had hamstrung the CIA, but instead blamed Hillenkoetter's shortcomings as a leader. Truman then began looking for a new DCI.

The last part of Hillenkoetter's CIA career was marked by the failure to predict the North Korean invasion of South Korea. On the very day of the invasion, the current intelligence people put out a report that contained all the indicators of attack—extensive troop movements, evacuation of civilians, suspension of civilian flights, movements of arms and ammunition—but they did not forecast what was coming. Evaluation was not their job. The long-term intelligence people put out a separate report, claiming that the North Koreans had only limited objectives.[53] Truman was so shocked and dismayed when news of the invasion came that he thought it was the opening shots of World War III.

Once again, Hillenkoetter was summoned to Capitol Hill. Once again, he ably defended the agency by showing reports that, in the words of one senator, "clearly showed preparations for an attack."[54] He also managed to convey the fact that his job, as the NSC had defined it, was to collect and disseminate, not to evaluate. Five days later, just over a week after the invasion, Hillenkoetter told the president that he wanted out. He had already heard rumblings about being replaced. The outbreak of war gave him an opportunity to request a return to sea duty rather than to resign outright. Truman had already picked his replacement. In May, when Souers (still executive secretary of the NSC) had asked him what he intended to do about the post, Truman seemed to pull the answer out of the blue: "How would Bedell Smith do?"[55]

General Walter Bedell "Beetle" Smith had briefly attended Butler University in 1912 but was forced to leave during his freshman year after his father became unable to work; Smith then joined the Indiana National Guard. From this meager start, he was probably surprised to find himself Eisenhower's chief of staff in 1942, and to find his picture on the front pages of newspapers around the world as he accepted the German surrender in 1945. An admiring George Marshall had given his career a boost.[56] During the war, Beetle Smith had, as previously noted, saved Donovan's widely disliked COI from utter extinction. After the war, when the president tapped Smith to be ambassador to Moscow, Smith found, much to his dismay, that he had been in uniform for so long that he had a "practically non-existent" civilian wardrobe.[57]

Veneration for Smith has been almost perfectly consistent, as are accounts of his temper and the tension he generated, which he called "some of the less attractive characteristics of my personality . . . acquired at a very early age as an infantry first sergeant." He was remembered as fair, but also feared. At the CIA, he liked to wander the halls, poking his head into random doors to ask questions like "And just what do you do, young man, to earn the taxpayers' dollar?"[58]

Smith's intensity had resulted in several ulcers. In an operation done at the Army's Walter Reed Medical Center in Washington, D.C., a large part of his stomach was removed, and Smith dropped from a powerful 185 pounds to 135. He was still recovering from the surgery when Truman offered him the job. The post looked like a surefire course to another ulcer, and Truman had to resort to a direct order and an appeal to Smith that stressed the gravity of the nation's situation. Smith then used the same technique to get the staff he wanted. For example, William Langer was quite happy back at Harvard after having served as head of Donovan's R&A division. He initially refused Smith's offer to serve as the head of the new Board of National Estimates. Smith wouldn't accept no for an answer. "What can you say to a fella like that?" Langer wrote in his memoirs. "He was ordered down here by the president, and he brought only half his stomach with him!"[59]

Smith simply cowed people by the force of his will, not by getting new NSC directives. As recalled by Fisher Howe, who had gravitated from OSS to the State Department, "He fulfilled his reputation. He could give anybody ulcers. He was imperious but he wanted to hear opposing views. He was just demanding that people be orderly and speak up and say what they meant and defend themselves."[60] The general rode OPC chief Frank Wisner mercilessly and unleashed General Lucian Truscott to, in Truscott's words, "find out what those weirdos are up to."[61] At a meeting of the chiefs of the various intelligence services, Smith was challenged by the Army's chief of intelligence, who had once been a colonel under Smith. "General Smith looked down the table at him, a slight smile on his thin lips," one witness recalled. "'Now, little Alex,' he said, 'you're not going to delay us with nit-picks like that are you?'"[62]

Smith had been on the job only two days when Truman asked him for a series of estimates to be delivered in two days, in advance of his trip to Wake Island to meet General Douglas MacArthur. MacArthur's landing at Inchon on September 15, 1950, was already being talked of as one of the greatest military successes in history. The war was certain to draw to a rapid close. The purpose of the meeting, according to Averell Harriman, then a special assistant to the president, was to ensure that the forthcoming military victory would result in a political victory on the world stage as well.[63]

Smith called the chiefs of the intelligence services to assemble for a meeting at seven that night, October 10, 1950. One of them complained that he had dinner plans, and learned firsthand about some of those less attractive aspects of the new DCI's personality. This was something completely new—a DCI was bossing around the head of an intelligence agency located in another department! Souers and Hillenkoetter would never have dreamed of doing such a thing. Vandenberg and Donovan might have but knew they wouldn't have succeeded. The only differences here were that Smith had direct presidential orders, and he was a former drill sergeant.

The chiefs of the intelligence services assigned each of the president's six requests to six ad hoc committees. Each worked overnight toward an 8:00 A.M. deadline. Although a CIA analyst supervised the teams and they relied on previous CIA reports, this was not a CIA project. The chiefs met in the morning to consider the results, and there was agreement on one critical point: "Barring a Soviet decision for global war," an all-out Chinese intervention in Korea was "not probable in 1950." The Soviets would not start a global war until they had enough bombs. Ever since the Soviet test, the date by which they would have "enough" had steadily moved up. Now, Truman read that "by 1952, [the Soviet] atomic stockpile would be enough to succeed offensively."[64]

In his memoirs, Truman recalled favorably the CIA's performance before the Chinese attack. In his recollection, the reports led him to conclude in early November that "they [the Chinese] were ready for general war."[65] The CIA's own self-assessment was not so forgiving: "ORE's [the analytic branch's] record was little less than disgraceful."[66] No matter what evidence they received, they found reasons to discount it. The initial judgment of the chiefs of the intelligence services that the Chinese would not attack prevailed not because it was convincing but because it was unanimous. The accumulating evidence to the contrary didn't stand a chance. Inside the CIA, the Far Eastern analytical branch placed "almost blind reliance on one individual," according to an internal review, because he'd been on the ground with OSS in China, "and knew personally some of the more important Chinese Communist generals." His experience told him that there would be no invasion, and, "having made up his mind early in the game . . . and having followed this line for a period of time, he continued to follow it in the face of evidence, perhaps from fear of admitting that he had been wrong."[67]

By November 1950, however, the evidence had battered preconceived notions enough for a shift in the CIA's estimate. The situation could "get out of control" as both sides gathered strength.[68] This was too subtle and too late. General Smith himself noted during an NSC meeting on November 9 that the Yalu River, the border between North Korea and China, would freeze over in two weeks to a month, allowing Chinese troops to pass without relying on bridges. He didn't realize that he'd just accurately predicted the timing of the invasion.[69]

On November 25, the attack came across the frozen river, virtually wiping out the Eighth Army, trapping eight thousand marines at the Chosin Reservoir and prompting the longest retreat in U.S. military history. Chairman of the JCS Omar Bradley felt that both the Joint Chiefs and the entire cabinet had "failed the President." Dean Acheson would later write that "none of us, myself prominently included, served him as he was entitled to be served."[70]

One of Smith's most ambitious goals as DCI was to do away with the emphasis on current intelligence and place more on long-term intelligence—specifically long-term estimates for the president. Given the series of failures and alleged failures that the CIA had already weathered, it's not surprising that the analysts were wary of a more predictive role. They knew that their conclusions, in the words of analyst R. Jack Smith, sometimes "would rest on very thin ice." In addition, in the early days of the CIA, several items had been taken off the table by NSC members attempting to protect their turfs. One of these was political intelligence, which was deemed to be the area of the secretary of state. Now, it is hard to do long-range estimates without getting into foreign policy. Souers and Hillenkoetter were not assertive here, and the CIA's long-range intelligence suffered. Smith tried a new approach. He simply told the secretary of state that the State Department had authority over political reporting, but allowed the CIA to stray into this area because the department's performance was lacking.[71]

One important example concerned developing events in Guatemala. Smith had agents on the ground who detected Communist infiltration into the government of Jacobo Arbenz Guzmán. The State Department, however, saw that same government as "qualified and encouraging from our viewpoint."[72] Smith filed a report without coordinating it with the community at large, suggesting that there was a real possibility of the present government falling under Soviet influence.[73] Similarly, Smith approved sending a report on Iran to Truman that differed substantially from a report that had been "coordinated with" (and rewritten by) the State Department. The people at State cried foul: The report was "almost completely political intelligence," and this had to stop. Smith's deputies, however, were instructed to pass such complaints to him. If there was a problem, it wouldn't be sorted out at the working level—it was strictly between himself, the secretary of state, and the commander in chief.[74] Smith's philosophy was simple—no one would stand between him and the president.

The one place Smith found he had to play by the rules was during meetings of the National Security Council. On one occasion he spoke up on a political topic during an NSC meeting. Much to the general's embarrassment, Truman reminded him that the secretary of state was present, and that he, Smith, was out of line.[75]

Just as the State Department wanted control over "political intelligence," the military insisted on following the precedent Souers had set of the DCI's remaining in the dark about the United States' military resources and capabilities. This made the CIA's job difficult, especially when the secretary of defense (by now George Marshall had come out of retirement to take the job) asked for an estimate on the likelihood of an attack on Japan. How do you accommodate such a request when you are, to use the words of one of the CIA's early analytic icons, Sherman Kent, "not permitted to introduce the thought that American forces were actually in the Far East"? Instead of letting Marshall's request die, though, Kent continued, "We shamelessly war gamed that estimate."[76] To his surprise, it went through the chiefs of the intelligence services. However, Smith and the director of naval intelligence fought over the conclusions of the report, with the admiral claiming that the Soviets wouldn't attack Japan unless there were a general all-out war with the Soviet Union, and Smith's arguing that they wouldn't attack even if there were such a war. Smith was in the minority. Usually, minority dissents were placed in footnotes. In this case, Smith simply told the chiefs that his opinion would be presented as the conclusion of the report. It was his estimate, and his opinion would go to the president.[77] This was a precedent, in my opinion, of great value to those of us who followed Beetle Smith.

Meanwhile, Smith was making semisecret Friday morning trips to the Oval Office to present Truman with a weekly briefing on Korea. In his packets of information was an order-of-battle map of Korea—exactly the kind of information the CIA was not supposed to provide the president without full coordination with the armed services. These briefings took place the day after the NSC meetings where General Bradley made his presentations on Korea. Truman was getting a second opinion from his DCI. At the NSC meetings, Smith kept his opinions about Korea to himself. However, claimed one CIA employee, "Smith's chief concern was to make himself letter-perfect on the situation in Korea and to make his Korean situation map more precise than General Bradley's." He must have received encouragement from the president; in contrast to the normal atmosphere of tension that surrounded Smith, when he returned from these meetings at the White House, he was "almost always in a jovial mood."[78]

In the spring of 1952, signals intelligence revealed formations of Soviet TU-4 bombers flying into Siberian bases in alarming numbers. Some thought it looked like preparation for an all-out attack. Smith helped convince Truman that they had to send in reconnaissance aircraft to see if a surprise attack was coming. Finally, in August, Truman looked at the plans. Although he denied it later, Truman had approved overflights of the USSR as early as the fall of 1950, without a lot of pressure on him. "Listen, when you get back there," he told an air force general as he signed off on the flights, "you tell General Vandenberg from me, 'Why in the devil hasn't he been doing this before?'" Soon there were as many as forty-seven planes in Soviet airspace at a time.[79]

In 1952, however, the situation was different. Previous flights had relied on gaps in air defenses; this one would be going directly over air bases. The commanding officer confessed that this mission made him feel like he was sending Christ to Calvary. The reconnaissance planes were chased but got out safely, and later intelligence revealed that the Soviet regional commander had been fired for letting them get away. The photographs revealed that bombers were not being massed. The mission seemed to prove how cooperation between the CIA and the military could give the president specific information about a possible surprise attack.[80]

Another of Smith's actions with far-reaching impact on the CIA was gaining control over covert action. No longer was there a split between responsibility and authority. In bringing this about, though, Smith invited the covert operations foxes into the hen house. While it was imperative to have the office of covert action be responsible to someone, once it was both in and of the CIA, it soon threatened to dominate the entire organization. In part this was because Smith hired Allen Dulles. He, along with Frank Wisner, oversaw an age of covert action led by the CIA. They moved to place espionage and covert action in the same organization, against Smith's express wishes. What concerned Smith was that covert operations could take over an intelligence organization and skew the intelligence in support of the operations.

In a 1951 staff conference, Smith indicated that operations were taking over, the intelligence side was losing out, and "we have almost arrived at a stage where it is necessary to decide whether CIA will remain an intelligence agency or become a 'cold war department.'" He repeated himself in 1952, stating firmly that "the Agency's primary mission was intelligence" and that he would "do nothing that militated against accomplishing this objective."[81]

At the same time, he had become quite aware of the limits of intelligence in prediction. "Despite the utmost vigilance . . . there is no real assurance that, in the event of sudden undeclared hostilities, certain advance warning can be given," he told the NSC in the last year of his directorship.[82] To a friend, he confessed that being DCI was "one of those jobs where one can never be right as the American people expect the incumbent to be able to predict with accuracy just what Stalin is likely to do three months from today at 5:30 a.m. . . . Furthermore, whenever there is a failure, everybody begins to shriek 'intelligence' and with a political November coming up, the immediate prospect is even more gloomy."[83]

Truman made one final contribution to the relationship between the president and the CIA by instituting intelligence briefings for the major political candidates. Recalling how little he knew when he took office, it's easy to believe that he was sincere in his desire to make sure the next president wasn't as burdened. Eisenhower at first declined this offer, sensing a political motive, which prompted an angry handwritten note from Truman (a prerogative of an outgoing president): "Partisan politics should stop at the boundaries of the United States. I am extremely sorry that you have allowed a bunch of screwballs to come between us."[84] Soon, however, Eisenhower was receiving briefings, and after the election Smith started to look forward to working again with his former commander.

"You know what I want," Smith told Eisenhower: "to be Chairman of the Joint Chiefs of Staff." Now, this was a lot to ask, and Smith knew it. But at the very least, he was willing to stay on as DCI. The incoming president threw cold water on his plans immediately. He wanted Smith as undersecretary of state. Whatever the reasons for this, none of them were convincing to Smith, who muttered as he returned to his office, "And I thought it was going to be great." Smith made sure to check in with Truman and ask if he had any objection to his DCI accepting a political appointment from an incoming Republican. When Truman later told this story, the memory of Smith's loyalty moved him to tears.[85]

Smith was to serve under the new secretary of state, John Foster Dulles, the brother of Allen Dulles, who was to become the new DCI. The stage was set for what became known as the golden age of covert operations—over a decade of skulduggery. And we are still adding up the costs.

CHAPTER THREE

DWIGHT D. EISENHOWER AND ALLEN DULLES

The CIA Is Thrust into Action

The directors of central intelligence who served Harry Truman had a president who was skeptical of the reliability, trustworthiness, and objectivity of his intelligence apparatus. Dwight Eisenhower, in contrast, was a president who appreciated the value of good intelligence, having actually employed it to military advantage. He had seen firsthand the invaluable insights into enemy intentions, plans, and dispositions yielded by communications intelligence like ULTRA (involved in breaking the German Enigma codes) and tactical intelligence from the field. He had also seen the consequences of intelligence failures, particularly during the Germans' Ardennes offensive, the Battle of the Bulge. So he had a sophisticated appreciation of the vagaries and limitations of intelligence data and estimates. Accordingly, he welcomed diverse views and took the intelligence provided him with an understanding of its limitations. Moreover, having participated in World War II in such a high position, he had a broad, long-term view of world affairs and wanted intelligence to match that outlook.

Having such a well-informed and positively inclined consumer of intelligence is just what encourages intelligence analysts to be open-minded and inquiring. Moreover, as it turned out, Ike and his DCI were in office together for eight years, as opposed to the previous five years during which four DCIs directed our intelligence. This continuity offered an opportunity for building a strong foundation under the incipient intelligence program established by the National Security Act of 1947, especially so for the analytic branch of the CIA.

Unfortunately, the opportunity did not materialize, because of the personality of Ike's DCI. Yet Eisenhower's choice, Allen Dulles, ended up setting a record by serving in that position longer than anyone before or since, eight years and nine months. He and I are the only DCIs to have lasted the entire term(s) of their presidents. Dulles was also the first civilian to be a DCI and the first of four alumni of the OSS.

In the OSS, he started by serving in New York but shifted to a post in Switzerland because he was tired of "a lot of generals looking over my shoulder." From Switzerland he controlled operatives conducting espionage behind Nazi lines. He proved to be a hardheaded pragmatist not above negotiating with Nazis if he thought he could get results. He loved the intrigue of his job.

Dulles was a relentless self-promoter. For instance, he made sure a tale of his early career entered into CIA legend. While serving with the American legation in Bern, Switzerland, in 1917, he received a call on April 11 from a Russian expatriate who demanded a meeting that afternoon. Dulles was alone in the office and dismissed the caller because he had a date with a young lady. The Russian insisted that a visit the next day instead was impossible, but Dulles stood firm and went ahead with his plans. The caller, Vladimir Ilyich Lenin, caught a train to St. Petersburg on April 17 and went on to establish the USSR.

When Ike chose Allen's brother, John Foster, to be secretary of state, there were people inside and outside the CIA who thought it was inappropriate for brothers to be appointed to those two positions at the same time. Only Allen's experience in the OSS and, more recently, in the CIA, got him through the confirmation process with the Senate. Ike was likely impressed with Allen's ability to acquire information, as demonstrated during his years in the OSS. Beyond that, Ike did want a strong link between the State Department and the CIA to make it less likely that the latter would fall under the sway of the military. Ike was intimately familiar with how the military could use and distort intelligence to suit its own ends—particularly when it came to getting more money from Congress.

The time Dulles served in the OSS should have been a great background for being DCI. There was a problem, though. His OSS experience left him well versed in espionage and covert action, but not the least versed or interested in managing a large organization. In fact, he had not been assigned to a managerial position in the OSS because Donovan, himself no manager, saw Dulles as "such a damned poor administrator."[1] Whereas Eisenhower brought a military discipline to the White House, with clear chains of command, Dulles broke those lines almost every day in micromanaging the CIA. "Allen's habit," one officer recalled, "was to reach down into his organization as far as he wanted to go." Of course, this caused problems, especially when he gave orders without passing them through the middle levels. When a CIA officer once pointed this out to him, "he turned on me and said, 'I am not going to be walled off from anyone in this organization. . . . I'm going to talk to whoever I want.'"[2] In this and many other ways, Allen Dulles and Dwight Eisenhower could not have been more different. Ike was shaped by the culture of the army officer class. Dulles had a far more "cosmopolitan" background in law and the Foreign Service.

With his background in espionage and covert action, it was no wonder that Dulles, as DCI, spent about 75 percent of his time on them. The remaining 25 percent was almost certainly not adequate to meet three other key demands on any DCI, over and above being the president's intelligence advisor: reviewing analyses and estimates; managing the Intelligence Community—that is, getting fifteen separate intelligence agencies to work together (see Appendix A); and shepherding new techniques of intelligence into being as technology made them available.

On this last responsibility, Dulles had become DCI at a time when intelligence was becoming much more technical and much more professional than it had been back in Donovan's days. Specialists were coming into the organization who had little time for the legendary, more colorful days of the gentleman spies and academics of the OSS. "You are taking all the fun out of intelligence," Dulles told one technical specialist during a briefing. According to one colleague: "Dulles measured things in terms of espionage—how hard would it be to steal?"[3] That was the kind of activity he loved. It was odd behavior and an odd career choice, he often remarked, for a man who had been raised by a Presbyterian minister.

With respect to the burgeoning technical systems for collecting intelligence, the president had a strong interest in signals intelligence. After all, he had employed intercepts of German messages under the ULTRA program to help defeat Germany in World War II. Ike also gave the go-ahead in 1954 for the development and deployment of the U-2 high-flying spy aircraft. Here, the president had seen the immediate operational value to a military commander of aerial photography. While Dulles, too, was thrilled with the U-2, he also saw it as competition for espionage. It is ironic that Dulles, a master of human spying, was leading American intelligence into a new era in which collecting data by technical means would grow greatly in importance. It is not that technical means were to become more important than human spying. Nor is it that they are more competitive, inasmuch as the costs of human agents are infinitesimally less than that of electronic listening and photographic systems. What was needed was to find ways to make technical and human systems complement each other, a job for which Dulles was ill-equipped.

Until the U-2 came on line in 1956, aerial photographs had always been taken at some considerable risk to the pilots. Cruising at about seventy thousand feet, the U-2 appeared to be invulnerable to antiaircraft fire. Nonetheless, Ike insisted on personally clearing every U-2 mission that flew over the Soviet Union. Perhaps this was because he assumed there would still be risks. Or perhaps the boldness of flying right over the heart of the Soviet Union was truly rubbing it in and he wanted to control when and how much of that we did. In my day we ran some daring submarine missions right into Soviet territorial waters to collect intelligence. (Similarly, I took each of these proposals to President Carter for approval. Our subs might have been detected operating illegally in Soviet territorial waters and possibly even attacked. It was simply beyond my pay grade to commit the nation to an activity that could have had consequences ranging from being seriously embarrassing to starting a war.)

On May 1, 1960, after almost four years and some twenty U-2 missions, Ike's fears were realized. Francis Gary Powers and his U-2 were shot down. Dulles advised Ike that there was no likelihood Powers would have survived ejection from such an altitude and, besides, Powers had been given a poison pill to take. This, though, was hardly Dulles's field of expertise; but his brother, Secretary of State John Foster Dulles, insisted that the Soviets would not want to acknowledge that a U.S. aircraft had been able to penetrate so far into Soviet airspace. The president immediately denied that he was personally responsible. Within two weeks, however, the Soviets displayed not only the wreckage of the aircraft but Francis Gary Powers, very much alive.

This incident tested a doctrine known as "plausible deniability"; that is, that a president can deny his personal involvement in something like a U-2 program and blame it on others. There was a time when heads of state could get away with such dissimulation. In this case, Ike finally had to acknowledge his responsibility because it was now an age when such actions as flying boldly into someone else's territorial air space or driving submarines into territorial waters could trigger a nuclear war. It would have looked bad for Ike to acknowledge that he was not in control of the risks we were taking.

In response to the Powers incident, the Soviets withdrew from a summit meeting between Eisenhower and Soviet Premier Nikita Khrushchev scheduled for Paris later in May. Ike, thus, had to pay what for him was a high price for this spying adventure. The summit was an opportunity he had wanted very much, and the cancellation left him very discouraged. Francis Gary Powers, then, very likely took down with him the doctrine of plausible deniability. After twenty-one months of incarceration in the Soviet Union, Powers came home in a trade for a Soviet spy we had captured, Rudolf Abel. The exchange took place at the middle of a bridge in Potsdam, Germany. When Powers died in a crash while flying a television news helicopter in Los Angeles on August 1, 1977, I represented the CIA at his funeral in Arlington National Cemetery.

With respect to another of a DCI's responsibilities, that of managing the Intelligence Community—the CIA and the fourteen intelligence agencies within the various departments—this was not what Dulles liked doing or was suited for. It also was not yet a developed concept. The National Security Act does charge the DCI with coordinating the efforts of all intelligence agencies; it does not, however, lay out any specifics about how to do that nor assign any particular authorities for doing it. Back in rather than later. This juxtaposition turned out to be unfortunate for the CIA. In the world of intelligence, there is always a clash between long-term forecasting and current reporting. The tendency is for the current to drive out the long-term. Decision-makers can easily become so busy that they will not take time to absorb a long-range estimate, and when long-range forecasters are not appreciated, the better ones look for a more rewarding career path. The CIA is then deprived of the institutional knowledge vital to the art of forecasting. While intelligence must focus on what is happening in the immediate present, it must also keep an eye on future possibilities and probabilities. During Dulles's tenure, with a president keenly aware of the longer term, he had an ideal opportunity to nurture the talents of those skilled at long-term forecasting. With a DCI who lacked interest in forecasting, it did not work out that way.

One controversial device of long-term estimating is what is known as "net assessment." Such assessments involve comparisons of us and them: for example, the strengths of our economy compared with Russia's, or the number of offensive missiles we have versus Russian missile defenses. In the army, Ike was accustomed to receiving commander's estimates, or net estimates, which took into account both enemy and friendly forces. Under Truman, the CIA had been blocked by the military from providing such assessments on the grounds that this was stepping beyond the realm of intelligence. Intelligence, after all, is about other people's forces and capabilities, not our own. Eisenhower wouldn't stand for such a restriction. During his term in office, the CIA had the opportunity to produce net estimates, but Dulles was either not interested or not willing to tangle with the military on this.

The prohibition on intelligence analysts doing net assessments under Truman reflected the original deal that Sidney Souers, as the first DCI, had made: that intelligence analysts would not share in or utilize data about our own forces. With Dulles not having seized the opportunity Ike

Dulles's time, he was not even chairman of the committee established to do coordination. It is understandable that the combination of Dulles's own proclivities and the incipient nature of the Intelligence Community led to his neglect of this function of the DCI.

As for the third responsibility of DCIs, that of producing intelligence reports and estimates, Dulles played his role in a strange manner. One way most DCIs do this is to debate differing interpretations of the same data by various agencies. The objective is to bring out the best of differing interpretations of the facts. Dulles, however, rather than debate and argue out differences, especially with the military intelligence services, was inclined simply to compromise. CIA analyst Ray Cline wrote in an internal memo that Beetle Smith's policy of overruling the military if appropriate "is never voiced now. . . . A threat from a single agency to dissent on a phrase is enough to send the Office of National Estimates into a desperate search for a compromise solution."[4] This procedure resulted in Ike's receiving reports in which the Department of Defense's perceived self-interest in overestimating the size of the threat had undue weight. He deserved to get the CIA's unvarnished opinion in addition to a military view.

When Ike read National Intelligence Estimates (NIEs) on military issues, he did not bother much with the numerous dissenting footnotes. These were almost always from the Air Force, Army, or Navy, and the president felt their dissents were self-serving and territorial.

Ike had problems even with the majority opinions he received. He found these were often watered down: "Is this the best they can do at bringing out the issues and resolving them?"[5] he asked; and he noted that one estimate "could have been written by a high school student."[6] As he saw it, the process of watering down estimates was leaving them with no bite. According to Ike's staff secretary, General Andrew J. Goodpaster, "Allen just didn't have the strength of position or personality to drive toward the resolution of differences. . . ."[7] That was a pity, because had

Dulles pushed for the CIA's view against that of the military, he would likely have had the backing of the president.

Another area of contention in which Dulles's disinterest in analysis was damaging was in his appraisal of the overall strength of the Soviet Union vis-à-vis that of the United States. He came at these estimates with preconceived views that were frequently at odds not only with his own analysts but also with the president. Dulles, nonetheless, continued to present Eisenhower with estimates maintaining that the USSR was growing much stronger strategically than it actually was, and much stronger than Ike thought it was. Dulles's alarmist view of the military balance with the Soviet Union conflicted not only with Ike's but also with the CIA's analysts'. When he thought those analysts were not alarmist enough, he would attach his own note, typically much more shrill, to an estimate rather than argue it out with them. This was an unfortunate approach, in my opinion. To begin with, it does not give the analysts the benefit of the DCI's insights into the issue, which may be informed from a wider, different perspective. Equally, it fails to help the DCI if he or she misunderstands the subject. It can be beneficial for a DCI to have to defend his or her view before a group of experts.

Typical of Dulles's disinclination to debate with his analysts was his response in 1953 to a CIA estimate that included the assumption that "there will not be a general war within the period of this estimate."[8] In the opinion of the estimate, the United States remained dominant. The growth rate of the Soviet economy would be high, but their output would be far lower than ours—a quarter to a third that of the United States. The gap was widening in our favor, and if that were not enough, the scientific assets of the United States would remain greater. Was time on our side? Without a doubt. But less than a month later, Dulles took it upon himself to put out his own position, stating, "If the USSR continues its present

policies it will close the economic gap now existing between it and the United States. From this point of view time is on the side of the USSR."[9]

One month later, Dulles had the CIA put out an estimate that stated the USSR would not have 180, but 200, heavy bombers in 1955. And this increase in military production would go on at the same time that the USSR increased production of consumer goods and embarked on an adventure designed by Khrushchev to increase wheat production—the "Virgin Lands" program. The USSR simply did not have the resources to do everything, and the economists at the CIA knew it. But when it came time to write the estimates, the military wanted to see pumped-up bomber figures. Allen Dulles, eager to avoid a fight with the armed services, let them have their way.

On the matter of strategic balance with the Soviet Union, Dulles, in taking a more narrow perspective than that of the president, was counting what the Soviets were doing at that time and extrapolating forward. In contrast, the president was looking at the long-term, underlying strengths and weaknesses of the Soviet Union. Eisenhower firmly believed that we would ultimately prevail. "I have pled with America to look facts in the face . . . to realize that we are 160 million of the most productive and the most intelligent people on earth; therefore why are we going around being so scared?"[10] When he looked at the Soviet Union's unbalanced, command economy, at America's technological edge, and at our vastly superior quality of life, he saw a one-sided battle. The way forward, he believed, was to keep a level head, a balanced budget, and not get carried away with defense spending.

There was, then, quite a contrast between a president who thought in terms of the long run and even acted on the basis of longer-term estimates and a DCI who was primarily interested in undertaking successful covert actions and espionage that would lead to productive results sooner

presented to reverse that position, the CIA did not move into the business of net assessment. The ethic of intelligence ever since—unfortunately, in my view—has been to stay away from net assessments.

Ike saw the value of receiving net assessments from his intelligence arm. He was also willing to nudge the DCI into giving advice on policy matters. This latter runs up against one of the most widely accepted ethics of American intelligence. That is, that intelligence officers eschew taking positions on policy matters lest it even appear that their intelligence estimates are slanted to support those positions. There is, though, another side to that coin. Almost all advisors to a president have policy positions they are attempting to sell to the president. A DCI can offer less biased, more neutral advice since intelligence agencies do not have institutional positions in favor of one policy or another. For instance, on several occasions President Carter took me aside and asked my opinion on some policy change he was considering.

An example of this practice was Ike's quest for what position the United States should take on Vietnam in 1953. Well before the French collapse at Dien Bien Phu in May 1954, CIA estimates said that the French situation was deteriorating rapidly. In trying to decide what the United States should do in response to this, the president found himself frustrated by the inadequacy of the ideas coming out of the normal decision-making process. He appointed a special high-level committee to come up with policy recommendations. Significantly, he included Allen Dulles on it. That could have been to ensure the committee always had the latest intelligence with which to work. It could also have been because he wanted Dulles's views to be included. As it turned out, one of the recommendations Ike received, encouraged by Admiral Arthur Radford, chairman of the Joint Chiefs of Staff and supported by Vice President Nixon, was to drop two or three nuclear weapons to clear out Ho Chi Minh's forces that were besieging Dien Bien Phu. Ike asked the CIA to forecast the expected reaction of the world community to such an attack. He was grateful for the CIA's report, which predicted that our use of nuclear weapons would ignite a third world war. This intelligence estimate, then, had a decisive impact on the policy process, helping keep the hawks at bay.

In fact, estimating foreign reaction to moves the United States might make is a quite legitimate part of intelligence. Policy-makers, indeed, ought to be interested in what others will say and do in response to what we do. Such estimating, however, is also a handy dodge around the idea that a DCI should not be involved in policy. If a DCI wants to oppose or support a policy, he or she can offer a view that some other country's reaction to it would likely be very bad or good.

One other area where Ike turned to the CIA for help was in economic forecasting. Early in his presidency, the CIA greatly overestimated the economic potential of the Soviets. What had happened was that in January 1951, during Truman's presidency, Beetle Smith had brought into the CIA an economics professor from MIT, Max Millikan. The CIA was badly lacking in economic expertise. Millikan was far from being an expert on the Soviet Union, but he saw it as an economic powerhouse.

By July 1953, however, the CIA's reports began to paint a much less frightening picture. While the Soviets' rate of growth was seen as astounding, it could not possibly continue; the technological advances would level off, and the economy would suffer from the government's emphasis on heavy industry at the expense of agriculture and consumer goods. This change in tone was due in large measure to Ray S. Cline, a CIA analyst who had recently returned from an assignment in London. Cline, like so many in the agency at that time, hailed from the Ivy League and the OSS. Unlike most of his swashbuckling colleagues, though, he was attracted to the analytic branch of OSS rather than that of covert operations and espionage.

The new tone Cline introduced clearly resonated with the president. After Ike had seen that the CIA could be objective with economic data, he directed that Cline and the CIA take primary responsibility for a recurring estimate of the Soviet economy. The Departments of State and Defense had previously handled this but had not given this area very high priority. As a consequence of the president's keen interest, Cline began making frequent trips to the White House at the side of Dulles. Dulles and Cline, then, deserve credit for directing the CIA into becoming the premier source of foreign economic data in our government. It was true of the CIA in my day, and I believe still is today.

At the same time, Dulles was never reconciled to a less than cataclysmic view of Soviet capabilities, be they military or economic. Flying in the face of the numbers that Cline's people produced, in 1960 Dulles told Congress that the Soviet economy presented the gravest danger our country had ever faced in peacetime. In light of this continuing philosophical difference between the president and his DCI with respect to Soviet power, and Dulles's disinclination to do the net assessments Ike wanted, it seems surprising that Ike kept him on as DCI. He did so even though Dulles refused to take the blame when it looked like America had been caught off guard during the Suez Crisis. Instead, Dulles leaked CIA reports on this to the press and publicly defended himself, causing the president considerable embarrassment. He also failed to admit that the CIA had been quite wrong in predicting that Hungary would not rise up against the Soviet Union, and took no responsibility for the fact that the CIA had actively mounted an operation, RED SOX/RED CAP, to encourage an uprising there while knowing that the United States would not back the rebels once things got going.

Another problem between the president and his DCI, one that had the potential to drive Eisenhower crazy, was that Dulles was not always terribly responsive. On one occasion, there was a serious delay in getting a critical piece of information to the White House. Eisenhower dispatched Goodpaster to explain to Dulles that if this happened again, the data had to be sent immediately. Dulles responded that his analysts always wanted to evaluate the information first. In fact, they insisted. This went through another round before Dulles was called on the Oval Office carpet. "[Dulles] used a very unfortunate term," Goodpaster recalled. "He said 'We can't let you have it.' "[11]

After the 1952 election, Truman had wondered out loud about how Eisenhower would deal with situations like this. "He'll sit here, and he'll say, 'Do this! Do that!' And nothing will happen. Poor Ike—it won't be a bit like the Army. He'll find it very frustrating."[12] Truman's prediction proved accurate at times like these. According to Andy Goodpaster, "Eisenhower was a man of terrific temper, and he was very proud of his ability to control his temper." But after Dulles told him he couldn't have the information he wanted, "this one time he really flashed up."[13]

Another time, after Dulles misunderstood Ike's wishes following a meeting, the president decided that Goodpaster had to be there for all of Dulles's Oval Office briefings. These were frequent, because Eisenhower liked to get to the bottom of things. He had plenty of questions about the statements made in National Intelligence Estimates and current intelligence reports, and in Allen Dulles's briefings for the National Security Council.

Dulles was expected to open each NSC meeting with a quick run-down of the world situation, but he was by no means given full ownership of the floor. Ike would frequently interrupt with questions—mostly along the lines of "How do we know that?" Since the answer often went to secret sources and methods, and Dulles did not want to reveal them in a crowded room, these conversations took place off to the side. Other times, Eisenhower would tell him bluntly that he'd held the floor too long: "Okay, Allen, let's go ahead."[14]

In late 1958, a commission headed by former secretary of defense

Robert Lovett surveyed the CIA. It came to a conclusion that there was a lack of administrative cohesion. Most particularly there was a lack of adequate internal communication. It recommended that Allen Dulles take on a strong administrator as a deputy. Dulles refused. This forced the president to choose between firing Dulles in order to acquire an administrator as the commission had recommended or keeping Dulles and ignoring the problem of administration. He concluded that Dulles's genius as an intelligence craftsman rendered him indispensable. Still another factor that made Ike accept Dulles's shortcomings was the friendly chemistry, even casual familiarity, between them. Dulles was even permitted to wear bedroom slippers in the Oval Office because he was suffering from gout. Eisenhower's loyalty to Dulles was impressive: "I have two alternatives, either to get rid of him [Dulles] and appoint someone who will assert more authority or keep him with his limitations. I'd rather have Allen as my chief intelligence officer with his limitations than anyone I know."[15] He seemed to accept the fact that well-coordinated reports and an authoritative DCI were not going to happen. He got a reminder of what this could mean in August 1957. Dulles reported to the NSC that there was nothing "new or dramatic" in the Soviet Intercontinental Ballistic Missile (ICBM) program. By the end of the month, the Soviets tested their first ICBM.[16] Two months later, *Sputnik I* was in orbit.

Where the two of them did harmonize most was on covert action. Eisenhower strongly wished to avoid a conventional military buildup. Covert actions were an alternative way to project U.S. power with minimal cost in both dollars and American lives. One of Ike's first expressions of interest in covert action came during the deliberations on Vietnam in 1953. Ike told the NSC that he "could not imagine the United States putting ground forces anywhere in Southeast Asia,"[17] but he was open to the covert route in Vietnam, maybe an air action using "a little group of fine and adventurous pilots"; or maybe through finding and supporting "a good

Buddhist leader to whip up some real fervor" (he then laughed when someone pointed out that "unhappily Buddha was a pacifist rather than a fighter"). The other problem, as Allen Dulles reported, was that most of the Vietnamese civilians supported the guerrillas.[18] Eisenhower kept the covert track alive long after he dismissed overt. He said that if we were ever to get involved in Southeast Asia, it would be ultra-secret, "and we would deny it forever."[19]

Eisenhower's and Dulles's first real use of covert action was in Iran in August 1953. Mohammad Mossadegh had been chosen to be prime minister by the Iranian parliament, the Majlis, back in 1951. He was, in our eyes and those of the British, more anti-shah than pro-Communist, but he was becoming more and more isolated from the non-Communist political spectrum. The British, whose oil interests in Iran had been nationalized by Mossadegh, urged Ike to join with them in toppling Mossadegh from power. The president readily agreed. When CIA operatives persuaded the shah to dismiss Mossadegh, the fat was in the fire. There were demonstrations and counterdemonstrations in the streets of Tehran. In the midst of these the shah got cold feet and left the country (something we were to see again when I was DCI). With the CIA using both persuasion and bribery on the side of the shah, however, the tide tipped his way. He returned to Iran and to the Peacock Throne and Mossadegh was ousted. It is worth noting that political conditions inside Iran were ripe for a change and Mossadegh's political base was weak. What the CIA had to do, and did well using only a few people and a modest amount of money, was to apply the final push.

When people talk about the CIA and covert action, the case of Iran in 1953 inevitably comes to mind because it was swift, neat, and successful. It was not long before it ceased to be covert, however. In the electoral campaign of 1954, Ike himself was boasting of what this action said about his administration's effectiveness and prowess. (There are those, however, who believe this covert action came back to bite us in 1979–1980, when anti-

American Iranians captured our embassy and held fifty-two Americans hostage for 444 days. The demonstrations in the streets at that time were focused on driving out "The Great Satan of the USA.")

With the success in Iran behind them, Ike and Dulles were soon at it again. This time it was in our backyard—Guatemala. Again we thought the president, Jacobo Arbenz Guzmán, was tilting toward the Communists. After several riots sparked by right-wing demonstrations, Arbenz banned anti-Communist demonstrations in the capital. He also proposed land reform, which would have taken money and property right out of the pockets of the United Fruit Company—former clients of the Dulles brothers' law firm. United Fruit threatened to pull out of the country, but also started providing support to a small group of rebels under Colonel Carlos Castillo Armas.

Armas was secretly preparing his rebel army in Costa Rica and crossed the border into Guatemala on June 18, 1954. The most meaningful part of the invasion, though, was a CIA-operated radio station. Masquerading as the rebels' tactical military network, it broadcast word of how rapidly the invasion forces were supposedly proceeding toward the capital and how strong these forces supposedly were. When the radio reported that the invasion force was nearing the capital, the government resigned and evacuated. The invaders were so far away they had to be flown to the capital for their victory parade. Here again, the government, which was overthrown, was pretty weak. And again, the question arises as to the propriety of our action. Guatemala has not had a truly strong, effective government since.

Once more, the covert action was not covert for long. Dulles's predilection for self-promotion got the better of him. He supplied the *Saturday Evening Post* with information for an article on the CIA's role in the coup (minus the mistakes and missteps). On July 4, trying to blunt criticism of the administration for not having prevented the fall of the French at Dien

Bien Phu, John Foster Dulles also took credit publicly for this coup in Guatemala. According to Goodpaster, Eisenhower became "very negative" about covert action after Guatemala, because it did not remain covert.[20]

A few short months after Guatemala, when Allen Dulles should have been at the top of his game, General James Doolittle submitted a secret report to Eisenhower on Dulles's management of the CIA. His committee was made up of four men who had ties to the Agency and who firmly believed in covert action. It was surprising that there was any criticism in the report. But it called Dulles's approach to intelligence "emotional" and suggested that the various "Cold War functions" of the CIA—for example, overthrowing governments—were distracting the Agency from its primary mission of collecting information. Dulles's centerpiece, infiltrating agents into the USSR, was painted as a lost cause. Dulles had been continuing parachute drops of expatriates behind the Iron Curtain long after the agents' short life expectancy was well established. Besides, the report went on, "the information we have obtained by this method of acquisition has been negligible and the cost in effort, dollars, and human lives prohibitive."[21]

Still, the covert action team went at it again in May 1958, in Indonesia. In this instance the operation was a total failure. One of the CIA's pilots was shot down after bombing a church. The resulting embarrassment caused the administration to do an about-face quickly and rush to support the dictatorship of President Sukarno with increased trade.

In his final months as president, Ike put out a signal that he wanted Patrice Lumumba of the Belgian Congo out of the way permanently. Dulles told the president he would take care of it personally. Future DCI Richard Helms arranged the details and an assassin was dispatched to Africa. Lumumba was ultimately killed not by CIA personnel, but by his political opponents days before Ike left office. Even though the CIA did not kill Lumumba directly, its hand was immediately suspected.

Finally, in the waning days of the Eisenhower administration, plans were hatched for a much more ambitious covert action: to overthrow a regime that was not weak and ready to be pushed over, even though the CIA may have mistakenly thought that to be the case—Castro's Cuba. Planning was well under way for the invasion at the Bay of Pigs in Cuba, to the point that Cuban dissidents had been trained and positioned forward. It is unclear how informed and involved Ike was in all this. Ike had confidence that his DCI was firmly in control of the CIA, but some felt otherwise. Dulles was, by 1960, "beginning to run on three cylinders instead of four," according to one officer, and "the agency was just beginning to go out of control."[22] But when Goodpaster told the president, "Sir, there is a danger here and that is if you organize this force [of Cuban expatriates], it may take on a life of its own," the president snapped, "No, by God, not while I'm here." To which Goodpaster was forced to point out, "Well, sir, that is the problem, you are not going to be here." That gave the president pause. "That's right. That is a real problem."[23] Preparations were well enough along and becoming sufficiently public, though, that it would have been difficult to call the operation off completely.

In assessing the Eisenhower-Dulles use of the CIA for covert action, I would note first that these actions implicitly told the world that it was an acceptable ethic of U.S. foreign policy to topple or interfere with duly instituted governments when doing so appeared to be in U.S. interests. Beyond that, neither of the two successful actions, in Iran and Guatemala, accomplished much. The best that can be said is that we continued to have a friend and ally in the shah for another twenty-six years. The operations in Iran and Guatemala, and even the attempts in Indonesia and Cuba, have had a profound impact on the image of the CIA around the world. Since none of these events remained secret, they have created an aura of power and mystique about the CIA. In one sense this is a benefit to the United States, as the threat that we might turn the CIA loose can be used as a tool of diplomacy. In another sense it is a handicap, as people will both fear us when we do not want them to and suspect us of actions in which we played no part. When, as DCI, I traveled overseas, I was always received by the head of state in any third world country that could possibly worry about a CIA covert action against it. Because of the aura of the successes of covert actions in Iran and Guatemala, and because of the attention Allen Dulles lavished on it, the Directorate of Plans (later changed to the Directorate of Operations), the branch of the CIA that housed both covert action and espionage, became the prestige element, really the personification, of the CIA. CIA personnel from today's Directorate of Operations (DO) have a deep respect for Allen Dulles, largely because of his preoccupation with espionage and covert action. That preoccupation, however, resulted in a lost opportunity to establish the analytic arm of the CIA on a firm foundation of long-term forecasting and net assessments when we had a president who wanted just that. Dulles's modest achievements in covert action and espionage do not offset his failure to handle analysis, technical collection, and the Intelligence Community well.

Most of all, in my opinion, Allen Dulles failed to leave the position of director of central intelligence any stronger than it was when he took over, despite having a president who would likely have supported making the position stronger. On the positive side, Allen Dulles oversaw a sizable expansion of the CIA and its establishment as a major element of the executive branch. It was during his tenure that the Agency moved out of a motley collection of World War II temporary buildings on the Washington Mall plus some space borrowed from the Department of the Navy. One of Dulles's last official acts was to show President Kennedy around the new headquarters building at Langley, Virginia, some five miles away.

CHAPTER FOUR

JOHN F. KENNEDY, DULLES, AND McCONE

Scandal and Confusion on the New Frontier

Three days before the inauguration of John Kennedy in 1961, Prime Minister Patrice Lumumba was murdered in the Belgian Congo. A CIA agent had been dispatched to this newly independent country with poison darts and a plan to assassinate Lumumba. The Agency had assessed him as a dangerous leader who would certainly be swayed by the Communists, if he was not already one himself. The plan for assassination was never activated, however. Instead, Lumumba was arrested and detained by his political rivals, aided by the CIA. He was transferred to a breakaway province, Katanga, where under a cloud of secrecy, he was murdered. When the world learned that Lumumba had been killed, few in Africa doubted that the CIA had been involved. Between his election and inauguration, Kennedy had not been warned that this assassination was planned or even that it had actually taken place.

There was not much Kennedy could do with respect to the Lumumba fiasco, but he did have to deal almost immediately with the very last of the Eisenhower-Dulles–era plans for covert action: ridding the world of still another Communist-oriented leader, Fidel Castro. This "covert" action was hardly covert at all. Hundreds of Cuban exiles training in Guatemala could not be kept secret. Despite the advanced stage of the planning and training, Eisenhower had not given his approval to the plan nor indicated that he was ready to have it executed. That he left to his successor. It was one of the first major items of foreign policy on John Kennedy's plate. A key item in the plan, which neither Ike nor JFK questioned adequately, was the CIA's forecast that many Cubans would rally to the side of the invaders. Unaware that this assumption was based largely on wishful thinking rather than on solid intelligence, Kennedy approved of going ahead with the operation.

April 17, 1961, was the date set for D-day, so at this early stage of his administration the young president was entrusting his prestige, possibly even his political future, to the CIA. The one critical operational decision that he made personally was to rule out the use of American airpower to support the landing force when it hit the beach. When the Cubans did not rally to our side, and without air support, the operation failed miserably. The misjudgment of how the Cubans would react to an invasion tells us that we should not allow the covert-action people in the CIA to be the only ones who assess what the responses of others will be to a given covert action. The views of the people who do analysis also deserve to be heard, especially as they are less likely to be swept up in enthusiasm for the action. Ensuring this is the case bears importantly on how we organize for covert action.

The man who led John Kennedy into the morass of the Bay of Pigs was Allen Dulles. While the president took responsibility, he was very angry with Dulles. He had opted to retain Dulles as DCI despite the fact that Dulles was a Republican. It may be that the young former senator from Massachusetts, who followed World War II's largest legend in the White House, just could not displace the Cold War's first legend in the CIA. It is generally agreed, however, that Kennedy decided to keep Dulles as DCI (and Hoover as FBI director) in order to placate the Republicans and southern Democrats in Congress. In fact, these two masters of intrigue were the first appointments Kennedy announced, right after the election. But Kennedy was also fascinated, even more so than Eisenhower, with the romance and excitement of secrecy, espionage, and covert action. In March 1960, with his electoral campaign barely under way, he hosted a party, invited James Bond's creator, Ian Fleming, and listened with rapt fascination to Fleming describe how Bond would deal with Castro. Fleming digressed into what sounds like pure fantasy, but the future president loved it. For example, Fleming offered up the idea of relieving Castro of his beard through clandestine chemical warfare.[1]

Another reason Dulles was retained, at this early point in the life of the DCI, was that it seemed logical not to change the apolitical office of DCI just because there was a change of administrations. This view persisted until Jimmy Carter replaced George H. W. Bush with me in 1977. It was, in my view, too bad that the tradition that DCIs can carry over between administrations was broken. The fault in this case, though, was Gerald Ford's. His appointing a DCI, Bush, who was politically partisan (as a former chairman of the Republican National Committee), just made it very difficult for a Democratic president to accept him as a key player in his administration.

After the fiasco in Cuba, in a meeting with Dulles and two of his deputies, Dick Bissell and Charles Cabell, Kennedy famously told them,

"If this were the British government, I would resign, and you, being a senior civil servant, would remain. But it isn't. In our government, you and Allen have to go, and I have to remain."[2] Arthur Schlesinger Jr. summarized the debacle: "I believe Allen Dulles was a frivolous man. He was most intelligent and a man of great charm, unlike his brother. But he was frivolous in the sense that he would make these decisions which involved people's lives and never really would think them through. He always left that to someone else."[3] Thus ended the career of a man who had helped shape U.S. central intelligence from the days of Donovan. On September 27, 1961, President Kennedy announced that Allen Dulles had resigned as DCI and nominated John A. McCone to replace him.

When Dulles departed the CIA for the last time, he got into the DCI's car, a special Cadillac equipped with bulletproof glass and armor, an encrypted phone, and two-way radios, and was driven off by his regular driver while his successor went home that night in a much more run-of-the-mill Mercury with only an ordinary phone. Dulles hadn't really left the Agency. He wasn't completely gone. He left in the DCI's car, with the loyalty of its best men.

At the end of November 1961, John McCone replaced Dulles. McCone had left public service as head of the Atomic Energy Commission just eleven months before. That he viewed with "alarm and concern" Kennedy's attempts to reach agreements with the Soviets was well known. Kennedy invited him to visit the White House and discuss those views. McCone refused, believing it was just an attempt to mute his opposition. But when the Soviets broke the nuclear test ban moratorium, he accepted a second invitation. Kennedy asked McCone for a report on the consequences of the Soviet resumption of nuclear testing. When he submitted this report, Kennedy asked him to be his next DCI.

McCone, a Republican businessman, was hardly an obvious choice. In the wake of the Cuban fiasco, it may be that JFK did not want to look weak by appointing a liberal-leaning Democrat. However, Kennedy was taking a bold step with this appointment. McCone followed two DCIs who had considerable experience in intelligence and three who, as military officers, had at least some acquaintance with it. He was the first business-man to fill the post, though he also had considerable experience in the government. McCone was a self-made man who had founded his own en-gineering firm, Bechtel-McCone, and had risen to be a director of Con-solidated Steel Corporation, Joshua Hendy Iron Works, and California Shipbuilding Corporation. Although he was an active Republican, he had entered public life under Harry Truman in the office of the secre-tary of defense and later was moved up to undersecretary of the air force. In 1958, Eisenhower appointed him to be chairman of the Atomic Energy Commission. As with Secretary of Defense Robert McNamara, Kennedy's choice of McCone reflected his preference for "organization men." In his view, running a bureaucracy wasn't all that different from running a business.

McCone was regarded as a man who was determined to play a major role in the administration and ensure the Intelligence Community also had a stronger, more effective voice. A large bloc of the CIA was opposed to his appointment, according to McCone, "on the basis that I was more of an outspoken anti-communist than should be in that position and I was incapable of making a fair evaluation and that my estimates would be slanted."[4]

CIA analyst Robert Amory, for one, threatened to resign. "I thought it was just the wrong thing; this was a cheap political move to put a promi-nent Republican in so the heat could be taken off the Bay of Pigs." How-ever, after Amory sat down with McCone, "I immediately decided I'd been wrong. . . . In the first sessions he obviously grasped things awfully fast and was not a reactionary, and was obviously going to work with the staff he'd got."[5]

Still, John McCone came across to many in the CIA as cold and hard, though also as highly intelligent and demanding. Those in the CIA who briefed the DCI had been accustomed to dealing with a distracted and scattered Allen Dulles. They were put under a spell by McCone's penetrating stare and dedicated focus. They invariably remembered McCone's "steely blue eyes," which, however, were actually dark brown.

Perhaps by the time I met John McCone he had mellowed some, but I found him anything but cold. When I became DCI in 1977, John McCone had been out of the position for twelve years. Three times during my tenure, however, he asked to see me when he happened to be in Washington. Each time I agreed, of course, out of respect. Each time, however, I was fidgety as he recounted old experiences. I kept thinking of the work I had to do and the time the meeting was consuming. Yet on each occasion, at about the end of the conversation, John McCone dropped a nugget of advice that made the loss of work time more than worthwhile.

He was, however, a bitter person in one respect over his time as DCI. Since his tenure, there had been much publicity about the CIA's dealings in Chile. He told me that his director of operations, Richard Helms, who was later a DCI, had not kept him informed about what the CIA was doing in Chile. That frightened me as I looked over my shoulder and wondered what might be going on that I was not being told about. Even today I wonder.

That uncertainty makes the job of DCI a unique challenge. John Kennedy, while trying to convince a major general to take the job of deputy director of central intelligence, said, "commanding an Army is an important responsibility and has many problems. Running the Defense Department has even greater responsibilities and more problems. But neither of these can even compare to the responsibilities and problems of running the CIA."[6]

Recognizing that only the president could make the DCI's job easier,

Kennedy instituted weekly meetings and made sure everyone knew that McCone was getting this face time. Even further, Kennedy directly ordered McCone to take the reins of the Intelligence Community, and he put it in writing. This was the part of the job most neglected by Dulles, most difficult for Hillenkoetter, and not given much attention by Souers and Vandenberg. Before McCone, only Bedell Smith had made a concentrated effort to be a real director of central intelligence.

"In carrying out your newly assigned duties as DCI, it is my wish that you serve as the government's principal foreign intelligence officer," Kennedy's letter read. The letter had actually been drafted by CIA hands. In an early version, the DCI was supposed to "coordinate and direct" all the intelligence agencies located in the different departments. But others in the CIA objected. "How does the director of central intelligence direct intelligence organizations that are responsible to members of the Cabinet?" asked CIA inspector general Lyman Kirkpatrick. The line was eventually changed to "coordinate and give guidance to."[7] More than forty years later, the same questions came before Congress as it considered the recommendations of the 9/11 Commission. The country was no closer to an adequate answer.

The 9/11 Commission also proposed another Kennedy-era idea, that of moving the DCI into the White House, where he would become more of a national intelligence director than a CIA director. Kennedy had resisted this move, which would have looked like politicization.

No massive restructuring was to take place under Kennedy. Many thought that a strongly worded letter was enough. "President Kennedy, by specifically stating in an unclassified document available for everybody to see and study, made it very clear that there was to be one focal point for the United States intelligence effort and one man to whom he would look for his intelligence information," Kirkpatrick concluded, while acknowledging that this status would require maintenance on the president's part.[8]

McCone, for his part, was directed to turn day-to-day operations over to his deputy, which he did more than Dulles had. However, it's hard for any DCI to cede complete control, especially an organization man like McCone. "There are some people that claim that it's impossible for a person to wear two hats like that," McCone recalled. "But I did my best."[9]

McCone was a close reader of estimates (one witness watched him pore over "each line" of an estimate "as if it were a corporate mortgage"). He put the brakes on the page inflation that had infected the National Intelligence Estimates (NIEs) during the 1950s. "I don't want you to write any long reports," he announced. "In this organization it seems that every time I ask for something I get a forty-two-page report with twelve annexes."[10]

But while he was taking control of the Intelligence Community and the estimates, he refused to view the NIEs as "his." He would criticize them, and attempt to bring dissenters over to his view, but he never used his power to rewrite estimates. Bedell Smith had once taken control of an estimate, but cautioned that it should not become a precedent. Overall, McCone believed that "the NIE system was bigger than he was."[11] If he had dissents, he could always count on a weekly private meeting with Kennedy to air them. As we will see later, by my time NIEs had come to be compromise documents, and I took a quite different approach to injecting my views into them in order to give them some real substance.

This restraint on McCone's part is usually presented favorably. But while McCone's view of his role in analysis was a prudent course at the time, in retrospect it wasn't always right. McCone went against the opinion of the entire Intelligence Community over whether Khrushchev would put nuclear-tipped missiles in Cuba, and he told Kennedy that "something new and different was going on."[12] The Intelligence Community proclaimed that "it would be incompatible with Soviet policy to introduce strategic missiles in Cuba," so the 150 round trips made by Soviet ships, they reasoned, must be up to something else. As a later estimate said, "The Soviets simply would not do anything so uncharacteristic, provocative and unrewarding."[13] Sherman Kent, an analytical legend in the CIA, told McCone that he could change the estimate if he disagreed, but McCone declined. Still, with McCone, the country got a DCI who was willing to manage the Intelligence Community, submerge his own views, and honor the CIA's real mission as an intelligence and analysis agency rather than one largely focused on covert action.

Covert action, though, has fascinated many presidents and their advisors. This was the case with the Kennedy administration, despite the early fiasco in Cuba. The Kennedy team arrived in the White House "aglow with new ideas and a euphoric sense that it could do no wrong," according to advisor Arthur Schlesinger Jr., and "promptly collided with the feudal barons of the permanent government, entrenched in their domains and fortified by their sense of proprietorship."[14] The Central Intelligence Agency stood in contrast to these stodgy bureaucracies—in fact, it shared many of the same gripes with "the system" that Kennedy's people did. To Kennedy, the CIA seemed to be the agency most prepared for his brand of government.

For a moment, though, it looked like covert action might have bombed out too many times to survive with this administration. In the Dominican Republic, the CIA had armed an assassination plot to take out President Rafael Leonidas Trujillo Molina. After the Bay of Pigs, Kennedy wanted the project stopped because it was too soon for another debacle. The problem is that once you encourage and arm a group of highly motivated locals, you can't just turn them off. Trujillo's enemies gunned him down dramatically, though technically speaking without U.S. help.

In Laos, the CIA backed the Hmong (then known by the derogatory name Meo) people of the highlands to fight a counterinsurgency. This set off a complicated three-way civil war that hit the Hmong hard.

In Ecuador, the CIA helped overthrow President José Velasco Ibarra.

His replacement didn't last long before the CIA turned on him, looking for greater stability and allegiance.

In British Guiana, the CIA stirred up trouble through the labor unions to take down the democratically elected Cheddi Jagan.

The centerpiece of all covert operations was Mongoose, a secret campaign against Castro.[15] The operation had been initiated during the Eisenhower administration, and neither the president nor his brother Robert, the attorney general, objected to its moving forward. "It was very simple," said one Mongoose task force member. "We were at war with Castro."[16] This was hardly an overstatement—Castro's security detail thwarted thirty-two assassination plots in the early 1960s. JFK was supportive; RFK appeared rabid; and McCone was concerned. "The subject you just brought up, I think it is highly improper," he told McNamara in a meeting after a discussion of the possible assassination of Castro. "I do not think it should be discussed. It is not an action that should ever be condoned. It is not proper for us to discuss and I intend to have it expunged from the record."[17]

The CIA's point man on the operation didn't have such qualms—or any qualms, really. William King Harvey, a short and wide man with poor manners and low charisma, carried a .38 in his pants on his first visit to the Oval Office, handing it to a shocked Secret Service agent at the door. "So you're our James Bond?" Kennedy asked. Kennedy's advisors "thought he was crazy," according to the CIA secretary for the group that managed the operations. "They didn't realize he was just drunk."[18] Out of wild-eyed covert action managers like Harvey came the famous list of ideas for killing Castro—the poisoned cigar, the exploding conch shell, the infected wetsuit—and the association between the CIA and known mobsters, contract killers, and the like. McCone, who early on spent about 80 percent of his time on broad Intelligence Community matters (according to an audit done by Kirkpatrick), wound up having to spend, according to his executive assistant, about 90 percent of his time on clandestine affairs.

McCone's organizational and managerial skills must have been very valuable at this point in the life of the CIA and of the Intelligence Community. After all, both organizations were new entities thrust into the governmental bureaucracy. There were no established procedures or traditions. In the first seven years there had been five DCIs, followed by the almost-nine-year tenure of Allen Dulles, who had not been a good manager. McCone is regarded as the DCI who built up and organized both the intelligence-gathering and analysis functions. Perhaps not surprisingly, this accomplished businessman took the CIA in the direction of tapping knowledge acquired by U.S. corporations operating overseas. He even went so far as to find ways to support them when they had problems with local governments.

A conspicuous example of this was Brazil. The CIA regarded Brazil's president, João Goulart, to be a Communist in the making, based on his record of favoring state ownership of important utilities. It looked as though Goulart's government was going to take over a phone company that was a subsidiary of International Telephone and Telegraph (ITT). Harold Geneen, ITT's president, appealed to his friend John McCone. McCone involved the CIA in waging what resembled a psychological warfare campaign. It included press releases that smeared Goulart, a joint effort by CIA and the Agency for International Development (AID) to persuade the AFL-CIO to establish training centers to teach Brazilian labor leaders alternatives to communism, funneling money to the Brazilian Institute for Democratic Action in an attempt to influence regional elections, and encouraging contributions from American businesses to Brazilian opposition parties.

These activities—tapping U.S. businesses for intelligence and providing them assistance with their operations overseas—are highly controversial. Some years after he left office, McCone claimed that when he was DCI it was CIA policy to refuse all offers of help from corporations and to adamantly tell U.S. corporations to stay out of local politics. That seems to be stretching the facts a bit, but with McCone's having gone to work for ITT after leaving the government, he may have been overly sensitive on this issue.

Early in my days as DCI, I had not even thought about turning to American businesses to obtain intelligence. Then, on my first trip overseas, I called on the chief of British intelligence, MI-6. To my surprise, the first question this "spymaster of spymasters" put to me was whether we were tapping the resources of the U.S. business community. His point was that it was a shame to use secret sources, often at considerable risk or expense, to obtain data that was available for the asking.

Actually, back in 1977, American businesses were shying away from any contact with the CIA. Congressional investigations had revealed some questionable contacts in the past between businesses and the Agency, such as with ITT in Brazil. Some shareholders were threatening lawsuits against their companies for having used stockholder resources to work for the CIA. I thought, and still think, that was an overreaction. If the American business community has information of value to the government, and hence to American citizens, we ought to find ways to share it. Yes, businesspeople should not get involved in conducting espionage, but there is little harm in reporting what they see and hear in the normal course of their business. Of course, there will always be a risk of slipping over the line between reporting and spying. And there is also a risk that such a relationship could result in the CIA, perhaps inadvertently, providing information to a business that would give it commercial advantage over other American businesses. It seems to me these potential problems are manageable, with one exception.

The exception is the media. Our media are extremely sensitive to being seen as adjuncts to or fronts for the CIA. During the Cold War, reporters feared that such identification not only would cut off their sources but also could expose them to arrest or even assassination. I thought that was an exaggeration. The Soviet Union, because it blatantly employed media personnel as spies, would assume we did also. In short, as far as our principal opponent was concerned, our media people would be suspect as spies whether they had a relationship with the CIA or not. My predecessor, George H. W. Bush, had issued a directive that the CIA would not use people in the media as sources of information. I rescinded that order. This raised a storm of protest from the media, but in time it died down. My reasoning was that if a media person came across information he or she felt to be of vital importance to the country, the CIA should not place an impediment in the way. We would not, though, solicit information from the media.

The other side of this coin, that of the CIA providing support to American businesses overseas, is even more controversial. We had good evidence that even friendly governments were spying on U.S. businesses in the United States to acquire commercial secrets. While I did not think we should do that, I was open to sharing with the U.S. business community commercial information we came across that might be of value. Soon after I suggested doing this, I faced a storm of protests from CIA professionals. They did not see helping business as being part of their mission of promoting national security. I argued that our economic health is the heart of our security. As a practical matter, though, the opportunity for the CIA to provide information to U.S. businesses is limited by a concern for not giving one U.S. business commercial advantage over another. I reserved the right to support businesses whenever we could avoid partiality, but such opportunities are rare.

John McCone almost certainly felt more strongly on this issue of mutual benefits between U.S. businesses and intelligence operations overseas. The fact that he and the Kennedy administration found it necessary to declare that they had a hands-off policy would seem to indicate, though, that there must have been considerable resistance back then to where McCone wanted to go. The fact that it was the same in my day might well indicate that there are systemic problems here. The question still applies today, though, as to whether we can afford not to tap all the resources of the country, business included, in the quest for intelligence on terrorism.

CHAPTER FIVE

LYNDON B. JOHNSON, McCONE, RABORN, AND HELMS

The Value and Price of Loyalty

Vice Admiral William "Red" Raborn, President Lyndon Johnson's second DCI, had barely moved into his office when he uttered the words that would be cited repeatedly by historians and commentators to characterize his short tenure from April 1965 to June 1966. Assuming the directorship smack in the middle of a crisis in the Dominican Republic, Raborn was on the phone to President Johnson, who wanted incontrovertible proof that Communists were on the verge of taking power on the island. What he really wanted was proof that the deployment of the Marines he had already made was justified. Vice Admiral Raborn seemed to click his heels when he closed the conversation with "Aye aye, sir!"[1]

There are two currents in the CIA's world of intelligence that are always at odds. One is unquestioning service to the president. The other is the belief that the Intelligence Community serves up the truth as best it sees it, no matter how inconvenient that is to the president. Ray Cline was of the latter opinion, and must have winced when he heard Raborn verbally salute LBJ.

The Dominican Republic had been unstable since Trujillo was assassinated while Kennedy was president. Hope seemed to appear briefly in the person of Juan Bosch, who was elected with 60 percent of the vote, but he lasted only seven months before a right-wing military coup ousted him. America, in general, didn't mind this sort of thing as long as the dictators weren't Communists. But a lot of Dominicans on both sides of the political spectrum did mind, and a countercoup started on April 24, 1965, four days before Raborn took office.

On that day, the American ambassador in Santo Domingo asserted that the countercoup was led by Communists and "Castro-type" elements. Johnson reacted. He sent American forces into the country. (We had been there before. U.S. Marines had occupied the country from 1916 to 1924, after the republic's government had virtually come apart at the seams. One of the many ironies of that occupation was that it set the stage for Trujillo, head of the armed forces we had helped to create, to take control.) Now the initial commitment of four hundred Marines on April 28 would swell to forty-two thousand. Johnson knew all along that he would have a very tough time selling this action to the American public, especially because he was upping the ante in Vietnam at the same time.

"Now, our CIA says this is a completely led, operated, dominated—they've got men on the inside of it—Castro operation," LBJ exclaimed to an advisor. Johnson was clearly very impressed with what he thought was deep CIA infiltration into the countercoup: "They say it is! Their people on the inside tell us," he shouted when the advisor suggested that it "may" be true. Johnson knew what he needed in order to sell this operation to the American people: "I think we ought to get the CIA, who have men right in these operations . . . to give us name, address, chapter and verse . . . and say 'This is a case of Cuba doing the job.'"[2]

To many in the CIA, this assignment looked like intelligence being cooked to please the president. It seemed to be a way for Johnson to back-stop his already-executed policy. Some highly placed sources were report-ing that the countercoup was backed by Castro, but Johnson overestimated these reports and assumed that they were the official CIA line. In fact, when the research was complete and a list of names of the countercoup plotters was released through the State Department, it almost immedi-ately came under fire. A few of the fifty-odd alleged Castroists were even found to be right-wingers. Both the CIA's and the State Department's in-telligence failed Johnson in this case, and contributed to his decision to embark on a risky and probably unnecessary military adventure.

Once, when Cline and Raborn reported to the White House to brief Johnson, the president was sick in bed. The meeting was supposed to have been canceled, but since they'd come in from Langley, they were told to report to the president's bedside. Things were not looking up. Johnson fi-nally exclaimed, exasperated, "How the hell can I get my troops out of this damned mess?" This was a policy question—not for the CIA—but Raborn cheerfully went along: "Maybe Dr. Cline has a suggestion!"[3] Raborn was just trying to be helpful to his friend and president, but he really misun-derstood the role of the CIA on policy. By enlisting the CIA in helping the president out of a politically difficult situation, Raborn lost the confi-dence of the Agency. By failing to deliver accurate information that Johnson was sure he was going to get (due to the "man on the ground" re-ports), he lost the confidence of the president. Worse, this president was already disposed to distrust the CIA. The CIA had done a number of things to earn Johnson's distrust. The Bay of Pigs certainly figured into it, as did the secret war against Castro that LBJ did not find out about until after he succeeded Kennedy. And what if, Johnson may well have speculated early on, Kennedy's death was blowback from one covert operation or another?

When Johnson stepped into office, then, the intelligence professionals found themselves in a quite different relationship with the new president. Truman, while skeptical of secret intelligence activities, oversaw the construction of the extensive intelligence apparatus we still have; Ike was an avid consumer of intelligence; and JFK staked his reputation on the CIA at the Bay of Pigs. Now, Johnson treated intelligence with disdain. Truman had wanted a daily secret newspaper. Ike and JFK had been genuinely interested in learning what was going on in the world. Johnson wanted only to have the intelligence apparatus confirm what he already believed.

By the time of the change in the presidency, John McCone had been DCI for two years. He had come to be highly respected within the Agency for his organizational acumen and for encouraging independent thinking. McCone made a bold move on Johnson's first day as president, the day after Kennedy had been shot. He announced that protocol under Kennedy had been for him to provide the regular morning briefing. Johnson agreed to see McCone every morning.

Just days later, Johnson witnessed what would become a theme with McCone. In an afternoon meeting on Vietnam with his main national security advisors, Henry Cabot Lodge, ambassador to South Vietnam, according to McCone, "left the President with the impression that we were on the road to victory,"[4] but McCone suggested Vietcong activity was increasing while the government in South Vietnam was in disarray; the future was bleak. Johnson hated getting two sets of opinions from his advisors. He wanted clear policy recommendations that he could either follow or not follow. So at this early meeting he set the tone, telling the group that several heads in the U.S. team in Saigon would roll, and plainly stating that he "wanted no more divisions of opinion, no more bickering, and any person that did not conform to policy should be removed."[5]

The message was clear, but Johnson confused the issue later by telling McCone privately that he wanted to hear honest assessments of what he thought was going on over there. Not only that, he wanted McCone's policy advice. This suited McCone fine, and it looked for one moment like this was the start of a beautiful relationship between Johnson and McCone. The patterns set during the first weeks of the administration did not hold for long, however. McCone found that "each man has to organize himself differently." Johnson "only wanted to see me when I had something particular I wanted to tell him. His door was always open, but he wasn't inclined to want to sit for a general review."[6] Johnson likewise avoided NSC meetings, preferring what came to be the famous Tuesday Lunches.

Johnson had learned from watching the Kennedy administration that "the National Security Council meetings were like sieves."[7] He felt just about anything discussed in these meetings was likely to end up in the morning papers. Paradoxically, it was Johnson who invited members of the congressional leadership to his first NSC meeting and allowed a photographer in while classified maps of Soviet missile sites were arranged around the room. But Johnson blamed his advisors for the general lack of secrecy: "I couldn't control them. You knew after the National Security Council meetings that each of those guys would run home to tell his wife and neighbors what they had said to the President."[8]

His answer was to keep the group small. So, Johnson would gather his secretaries of state and defense, his national security advisor, the chairman of the JCS, maybe his attorney general, and usually his press secretary (to take notes). The setting, lunchtime on Tuesdays, was deliberately informal to put participants at ease. Those in attendance would sip sherry in the family living room. "Clashing, exploratory, or even frivolous views could be expressed with little bureaucratic caution and with confidence no scars would remain," remembered National Security Advisor Walt Rostow.[9] This type of meeting suited Johnson's style of operating, and he reveled in it. "He was not, I don't think, ever particularly good at dealing with people he didn't know. . . . He didn't know what they stood for. Therefore he didn't know whether he could say certain things," recalled Richard Helms, Johnson's third DCI.[10]

But because these informal meetings worked so well (Johnson bragged that nothing had ever leaked from a Tuesday Lunch), they provided a crucial means for Johnson's advisors to make their views known to the president. By the middle of 1964, Johnson was holding the lunches right after the NSC meetings. People who knew they were going into a more private setting later held back in conversation, saving their best ideas for the meeting that really counted. The lunches became the place where the actual decisions were made, but "the informality of the meetings fostered consensual fuzziness rather than hard choices," a congressional investigating committee would remark later.[11]

The other problem is that an invitation to the meeting came to signal presidential favor. If you had it, you were having an impact on policy. If you didn't, you were just another line worker. And that was a problem for McCone because he didn't have an invitation. This was particularly galling when coupled with the fact that McCone had lost his regular weekly meeting, the important status symbol he'd received originally from Kennedy.

McCone had trouble getting regular meetings with LBJ, and he had trouble getting feedback from him on the CIA's publications. McCone has said that Johnson would not read estimates on Soviet capabilities. The bigger problem, though, was that LBJ was just not that interested in the CIA. "I do not believe that he really had the faintest idea of how the Central Intelligence Agency was organized, or how the Intelligence Community was organized," recalled DCI Helms.[12] He never made the trip out to Langley, and never took it upon himself to learn how the publications he read (or not) were produced. There were a number of reasons for this.

Early in his presidency, Johnson was simply much more interested in domestic issues than in foreign affairs. He wasn't enamored of covert action. And when he did become interested in foreign affairs, they were almost all related to Vietnam. But he also came to the Oval Office with a legislator's mind-set. He preferred to think things through on his own, build ad hoc committees to work on problems, and rely on his gut. Richard Helms remembers that he was surprised, and then almost ashamed at his own naiveté, when he realized that "a President of the United States doesn't make his important decisions in an orderly way or the way the political scientists say they should be done or the way the organization experts would like to see them done or, in fact, the way 99 percent of the American people understand that they are done. This is a highly personal affair."[13]

Since decisions on Vietnam were personal, McCone fell from the short period of favor he had enjoyed. As unity on Vietnam became all-important for Johnson, he became increasingly suspicious of McCone. Johnson's advisors jumped into the breach, making it even larger. National Security Advisor McGeorge Bundy called one CIA report on Vietnam "a shade blue, not quite balanced account. They are a little bit covering their flanks over in the Agency and making sure that they are the ones that are giving the gloomy news first." On a trip to Saigon where McCone was part of the visiting group, Bundy remarked to LBJ that they didn't "want anybody on this trip coming back with two different plans. . . . John McCone, especially, has a way of saving his skin—to be blunt about it." Johnson responded, "That's right." Later, it was Johnson who pointed out to Bundy how important it was to deal with the "Stevensons," "dissidents," and "McCones"—that is, "anybody who might get off board later—very carefully so we don't get a government that's divided. That's the great danger we face here."[14]

The problem wasn't just that the CIA estimators were painting a gloomy picture of the situation in Vietnam. That would have been easy enough to ignore. But McCone, following up on Johnson's suggestion that he make policy recommendations, had developed a six-point plan on Vietnam that was very unlike McNamara's plan. For one thing, it called for far more troops. This alternative plan was a real danger to Johnson politically as he tried to get the American people to accept even modest troop numbers. And Johnson saw McCone increasingly becoming a pest, always asking for meetings. Another irritant to Johnson was McCone's reminders on how right and persistent he, McCone, had been on the Soviet placement of missiles in Cuba. He wore out his welcome. When Johnson mentioned all this to Bundy, the advisor suggested that McCone might be placated by a few rounds of golf with the president. LBJ ended up responding to McCone's complaints by having research done on just how much face time the DCI had received. It turned out he'd had eighty-nine meetings with the president—on average at least one meeting a week—even though they were not a regular part of the president's schedule.

No, the problem wasn't meetings—it was policy. McCone was going too far. McCone claimed that the "slowly ascending tempo of air strikes" had to be measured against the "increasing pressure to stop the bombing. This will come from various elements of the American public, from the press, the United Nations, and world opinion."[15] In making his views known to the president he was advising not only on winning in Vietnam, but on managing public opinion at home and abroad. McCone was proven right in time; but he was out of line, even foolish, for trying to advise a master politician on how to do politics. It was more than the president could stand. One evening, in a meeting with McCone and his military advisors in the White House, Johnson finally snapped after hearing about how to handle American public opinion one too many times: "Listen, you sons of bitches, don't tell me what the American people will stand for. That's my responsibility. I want to know whether we can win this war or not."[16]

Richard Helms remembered that the reason McCone decided to leave was that "he was dissatisfied with his relationship with President Johnson. He didn't get to see him enough, and he didn't feel that he had any impact and he didn't have sufficient influence. This just didn't suit John McCone's way of life or interest."[17] McCone claimed that Johnson wanted him to stay (but he probably just wanted him to stay until after the election). And so began McCone's long lame-duck session—from June 1964 to April 1965. Typically neglectful of the CIA, Johnson simply didn't consider who would replace McCone.

It was during this time that the CIA abandoned Harry Truman's "Daily Summary" and produced the "President's Checklist." This is one of its most successful and longest-running publications, although its name has changed to "President's Daily Brief" (PDB). Because of concerns about the sensitivity of the content and the fact that McCone was finding the only sure way to get to the president was in writing, the Checklist/PDB became a newspaper-style publication for only the president and a very few top officials, such as the secretaries of state and defense.

Johnson may not have understood intelligence, but he knew politics, and during the run-up to the election in 1964, he had a strictly political question for the CIA. Johnson didn't often sidestep the chain of command as did Kennedy, but on this occasion he made an exception by having Bundy call Ray Cline directly. The question: Could South Vietnam's instability "result in an irretrievable loss of South Vietnam before Election Day in November"? Why would Johnson need to know that? LBJ was scoring political points by taking swipes at Barry Goldwater, labeling him a hawk and claiming he would get our boys killed in Vietnam. Now he wanted to be sure: If he continued his current policy, would South Vietnam last until the election? Bundy pointed out to Cline, "Old friend, you can understand I don't want anybody to know this question ever got asked." Cline explained that he would have to let at least McCone know that the question had been asked and answered. Johnson could get away with doing the minimum in Vietnam for now, but, left alone, the situation would get worse. After the election, Johnson would have his "back to the wall."[18]

After the election, McCone continued to express reservations about the president's Vietnam policy. On April 2, 1965, he fired off a memo saying not only that McNamara's planned land war would fail, but also that the bombing was ineffective. That same day, Johnson turned his attention to replacing McCone.

His conversation revealed a lot about what he was looking for, and what he would miss in McCone. "Is he mean enough to mix up that hamburger and that pepper?" LBJ asked about one candidate. Toughness in the face of morally questionable operations was a premium in a DCI. "You know what some of those guys do, don't you? . . . What I want is a careful man and an analytical man, and a good man, but one that can light the fuse if it's just got to be done to save his country. And when you go strike that match and setting off dynamite, a lot of them hesitate."[19]

The person Johnson selected to replace McCone, Vice Admiral Raborn, was a driven man. During the war in the Pacific, he had watched a suicide attack cripple the aircraft carrier he was serving on and cause a terrible number of grisly deaths. Like many who lived through that war, he worked to prevent it from happening again. His method was to guarantee mutual assured nuclear destruction through submarine-based intercontinental ballistic missiles—the Polaris system. Raborn worked himself into a frenzy and a heart attack on this technically difficult problem. Ultimately he created an impressive system and propelled the navy into the forefront of nuclear strategy by assuring that the Soviets could never destroy all of America's second-strike capabilities. His career definitely left a mark, but not on the CIA.

The only thing that set up Raborn for a second career in intelligence was his political support of Johnson. In Johnson's mind, Raborn was not only someone who would remain loyal but a fixer who could knock the Agency into shape. "I have told you before but I cannot repeat too often," Johnson wrote Raborn in a memo that attempted to boost his morale while taking a swipe at the Agency, "that we must make every possible fresh, imaginative effort to get the best out of the talent assembled at the Agency. . . . I know you are not a man to rest on laurels of the past—and we don't have many laurels in the intelligence field."[20]

Johnson didn't offer much guidance about what to fix; he didn't seem to ever develop a clear idea of what was wrong at Langley, if anything. But regardless, he placed Raborn in a terrible position. Raborn simply didn't have the right skill set to fix the CIA. His predecessor noted that while Raborn was "hard-driving" and "technical," "the CIA requires a different kind of mentality": namely, the ability to balance the operations people against the analysts.

So instead of enjoying the success of the Polaris program and wrapping up a successful career, Raborn became a laughingstock at the CIA. His tenure was marked by one unfortunate episode after another. "How are we doing in the Dominican Republic?" he shouted into his intercom one day. Silence. He tried again: "What's the word from our agents?" The answer: "Admiral, I think you've got the wrong office. This isn't Operations." His answer: "Oh, sorry. I've got so many buttons up here I never know which one to push."[21] He reportedly mistook "Kuwait" for a code name and demanded to know what it meant. He gave a group of officers a long, sprawling, irrelevant report on Polaris. When it was finally over, one CIA officer wondered out loud if Polaris actually worked.

One day, in 1965, Cline, who said he had "nothing but sympathy for him," heard Raborn insist that something he'd read about friction between China and Russia "really is really important." He demanded a paper on the possibility of a split between the two Communist superpowers. Cline had been working on this since 1956. The CIA had accurately predicted the Sino-Soviet split. It was fairly amazing that anyone in Washington thought that China and Russia were still friends. But Raborn persisted: "You're not taking this seriously. . . . I want to see all these studies." Cline: "Well, what do you want me to use, a wheelbarrow?"[22]

Having foisted Raborn onto the CIA, Johnson disappeared from the scene, leaving his loyal friend adrift. And due to the increasing commitment to Vietnam, the CIA's responsibilities in the areas of both covert action and intelligence reporting were increasing. The reporting wasn't really getting any more optimistic, and the covert actions weren't producing any magical results. Johnson relied more heavily on Clark Clifford as an outside advisor, and Clifford's remark that he was "genuinely and deeply worried about the leadership problem in the CIA" carried immense weight.[23] Raborn, in the job for less than a year, would have to go.

During Johnson's first years as president, two currents of loyalty and honesty ran from one end of the spectrum to the other through his DCIs. McCone had continued to speak his mind to Johnson just as he had to Kennedy, and CIA morale was high. Then Johnson picked a man whom he knew was politically and personally loyal to him, and CIA morale plummeted. Then entered Richard Helms, who became, twenty years after the CIA was created, the first true career intelligence professional to head the Agency. Helms didn't directly attack LBJ's policies as McCone had, but neither did he seem overly loyal. And he could not fail to inspire confidence in the Agency; he was one of them.

And so the position of chief intelligence advisor had gone through a variety of personalities—from the dashing but scattered Donovan to the growling Smith to the suave Dulles to the organized McCone—and now the torch was passed to a consummate bureaucrat. Allen Dulles searched for words to describe Helms, finally settling on "useful," and pointing out that he "knew how to keep his mouth shut."[24] Helms characterized himself as "the fact man" who sat at the elbow of the president. He believed his place was always in the president's shadow, and he made only one public speech during his tenure.

Helms had started out in journalism, but joined OSS in 1942. From that time on, he had known little other than intelligence work. And within this narrow world, he worked entirely in operations, a protégé of Frank Wisner (the early, charismatic leader of the espionage and covert action branch of the CIA who suffered a nervous breakdown and committed suicide) and of Richard Bissell (another early head of the espionage branch whose career ended with the Bay of Pigs). Unlike many in operations who reveled in the excitement or the tacit permission to do questionable things in the name of good, Helms's tendency was against paramilitary-type violence. This was not because it was, as he saw it, wrong, but because it was messy and often ineffective. But his heart was in CIA espionage operations, not in analysis or in managing the Intelligence Community. As it did under Dulles, the management of both the CIA and the Intelligence Community suffered.

As he rose in the organization, he came more into contact with the analysts, but he was clearly not one of them. Helms did not think he needed to do analysis—he had an entire branch of the CIA to do that for him. His job was to make sure differing opinions came to a consensus. What was important was that the Agency present a unified estimate to outsiders. He rarely came into the debate until a deadline was looming. At that point, he would often approve one version or another without much by way of explanation, editing out inconvenient information and making other decisions that some in the CIA saw as arbitrary. Others saw it as cooking the books to Johnson's taste.

In the later days of his tenure, McCone took Helms to meet Johnson, for no apparent reason. They had a brief conversation in the Oval Office, then Helms sat in on a National Security Council meeting. Helms surmised that he was being considered for a job. Days later, he got a call. Come to the White House; don't tell anyone. He learned from Johnson that Raborn would follow McCone, and he would be promoted to the number-two spot. Johnson didn't know how long Raborn would last, but Helms should be ready to become DCI whenever Raborn left. Helms thanked him and left. For the next ten months he concentrated on helping Raborn. Then, one day, he found out to his shock that he was DCI. "When he [Johnson] announced my appointment," Helms remembered, "totally to my surprise at this press conference, (a) I didn't know he was going to announce it, and (b) he didn't tell me he was going to announce it." It's remarkable, but Johnson "had not communicated with me about it, at any time."[25]

Helms, and a few of his subordinates, viewed his working relationship with President Johnson as anywhere from good to "golden." Helms claimed that "once our relationship developed, I could not have asked for a more considerate chief and taskmaster than President Johnson." But he also claimed, like the true bureaucrat that he was, that the relationship was irrelevant. What mattered was how much Johnson valued the information Helms brought him.[26]

So Helms didn't mind if he wasn't invited to the Tuesday Lunches. He didn't complain as McCone had when he didn't get a regularly scheduled meeting. He didn't take it personally when Johnson became "impatient in the extreme if any oral briefing lasted more than a few minutes."

Instead, he adapted. "I would subside into delivering a few sentences fash-
ioned like the lead in a newspaper report—who, what, where, when, why,
and how."[27] Most of the time, it was the reports that mattered: "[Johnson]
was far better served by having the written word than he would have been
if I had come down there every day." Helms was not in the inner circle,
not confided in, not often talked to, but "the President of the United
States paid attention to what his intelligence officer gave him to read, and
this is the most important relationship you can have, in my opinion."[28]

Behind Helms's stringent focus on the job rather than the personalities involved was his intense "feeling of awe" for the office of the president
and his loyalty to that office: "Like most Americans, at least at that time, I
had grown up in awe of everyone who ever occupied the chair behind the
desk in that office. I've never lost this attitude, and it was an effort to conceal it."[29] When he was having trouble in his marriage, Helms went to
Johnson, concerned that his personal life might embarrass the administration. Johnson waved him off.

Helms was in Albuquerque on business when Johnson got wind of an
exposé in *Ramparts* magazine about CIA excesses in the propaganda field.
The leftist publication revealed CIA funding of the National Student
Association, the Congress for Cultural Freedom, the National Education Foundation, the American Newspaper Guild, and the American
Political Science Association, among other media, academic, and labor
organizations. To recruit students, the CIA dangled draft deferments. It
also funded organizations that produced CIA propaganda and anti-
Communist views. This wasn't as bad as earlier exposures of assassination
plots, but the draft deferments touched a nerve and the clandestine infu-
sion of government funds in the free press and universities made many
deeply uneasy.

Helms got a call from the White House that Johnson wanted him back in D.C. right away, and he complied. But as the scandal unraveled and as Congress howled, Helms claimed, "I never had any conversation with [Johnson] about the whole episode."[30] Johnson drew a line between himself and the CIA, refusing to ally himself with an organization that was very vulnerable to investigation.

The CIA didn't even defend itself during this time, though McCone, who had firsthand knowledge of how the funding was used, felt a defense would have been possible. He didn't see anything wrong with helping American students express their anti-Communist views at international conferences. But "we were in a period when there was sort of an inclination, if an accusation was made about the CIA, not to analyze it at all but to crawl under the table and hope that it goes by."[31] Even worse, the CIA and the president were of a mind to deal with the problem clandestinely. Johnson wanted the staff of *Ramparts* investigated. Helms sent up a report that failed to find any foreign funding for the magazine or the story. But two of the staff, Helms revealed, were "active Communists."[32]

The CIA investigation of the staff of *Ramparts* was definitely illegal. It was also just a small part of a much larger Johnson-initiated project that went by the codeword CHAOS. Johnson assumed that the antiwar protesters and inner-city rioters were funded and organized by overseas Communist sources. Why else would they question their president in a time of war? Why else would they burn their cities? Helms was of the same mind. During much of his career, Helms had supported agitators in Communist countries. Why wouldn't the Soviets do the same to us? To Helms's credit, he claimed he did warn Johnson that what they were doing was illegal—the CIA's spying was supposed to be strictly foreign. "I'm quite aware of that," Johnson replied. "What I want is for you to pursue this matter, and to do what is necessary to track down the foreign communists who are behind this intolerable interference in our domestic affairs."[33] But when Helms, who fully expected to find a connection, found nothing, Johnson wanted him to keep looking. Helms felt that he had no right to reject an order from the president or to blow the whistle on him. So his CIA created patently illegal files on 7,200 Americans and set up the CIA for an intense and highly damaging investigation two presidents later.

Helms claimed that the high point of his career was the Agency's accurate prediction in 1967 that if Israel were attacked, it would defeat the Arab states allied against it in six to ten days' time. The very name of the conflict that followed—the Six Day War—enshrined the accuracy of the prediction. But Helms's pride over this achievement stemmed from more than just being right. In his view, he helped guide Johnson's decision-making, convincing him that he could afford to stay out of the war. Interestingly, Johnson apparently had forgotten how intelligence could help him, as Helms recalled it. For instance, the CIA had previously helped him by accurately predicting the first Chinese nuclear test, and that Soviet nuclear strength was less than we had been assuming, helping Johnson argue against a strategic nuclear buildup so as to keep resources available for the Vietnam War and his domestic programs.

In any event, Helms repeatedly trumpeted the prediction of the Six Day War in his interviews and memoirs, saying he was finally invited to the coveted Tuesday Lunches (one Johnson advisor, however, recalled his attending a year earlier). His focus on this one episode is a small crack in his veneer of bureaucratic obedience, since Johnson's personal attention, praise, and appreciation really did matter to Helms. The job was more than getting the president to read written reports.

"On no occasion in all the meetings I attended with [Johnson] did he ever ask me to give my opinion about what policy ought to be pursued by the government," Helms recalled. But he added that the same could not be said for Johnson's advisors and appointees, "who frequently challenged our work with infuriating suggestions that we 'get on the team'—that is, trim our reporting to fit policy."[34] And there were a number of cases where Helms served in his role as "fact man," like the time the chairman of the JCS claimed that the power grid in Hanoi had been destroyed by bombing. LBJ asked Helms to confirm this by checking the facts on the ground. It didn't take a long process of damage assessments and analysis for Helms to find out that the bombing wasn't as effective as the military claimed—the lights were still on in Hanoi.

When Johnson's advisors, especially McNamara, finally started questioning the assumed truths about Vietnam, Johnson called in a new group of outside advisors—old-timers known as the Wise Men[35]—to take another look. The Wise Men naturally wanted to hear from the CIA. By then tensions at the lower levels of the Agency threatened to bubble over if more attempts were made to deliver a diluted message. One analyst remembered shaking his boss by the lapels and warning of open rebellion in the CIA's ranks if their briefing was in the least bit sugar-coated. Finally an unfiltered message got through.[36]

It was a terrible moment of truth for Johnson when he heard from the Wise Men that his Vietnam policy was a failure. After losing the New Hampshire primary, and now convinced that he could not defend his Vietnam policy, he withdrew from the race for the Democratic nomination, stopped the controversial bombing of North Vietnam, and removed General William Westmoreland as Commander, U.S. Military Assistance Command, Vietnam (COM USMACV).

Why had Johnson never been given such a frank briefing by his DCI? Unlike McCone and Smith, who drew strength from their effective management of the Intelligence Community, Helms's only source of strength was the president. To displease him by presenting the CIA's opinion (which ran counter to LBJ's policies and to opinion in the rest of the Intelligence Community) would have diminished his standing and completed his isolation. And then there was Helms's "feeling of awe" and "respect and admiration" for the president. How could he have sustained a course that would have undercut his president's policies?

Helms's loyalty ultimately served his president poorly. But the president didn't forget him. Richard Nixon repeatedly inquired about Helms in conversations with the lame-duck Johnson, especially about his political leanings. Johnson called Helms in to let him know that the incoming president had been asking questions. "I told him, 'Helms was a merit appointment. I've no idea how he voted in any election and I have never asked what his political views are. He's always been correct with me and has done a good job as director. I commend him to you.'"[37] With that, Johnson dismissed Helms from the Oval Office, and Helms kept his job under Nixon, at least for a while.

CHAPTER SIX

RICHARD NIXON, HELMS, SCHLESINGER, AND COLBY

The CIA Despised

"What the hell do those clowns do out there in Langley?" Nixon once complained to John Ehrlichman. "What use are they? They've got forty thousand people over there reading newspapers."[1] According to Nixon, "The CIA tells me nothing I don't read three days earlier in the *New York Times*."[2] With the arrival of Nixon in the White House, the DCI-presidential relationship reached its lowest point ever, before or since. During the Johnson administration, the CIA was often an annoyance. But Nixon came to the job already despising the CIA; he never gave it a chance.

Most people close to the situation believed the reason for Nixon's deep distrust was simple. In the view of his assistant for national security, Henry Kissinger, "He felt it imperative to exclude the CIA from the formulation of policy; it was staffed by Ivy League liberals, who behind the façade of analytical objectivity, were usually pushing their own preferences."[3] Lieutenant General Brent Scowcroft, USAF, then assistant to Henry Kissinger and later assistant to the president for national security, summed up: "It was less anything that really happened than the sense that the Intelligence Community was manned by and large by Ivy League people. He had an inferiority complex."[4] Following along these lines is the story that Nixon believed the CIA helped engineer the election of JFK (an Ivy League liberal) by allowing the missile gap fallacy to persist until after the election. Was that all there was to it? Nixon was a complex and private man, and others got only a glimpse of the inner workings of his mind when he was venting his rage—just the moment when he was likely to take a shot at the Ivy League gang.

One of the CIA's earliest services to Eisenhower was to give him an accurate picture of the rapidly deteriorating French military situation in Vietnam. Eisenhower's thinking on the situation was closer to the CIA's than to that of his vice president. So it appeared that the CIA helped to sabotage Nixon's first attempt to influence foreign policy. As the decade continued, Nixon watched as the Dulles brothers dominated foreign policy discussions while he was sidelined.

The first time Nixon met Richard Helms was in 1956, when another cloud was gathering over the Agency. Allen Dulles and Helms briefed Nixon on the Hungarian revolt before Nixon flew to Vienna to address Hungarian refugees. There was plenty of evidence even then that the CIA had encouraged the Hungarians to revolt, even though the Agency had no plans to support their revolution. After meeting with the refugees and hearing their stories, how could Nixon not blame the CIA and its provocative broadcasts, or more specifically Allen and John Foster Dulles, for the tragedy?

Later Nixon could easily see how the CIA had done a disservice to

Kennedy and Johnson at the Bay of Pigs, in Vietnam, and by failing to predict the Soviet invasion of Czechoslovakia in 1968. With his knowledge of world events, and with Kissinger at his side, did he need the CIA? Paranoia and overconfidence co-existed in Nixon's dislike of the Agency.

Why, then, did Nixon keep Richard Helms in the director's chair? And why, after a brief experiment with James Schlesinger as DCI, did he appoint William Colby, another career CIA man who had also started out in the OSS? When Helms first met President-elect Nixon, whom he knew had been asking about him (and especially about his politics), Nixon told him that he believed in the apolitical nature of the CIA. A new appointment could appear to politicize the job. So despite his contempt for the Agency, even Nixon adhered to one of its central guiding philosophies, all the while believing that the CIA was not itself remaining apolitical in its reporting.

"Whatever Nixon's view of the Agency . . . ," Helms remembered, "he was the best prepared to be President of any of those under whom I served—Eisenhower, Kennedy, and Johnson." However, in Helms's view, Nixon's relations with the CIA were "cranky" on a good day and much worse on most. The problem was, according to Helms, that Nixon did not want "an independent intelligence service," but instead a CIA supportive of his policies.[5] And even though Helms respected Nixon, he felt that the president's contempt for the CIA and his "persistent deriding of many who were in the best position to serve him" had an explanation, but it was one "best left to board-certified medical specialists."[6]

Johnson had been known to explode when he got bad news and he might argue with it, but Nixon took steps to make sure bad news didn't even reach him. "Incoming intelligence was closely monitored and its distribution controlled by Kissinger's staff to keep it from embarrassing the White House, and the national estimates function fell into comparative disrepute and neglect," according to Ray Cline.[7] At the very first meeting between Helms and Kissinger, this became clear: All reports and briefings were to go through Kissinger, even the National Intelligence Estimates. And Kissinger wasn't done. He wanted Helms to leave after briefing the National Security Council—he was not to be present during the discussion that followed. Helms had only recently gained access to Johnson's lunches. Now he was being squeezed out of Nixon's NSC meetings. And the NSC was increasingly centrally controlled. Some of the best—and most conservative—minds in the CIA and State Department were made NSC staffers. Their ranks swelled the NSC staff to four times its previous size, giving Kissinger a small army of analysts and policy wonks.

Helms appealed to the secretary of defense, Melvin Laird, who prevailed on Kissinger. The DCI simply had to be at the NSC meetings, and it made no sense to exclude him. The decision was reversed, but no one told Helms. As he was dutifully preparing to leave after his first briefing at an NSC meeting, Nixon invited everyone in the room to lunch. Helms couldn't decide if Nixon had forgotten or changed his mind, but he went.

Since Johnson wouldn't often take briefings, Helms contented himself with the thought that at least the president read the reports—especially the President's Daily Brief. So Helms was understandably concerned when he received a call from R. Jack Smith (who had been in current intelligence since Truman), telling him that Nixon wasn't reading his PDB. So Smith set up a meeting with Kissinger to figure out how to tailor the publication to Nixon's likings. Smith bravely faced Kissinger and Attorney General John Mitchell and asked them to critique the PDB. Too encyclopedic, they thought. Nixon didn't want to know what was going on in every corner of the world. Too opinionated, they added. The president just wanted the facts. Smith took this back to Helms, who had always strived to meet the needs of his consumer. But there's no evidence that Nixon took to a more "customized" version of the President's Daily Brief.

During his briefings of the NSC, Helms caught the brunt of Nixon's contempt. The president often interrupted him, corrected him, or badgered him with as much condescension as possible. This happened regularly, not just on particular issues. Other participants were aghast, some deeply embarrassed for the president, but no one could intervene. Kissinger held back even less than Nixon. "This isn't what we want!" he once screamed in the middle of a meeting while waving an NIE at Helms.[8]

Even worse, Nixon wasn't consistent. He seemed to reserve his gall for Helms, rather than direct it at all CIA officers. Once, he bid farewell to a pair of CIA officers who had just given him an account of sensitive operations with a jovial, "But don't get caught!" And when meeting Helms in private, Nixon was, Helms claimed, "often affable and always businesslike."[9] This gives Nixon's behavior in NSC meetings the appearance of a performance staged for the benefit of the rest of the national security team, as if Nixon had to put Helms in his place regularly.

Not that Kissinger and Nixon didn't have genuine trouble with Helms. The estimates had always been written so as to obscure the sources of information and to reflect the judgment of the analysts, not just present the facts. Kissinger and Nixon wanted to be given the raw materials, from which they could draw their own conclusions. Helms dutifully ordered a new approach to the Annual Survey of Soviet Intentions and Capabilities that would include the raw material—and it grew to hundreds of pages. Similarly, when Nixon asked for a briefing on China (to support his secret diplomacy), he got a top-to-bottom, encyclopedic report on the population, square miles, history, and so on, with little analysis. Nixon was visibly annoyed; Helms's attempt to please the consumer with "just the facts" had gone too far and backfired.

Helms's desire to appease Nixon's and Kissinger's appetites for knowing sources sometimes caused problems. As India and Pakistan drifted toward their third war in 1971, the CIA had a high-level asset providing solid intelligence from within the Indian cabinet. This agent uncovered the reason that India hadn't recognized Bangladesh, which was then breaking away from Pakistan: The Soviets had signed a secret agreement with the Indian government that extracted a promise from it to delay recognition. When the CIA identified its source in a report to the president, as it was increasingly required to do, the information leaked to a *New York Times* reporter, who wrote a story on the secret agreement. Helms told the White House that lives were at stake, and was in turn told to start an investigation of the reporter.

Then, as Indian forces fought Pakistani forces in Bangladesh later that year, the agent in the Indian cabinet sent a cable informing the CIA that India would attack Pakistan in twenty-four hours. The White House had been pressing for this information, so Helms sent the cable directly to Nixon, who called it one of the few useful and relevant pieces of information ever provided by the CIA. But the cable was passed around the White House, and the agent's career was over.

However, wars involving India were peripheral. As Nixon told Helms, "Look, don't talk to me about this, that, and the other thing. There's one number one problem hereabouts and that's Vietnam—get on with it."[10] The CIA had already been focused tightly on Southeast Asia for years, but without great success in either operating on the ground or getting its intelligence estimates considered by policy-makers. Now the situation was complicated by flaring tensions between the CIA and the military. "At that time there was a great contempt for military intelligence in the DI [the CIA's analytic department—the Directorate of Intelligence]," recalled James Schlesinger.[11] To some extent this was justified—the military had definitely given precedence to intelligence that backed its own policies.

Schlesinger and others cited an episode involving Sihanoukville, Cambodia, as a classic example of the differences between the CIA's thinking and the military's. The CIA kept saying that it had no evidence that the Chinese were shipping significant amounts of arms through the Cambodian port, but the military saw things differently. As Schlesinger put it, the military view was "We know how much is being shot at us, and that stuff that is being shot at us came from somewhere."[12] The two ways of thinking reflected two cultures—the CIA was devoted to dispassionate reasoning that resisted jumping to conclusions, whereas the military was more tied into the experiences of their colleagues on the ground who were catching the bullets.

The CIA analysts found that they were wrong and the military was right. Solving the problem of supplies going through Sihanoukville meant going into Cambodia with military force, which Nixon eventually did under a cloud of secrecy. He instructed Helms not to tell anyone else in the CIA of the plan, and Helms followed orders. Even further, Helms held on to a CIA report that warned of the dangers of invading Cambodia. Instead of sending it to Nixon and Kissinger, he returned it to the Office of National Estimates with instructions: "Let's take a look at this on June 1st, and see if we would keep it or make certain revisions."[13] Later, Helms said he didn't pass on the warning because Kissinger's and Nixon's minds were clearly made up. The report would have just angered them.

But in this double-edged dilemma, Helms could not, and did not, win any credit. Although the CIA admitted its mistake about Sihanoukville, the administration continually reminded Helms of it whenever his reports took a controversial position. And because he didn't forward the CIA's estimate on the risks of going into Cambodia to the decision-makers, his own Office of National Estimates began to distrust him. "Vietnam," Helms said, "was my nightmare for a good ten years."[14]

Edward Korry, ambassador to Chile, walked into the Oval Office one day in the fall of 1973. Nixon was in the middle of a rampage: "That son-of-a-bitch! That son-of-a-bitch!" Then, sensing that the ambassador might take this the wrong way, he added, "Not you, Mr. Ambassador. I know this isn't your fault and you've always told it like it is. It's that son-of-a-bitch Allende."[15] Kennedy had Castro and Nixon had Salvador Allende, just as Reagan would have the Sandinistas. And involved in each of these executive obsessions was the CIA.

By the time Ambassador Korry walked in on this tirade, the president had completely lost faith in the CIA's ability to do anything about the "problem" of a democratically elected leftist president in Chile. The episode produced some of the most famous quotes and reflections of the era— Nixon's wanting the CIA to make the Chilean economy "scream"; Kissinger's saying that he couldn't see why the United States should let a democratic Chile adopt a leftist stance just because the people wanted to; and Helms saying that if he ever carried a baton from the president it was that day in 1970 when he left the Oval Office with orders to prevent Allende from assuming power (he later regretted saying this).

Here again, Helms was in a situation where he could not win. Nixon wanted dramatic results quickly with maximum secrecy. Helms had been involved in covert action his entire life and knew that what Nixon demanded was not possible—it would not be clean, quick, or quiet. He received his marching orders in a fifteen-minute conversation. He claimed that he tried to point out the problems with Nixon's course of action, but the president and Kissinger had already made up their minds. They were serious.

Helms's track record of failing to warn Nixon about the problems inherent in an invasion of Cambodia, and his admitted awe of the man in the Oval Office, do suggest that he didn't do as much as he could or should have done to prevent the United States from becoming involved in activity of questionable strategic value in Chile. "I tried to give him some idea of the problems and risks involved. Standing mid-track and shouting at an oncoming locomotive might have been more effective," Helms re-called.[16]

Nixon was full of complaints about the CIA when, at the turn of the year 1970–1971, he sent James Schlesinger of the Bureau of the Budget to look at it. Schlesinger reported back on the perennial problem of U.S. intelligence: that the DCI did not have control over the wider family of agencies that made up the Intelligence Community. "A year later, when . . . George Shultz was the director [of the Office of Management and Budget], [and] I was the Assistant Director for National Security," Schlesinger said, "Shultz came bursting into my office, as it were, saying he had this great idea that the President was interested in restructuring the Intelligence Community."[17] In November 1971, Nixon did restructure, by enhancing the authority of the DCI as leader of the Intelligence Community. He explicitly required him or her to "prepare and submit each year, through OMB, a consolidated intelligence program budget, including tactical intelligence."[18] He told his DCI, "If you have any trouble doing this, let me know."[19]

Of course Helms had trouble, as had every last one of his predecessors. Those who had made some headway—Smith and McCone—had done so because the president had clearly and consistently signaled his support of the DCI and welcomed him into the Oval Office. Nixon did the opposite, and, to make matters worse, he had a DCI who was, as Schlesinger put it, "very, very cautious in exercising any authority outside of the CIA, [or] with the DOD."[20]

During discussions over the SALT I arms control treaty, for example, Helms came under pressure from both the White House and the Department of Defense. In meetings of the U.S. Intelligence Advisory Board, where NIEs were discussed and "coordinated" with the wider Community, Helms would close the meeting whenever the discussion got too hot and send the NIE back for revision. Helms's acquiescence in this case was especially unfortunate—arms control verification is one of the most important functions of an independent intelligence service, a place where the CIA must seriously question military intelligence.

In 1969, Helms and his deputy director for science and technology, Carl Duckett, testified before the Senate Foreign Relations Committee about the need for an antiballistic missile (ABM) system. Kissinger and Defense Secretary Melvin Laird were for the system, claiming that the massive Soviet buildup of intercontinental ballistic missiles revealed that their intention was to create a first-strike capability. The prevailing view at the CIA was that the Soviets were building toward a nuclear balance; that they were just trying to catch up to the Americans. The difference of opinion reveals the grayest area in intelligence—trying to deduce a rival's intentions from his capabilities.

The Soviet buildup was concentrated on the SS-9, an ICBM the CIA felt was several generations behind the U.S. Minuteman missile. The CIA saw the SS-9 as an adequate deterrent from the Soviet perspective, but not accurate enough or plentiful enough to wipe out the United States' retaliatory force in a first strike. So, according to the CIA, the Soviet buildup had merely aimed for the balance of mutual assured destruction envisioned by former defense secretary Robert McNamara. Kissinger and Laird, however, believed that the SS-9 was a MIRV (multiple independently targetable reentry vehicle), a missile that carried several warheads, each targeted on its own destination with pinpoint accuracy. If this were true, the Soviets had a greater capability than that claimed by the CIA.

When Helms and Duckett were done with their testimony, Senator J. William Fulbright remarked that they had presented a very different picture from that of the secretary of defense. When Kissinger learned of this, he flew into a rage and called Helms onto the carpet. He ordered a revised report on the SS-9. The requested report contained more data—much more—but the conclusions were the same. The analysts, drawing not only on hard intelligence about what they knew of the missile but also on economic and political intelligence, decided that "we consider it highly unlikely that [the Soviets] will attempt within the period of this estimate to achieve a first-strike capability." The costs to their economy were too high. The chances were slim that they could succeed. And they knew that the United States would detect any attempt to develop a first-strike capability and then match it. The report didn't mention the ABM proposal, but without a credible threat, Kissinger knew that support in Congress would vanish.[21]

At Kissinger's direction, Helms removed the paragraph that speculated on Soviet intentions. The data remained the same, but the analytical contribution of the CIA was stripped. Helms himself played down this manipulation of CIA reporting, but Kissinger was bluntly informing Helms that in this administration the CIA was to provide information only. The White House would take care of interpreting it. The ABM program squeezed through the Senate by one vote. It was years, though, before the Soviets added MIRV capability to their missiles.

In 1972, under the pressures of the presidential election and the lack of progress in Vietnam, Nixon commented that he was "thoroughly disgusted with [the CIA's] performance in North Vietnam," and noted that "the problem is the CIA is a muscle-bound bureaucracy, which has completely paralyzed its brain." He stated, "I want a study made immediately as to how many people in CIA could be removed by Presidential action." Then he revealingly added that he wanted the CIA to "quit recruiting from any of the Ivy League schools or any other universities where either the university president or the university faculties have taken action condemning our efforts to bring the war in Vietnam to an end."[22] According to Chief of Staff H. R. Haldeman, Nixon said, "Helms has got to go. Get rid of the clowns—cut personnel 40 percent. Its info is worthless."[23]

There is no doubt Helms would have lost his job even if Watergate had never happened, but that episode showed Nixon that Helms's loyalty was to the office of the president, and not to him personally. This was clear when Nixon asked Helms to help quash an FBI investigation of Watergate that was getting too close. All Helms had to do was say that national security was involved, and the FBI would have to back off, Nixon reasoned. Helms refused, making perhaps the best and most courageous decision of his career. Nixon complained, "Helms's ass is out there. His whole career is out there," but "he's never going to say that he participated in a cover-up."[24] Helms didn't hear this conversation, but he could have surmised that his refusal would cost him his job.

Unbelievably, Helms didn't see it coming. In November 1972, after the election, Nixon summoned him to Camp David. Nixon, according to Helms, often had a rambling way of speaking, even during discussions of deeply important topics. This conversation started out that way, before Nixon moved on to a reflection of Helms's service and pointed out that he was a Democratic appointment in a Republican administration. Then he finally told Helms that his career in the CIA was over but he could have an ambassadorship.

Helms wanted to stay on until March, when he would turn sixty and reach retirement age. Nixon agreed. But Helms was surprised when his successor, James Schlesinger, was sworn in on February 2. Helms was undone: "A few days later, I encountered Haldeman. 'What happened to our understanding that my exit would be postponed for a few weeks?' I asked. 'Oh, I guess I forgot,' he said with the faint trace of a smile. And so it was over."[25]

Helms had been surprised when Johnson announced he was to be the

DCI, and surprised again when Nixon took him off the job. It is tempting to use these bookends to sum up Helms's tenure as one of bland service and lack of communication with the president. The CIA professionals remember him another way, however. He was one of theirs. He stood up to the president when asked to employ the CIA in a cover-up. He also cared for and looked after his people. Years later, when George Tenet became DCI, he moved the portrait of Helms from a gallery of DCIs into his office, indicating how much support and respect Helms retained in the Agency.

Nixon would have hated any comparison to Kennedy, but in replacing his DCI, he took a similar path. Both removed a man closely associated with the Agency and handed the reins to an outsider who was expected to fill the role of troubleshooter. In Nixon's case the outsider was James Schlesinger, the man who had already performed a survey of the CIA and made some controversial recommendations about reforming the intelligence apparatus. Now he was expected to implement them on a demoralized Agency.

"He is an impatient man, and there is nothing wrong with that," insisted one former CIA officer. "There are ways to be impatient and there are ways to implement the impatience."[26] Perhaps one way not to get started was the announcement Schlesinger made to the Board of National Estimates: "I understand that this is like a gentleman's club. Well, I want you to know that I am no gentleman."[27] Indeed, there was to be little protection for the CIA employees whom Schlesinger saw as clogging the system.

"The age profile of the Agency by that time had become either the oldest or near oldest in the federal government," Schlesinger claimed. "You had as a result this layering on top of the agency in which the same pals switched posts around." This kept new talent from rising to the top and kept in control the same folks who had been there since the OSS days, "this older generation that felt itself to be anointed."[28] These were the people that Schlesinger wanted removed.

The purge that removed a thousand employees in a matter of weeks was not appreciated. "The usual death threats came in through the security people," Schlesinger recalled.[29] The Agency's internal security put extra bodyguards on Schlesinger's detail. Once, when Schlesinger was hosting a tour, he guided his visitor away from the Technical Services Division (which was the R&D center for the CIA's 007-type gadgets). "I can't take you through there. I don't think either one of us would emerge alive."[30]

This painful process of thinning the CIA's ranks targeted the same people Nixon saw as part of the Ivy League liberal conspiracy. So even if that wasn't Schlesinger's intention, he could always count on distant support from the president. On one occasion, when a group of high-level officers were threatening to rebel, Schlesinger called them into his office and got Nixon on the phone. He explained to the president that his purging operations might have unintended consequences. Disgruntled employees might leak, sue, or otherwise malign the Agency. Nixon told him he would back the DCI no matter what, and the officers fell, more or less, into line.

Schlesinger's deputy director of operations (he got rid of the euphemism "directorate of plans," which had long been the name for the espionage and covert-action wing of the CIA) was William Colby, an OSS veteran who would become the next DCI. As investigations of Nixon's cover-up continued, Schlesinger found that the CIA had been involved in the burglary of Daniel Ellsberg's psychiatrist's office. Schlesinger hit the roof. He thought he'd been fully briefed on what the Agency had and had not done vis-à-vis Watergate. Colby caught the brunt of Schlesinger's anger, with the DCI threatening to "tear the place apart and fire everyone if necessary."[31] "His anger over this had to be experienced to be believed," Colby recalled, "and I experienced it, both barrels."[32]

Schlesinger didn't want any more surprises and ordered Colby to make sure there weren't any. But Schlesinger's memo to Colby "did not

specify Watergate," as he recalled. "It alluded to recent troubles or something like that." All CIA officers were to report what they knew to the inspector general. Schlesinger said he didn't intend this to be taken literally,
but that was what happened. The CIA spilled its guts en masse, and the
inspector general ended up with a collection of 683 incidents spanning
CIA history that could be considered illegal or against CIA policy and directives. "Well, it did not occur to me that anyone would think of dragging up all of the stuff in the Agency," Schlesinger stated, blaming
William Colby for what happened. "I think that was Bill's intention,
though, because when I left he kept dragging these things up, not about
Watergate, but about all these things."[33]

Someone in the CIA dubbed this collection the "Family Jewels." Its
very existence had the potential for destroying the Agency, but too much
damage had been done and too many people knew about the collection for
it to be simply destroyed and forgotten. "I don't think [Schlesinger] had
anything malevolent in mind," Brent Scowcroft recalled, "but once he had
collected all this stuff, he had a bomb."[34] All this was going on as
Schlesinger was on his way out. Nixon decided, somewhat abruptly, that
Schlesinger would be a better secretary of defense, and selected William
Colby to succeed him as DCI.

When Colby became DCI, the president was in the middle of Watergate, the CIA was in the midst of a traumatic restructuring, and the country was tasting the bitter fruits of the final stages of the Vietnam conflict.
No other DCI has assumed the reins during such a difficult time. Colby
may have been the most qualified within the CIA to deal with these problems, as he had firsthand experience with them all.

Like Helms, Colby was an old OSS hand and had spent his life in the
espionage and covert-action wing of the CIA. Colby had been in the field
for many years, including Vietnam, and had a bit less of the bureaucrat in
him. During World War II, he had parachuted into France in advance of

D-day, and later skied about Norway with a team of commandos blowing up bridges while evading Germans. He knew at the time that his efforts were not having much of a strategic impact—they were not winning the war. However, he wrote, "the political fact that Americans had fought and died in Norway dramatized the new alliance between America and this fatherland of so many of our citizens. . . . In this field . . . the actions of a few could produce potent political results, independent of their physical contribution. Thus, the final worth of the bravery of our men lay in the political dimension."[35]

Colby started his first day as DCI by driving his own car to work instead of being driven in the armored limousine. He parked in his normal spot, came in through the usual entrance, and ate in the cafeteria. He would regularly visit people in their offices rather than call them up to his. He carefully tried to remain one of the guys. It is difficult to tell if this was an employee relations scheme or whether he was actually uncomfortable in his exalted position. In any case, events would soon conspire to put a real wedge between him and the Agency that no such gestures could mend.

CHAPTER SEVEN

GERALD FORD, COLBY, AND GEORGE H. W. BUSH

The CIA Under a Microscope

President Gerald Ford took the call on an open, nonsecure line aboard Air Force One. He was flying to Colorado for his Christmas vacation in 1974. On the other end was his DCI, William Colby. The circumstances, timing, and urgency of the call portended a crisis. Had a government fallen? Had a new offensive opened in Vietnam? The use of a nonsecure line suggested that the DCI had thrown caution to the wind. But it was neither. The issue was an article in the *New York Times* written by Seymour Hersh and published on the front page on Sunday, December 22, revealing secret CIA activities—ones the executive branch did not want to be known. Because of this newspaper article, a ripple of events would bring the CIA under intense scrutiny by Congress and the public for the first time.

For a man like William Colby, who was used to life in the shadows and who once said, "I think family skeletons are best left where they are—in the closet,"[1] this was an incredibly emotional time. Secrecy was critical to the personal and physical protection of many in the CIA. At times it protected their lives, at others their ability to work in the future, and often their sources overseas, whose lives depended on the CIA's being able to keep their identities secret. But at the same time, it could conceal the misdeeds and the incompetence of some in the CIA. For a while, it looked like the secrecy on which so much depended was all going to end. Many in the CIA thought that their own DCI was rushing to make this happen.

When Gerald Ford, the first president who had not been elected either as chief executive or vice president, moved into the White House, he chose a portrait of Harry S Truman to hang in the Cabinet Room; and in the Oval Office a bust of Truman sat perched behind his desk, peering over his shoulder. Ford, who had been thrust into the presidency unexpectedly, felt a bond with Truman that transcended partisanship. He later admitted that, much like Truman, he did not feel ready to be president.

Ford had gone to college on a football scholarship and could have gone pro if he had seen any future in it. Instead he went to Yale Law School and served in the Pacific as an officer in the U.S. Navy during World War II. After the war, he had barely started his law career before he ran for U.S. representative in a district centered in the heavily Republican section of Grand Rapids, Michigan. His career in Congress spanned more time than even LBJ's—twenty-five years—and it was remarkable for how few enemies he made. Ford liked to say that he had only adversaries, not enemies. He was universally respected, with a reputation for nonpartisanship and honesty. He was one of those rare characters who attain leadership through merit rather than politics. But after a career that included twelve years on the House Appropriations Committee, service on the Warren Commission that investigated the Kennedy assassination, and serving as House minority leader, he was ready to retire in 1973. The Republicans had failed to get a majority in the House in 1972. It seemed he would never be Speaker of the House.

Then came a chain of events that would alter his life. First, Nixon's vice president, Spiro T. Agnew, was forced to resign in the fall of 1973 when it was revealed he had been taking kickbacks from some Maryland businessmen. On October 12, 1973, Nixon nominated Ford to replace Agnew. Then, on August 9, 1974, Nixon resigned and Ford became president.

Much like Truman, Ford had been picked for vice president largely because he was an uncontroversial figure. After the scandal of Spiro Agnew, Nixon needed a calming, if bland, second in command. When Ford came into office, he expected that his would be a short and typically uneventful vice-presidency. But by the summer of 1974, it began to seem possible, if not likely, that he would become president. When Nixon resigned from office in August, at the height of the Watergate scandal, Gerald Rudolph Ford became the thirty-eighth president of the United States.

Ford struck a chord with the public as he preached the need to restore trust in government. But a month after he became president, he decided to pardon Nixon, and suddenly the honeymoon was over. Accusations that there had been a deal could not be proven, but Ford could not shake the suspicion that his rhetoric about honest government was just rhetoric. Following the pardon, Ford was unfairly labeled as blundering and unintelligent. He couldn't escape LBJ's line that he was so dumb he couldn't "fart and chew gum at the same time,"[2] and he bore the unfortunate distinction of being the first president to be lampooned on *Saturday Night Live*, which launched during his presidency.

He always claimed that his real reason for pardoning Nixon was to attempt to save the presidency. There's no evidence to the contrary, and his record from that point on was perfectly consistent with that motivation. He battled incessantly with Congress over presidential prerogatives, used the veto more than any president before him, and was, according to Kissinger, even more closely involved in directing the details of foreign policy than Nixon had been.

Ford's desire to save the presidency guided him during the "Year of Intelligence," 1975. It brought him into conflict with William Casey, a future DCI and a man he probably would have gotten along with well under different circumstances.

Ford loved to talk things over. He would smoke his pipe during Oval Office meetings, leaning back and listening to whomever was speaking. When he was ready, he'd remove the pipe, lean forward, and quickly summarize what he'd just heard. He "preferred to have contact with people," recalled one aide, "to talk it over at the table and have a lively debate."[3] He saw "a lot of people in making a decision," recalled his staff secretary, "while President Nixon saw few or none."[4] It was very curious, then, that he and Colby met one-on-one only twice during 1975. Colby usually sent someone else to the White House with the daily brief. Because Ford was aware that he had a rather distant managerial style, he felt he was perhaps too easy on people who worked for him, giving them too many breaks and overlooking too many mistakes. Curiously, though, Colby received no breaks and Ford overlooked nothing.

Still more curious was how quickly Ford dropped an initial promise to the country. "I expect to follow my instincts of openness and candor with full confidence that honesty is the best policy in the end," he proclaimed in 1974. Regarding Congress, he promised "communication, conciliation, compromise, and cooperation."[5] It was only a few months later that Colby was being excoriated for being too open.

Although Ford admired and looked to Truman as an example, he had a different idea of the CIA's purpose. While Truman wanted the CIA to provide him with a "newspaper" that gave him the facts without independent judgments, Ford saw the CIA as a body that was set up as a "think tank for the President to get independent judgment." The CIA, during Ford's time, was capable of producing such judgments, but it had a difficult time getting them delivered to the president. "I would say I got as much of my intelligence briefing through Kissinger as I did through Colby," Ford claimed. "Henry was the conduit, basically."[6]

Getting an objective, independent judgment delivered through someone as policy-driven as Kissinger was unlikely. He was both secretary of state and assistant for national security. He dominated the NSC process and could control what intelligence flowed in and out of it. By the end of 1975, even Republicans in Congress were claiming that intelligence was coming to them "through a screen of policy-making officials." The Pike Committee, investigating the CIA, accused Kissinger of "political control of intelligence."[7] Ford, who liked to get deep into the details of foreign policy (according to Kissinger), was getting the Kissinger-filtered version of intelligence before he made decisions.

Ford wasn't fully aware that Kissinger had brought some baggage along with him from the Nixon administration. Accusations about CIA involvement in Chile broke in the *New York Times* just a month after Ford took the presidency. They made it look as though Nixon had lied to the people and misled Congress. For former DCI Richard Helms, who didn't yet have the benefit of a presidential pardon, things looked much worse. Helms had deliberately misled Congress about Chile on two occasions—when he was before a Senate committee on multinational corporations, and again when he was being confirmed as ambassador to Iran. In his view, in both instances it had been necessary to preserve secrets. Now, with the cat out of the bag, Colby started hearing rumblings in the CIA that Helms had perjured himself. The CIA's inspector general wanted to know what to do. Stuck between the law and loyalty to a friend, Colby sent the matter to an internal CIA legal panel. At issue was whether there was enough evidence of perjury to warrant a referral to the Department of Justice, a referral that Colby was legally bound to make if he suspected the law had been broken.

The panel split on whether Helms had committed perjury, which was not helpful to Colby. But they did recommend that the matter go to the Justice Department. Colby tried to hold fast and keep the matter under wraps, but the members of the panel started crying foul, so he paid a visit to Justice. There, he planned to get advice on procedure, not turn in his friend, but when the people at the Department of Justice got wind of what was going on, they forced him to name names. Without hesitation, the Justice Department took the matter into its own hands.

Thus, at the very beginning of what would become a year of probes and subpoenas, Colby had made a move that backfired and made it look as if he had betrayed the CIA, a president, and a friend. Colby and Helms had lunch in January 1975; it was their last social meeting. Helms, who later pled no contest to charges of failing to testify accurately to a Senate committee, never forgave Colby, nor did many others. "I was quite angry about his role in nailing Dick Helms," recalled James Schlesinger. "It was a disgrace. . . . Bill was intent on this cleansing operation and so he had gone to the Department of Justice. . . . It was bloody awful."[8] In these and similar statements, no one seemed to mention that Helms did, after all, lie. Colby was under the same obligation to tell the truth, but he felt it more deeply.

When Colby first learned of the impending publication of the *New York Times* article, he went to Kissinger and filled him in. The crux of the article was that the CIA had been involved in domestic spying against antiwar protesters. Collecting intelligence about Americans was outside the CIA's mandate. The CIA justified its actions by claiming it had limited itself to investigating possible foreign involvement in the antiwar movement. None were ever found.

But when Colby briefed Kissinger on the article, he did something he should have done a long time before. Although he had informed members of the House and Senate oversight committees of these reports on CIA misdeeds, the so-called Family Jewels, in hopes of heading off the very sort of investigations that would do great damage to the Agency, Colby had not told the White House. Nixon and Kissinger, as well as Ford, been left in the dark. Now it all came out.

Once he was informed, Kissinger's reaction and advice to Ford was to "not act in such a way as to give credence to the allegations . . . and create an impression that a major problem actually exists and that the Ford administration is confronted with a scandal of major proportions." The White House largely believed that this problem would blow over. But that was a severe misreading of the mood in the country and the seriousness of the allegations. Besides, the press didn't even have the whole story. The real scandals remained locked up in Langley. But it was a serious miscalculation to think that the press or Congress would not get excited about the "Family Jewels" sooner rather than later. In days past, the leadership in Congress would have been inclined to accept the CIA position that, as a general rule, secrets should remain secret. But after Watergate, Congress was not as disposed to be protective of the Agency. And now Ford found out about them from Kissinger, who agreed that "some few of them clearly were illegal, while others . . . raise profound moral questions."[9]

When it started to look as though the controversy stirred up by Seymour Hersh would not just go away, Ford shelved Kissinger's original idea of not responding. He did what politicians normally do when confronted with dangerous allegations—he formed a commission. But in this case, the commission had deeper purposes than stalling and obfuscation. By starting an investigation, the White House hoped to prevent Congress from doing the same. It also helped Ford address the issue without taking a stand. For nearly thirty years, presidents had risen to defend the CIA publicly. Now, the president's own chief of staff, Richard Cheney, recommended that Ford neither defend nor condemn the CIA. Colby and Ford did not meet between the publication of the Hersh article and the establishment of the commission. Ford was sending a clear signal that the DCI was on his own. The CIA professionals had distanced themselves from the White House during Watergate. Now it was their turn.

The president formed a commission on CIA activities within the United States, known as the Rockefeller Commission. It was heavily weighted in the president's favor. First and foremost, his own vice president, Nelson Rockefeller, chaired it. Most recognizable on the commission was Ronald Reagan, former governor of California. There was no love lost between Reagan and the war protesters who were the real victims of the CIA's domestic spying, for as governor, he had turned the National Guard on them in his home state. The commission also included General Lyman Lemnitzer, who had been an Eisenhower appointee as chairman of the Joint Chiefs of Staff; C. Douglas Dillon, who had been Ike's ambassador to France and undersecretary of state, as well as secretary of the treasury under Kennedy and Johnson, and so had an appearance of nonpartisanship; and John Conner, Johnson's secretary of commerce, who had resigned over Vietnam and whose previous experience with intelligence had been as an assistant to James V. Forrestal during the drafting of the National Security Act of 1947, which had created the CIA. Erwin Griswold, former U.S. solicitor general, added legal weight to the group. And finally, David W. Belin, investigator for the Warren Commission, became the executive director of the commission's staff. In all, the commission had the appearance of a group of serious public servants. However, none of them were really likely to question presidential prerogatives or to dig too deeply, or so Ford thought. The commission had a very narrow mandate to investigate the Hersh allegations only.

Once these rapidly made selections were announced, Ford finally sat down to meet with Colby on the evening of January 3, 1975. The two had not had a chance to develop a working relationship. One reason was that there simply had not been time. Another was that Colby typically did not force himself on those in power. It wasn't his style and it wasn't the way he had risen through the ranks of the CIA. In retrospect, though, he knew he should have tried for more face time with the president. By now the CIA was political poison. This short and sharp meeting between Colby and Ford convinced Colby that he would be on his own.

Colby's first appearance before the Rockefeller Commission was on January 13. He did not clear his testimony or his opening statement with the White House, but he did stop by afterward and let Deputy National Security Advisor Brent Scowcroft know what had just transpired. Colby later realized that not handing over his opening statement before going to the commission looked bad. He made things worse for himself by giving the commission just about the same information he had given to the president when the story was about to break and immediately after it ran. Kissinger was not at all pleased that he and the president knew no more than the commission, and that Congress had gotten a look at the "Family Jewels" before he did. Colby was not reading the political landscape well and was off to a rough start.

Soon, though, Ford committed one of the biggest presidential gaffes. At an informal meeting with the editors of the *New York Times,* a meeting that was totally off the record, Ford explained that he didn't want America's name and standing dragged through the mud by a series of investigations into and revelations about the "cesspool" of foreign intelligence. Was it as bad as it looked in the Hersh article? Worse, the president admitted. Somehow, in this casual atmosphere Ford let slip that the CIA had been involved in assassinations. This one gaffe changed the whole game. Although the *Times* editors decided they couldn't pursue it, the president's statement made it into the gossip circles and was eventually pursued to its logical conclusion by CBS's Daniel Schorr. The House and the Senate both voted to open probing and long-running investigations of the CIA.

Ford even started to lose control over his own presidential commission. Belin, the staff director, put assassination on the Rockefeller Commission's agenda, taking it far beyond its original mandate. He was backed in this by Ronald Reagan, who practically insisted on a full investigation of CIA misdeeds, not just of domestic spying. The commission took it to a vote, and Nelson Rockefeller, who wanted to continue with a limited mandate, lost. Later, as more CIA misdemeanors came out in the congressional hearings, Ford gave his blessing to an expanded investigation by his own vice president's commission. By then, the dike was breaking and there was no sense in trying to plug up the holes.

After one of Colby's sessions with the Rockefeller Commission, the vice president approached the DCI. Could he be a little less forthcoming with the commission? Did they really need to know all this? According to Colby, they did, and the Agency needed them to know it. Colby saw the very existence of the CIA threatened, and he believed that the best way to save it was "to lift as much as possible that thick cloak of secrecy that had traditionally veiled the Agency."[10] Although it was a recent memory, few in the national security firmament had learned a lesson from the fact that Nixon fell not because of the crime, but because of the cover-up. Colby did remember. It was better, he felt, to give a complete picture, so that the misdeeds of the CIA could be viewed in context. And besides, he wrote, "I also believed that any other approach just wouldn't work."[11]

Although the Rockefeller Commission had taken on a new magnitude of responsibility, it got only another two months from President Ford to complete its work. Belin did a massive amount of research on possible CIA involvement in the deaths of Patrice Lumumba of the Belgian Congo (Zaire), Rafael Trujillo of the Dominican Republic, and President

Sukarno of Indonesia. But he also naturally gravitated toward the Kennedy assassination due to his days on the Warren Commission. The information he gathered on the deaths of foreign leaders did not make it into the final report. "The Commission's staff began the requested inquiry," the final report stated, "but time did not permit a full investigation before the report was due. The President has therefore requested that the materials in the possession of the Commission which bear on these allegations be turned over to him. This has been done."[12]

The unfinished report was now heavily edited in secrecy by the White House staff. For example, Kissinger didn't like a section on interception of communications of the USSR. It might have complicated his détente project. Other parts of the report were toned down. Even some of the recommendations were revised. In the end, the report was not a complete whitewash, but neither did it add much to the ongoing debate. But that was not its real purpose. "I thought I had to have an independent group to counteract Pike and Church [the leaders of the Congressional investigations]," recalled President Ford. "I think they [the commission] gave us a backup to refute many irresponsible legislative intrusions."[13]

Those "legislative intrusions" were the investigations chaired by Senator Frank Church and Representative Otis Pike. Church was a feared and practiced debater who had long harbored presidential ambitions. But his fight with the Ford administration should not be interpreted merely as an attempt to seek publicity. Church was a longtime Vietnam dissenter and honestly believed in the dangers of the "imperial presidency." Presidents, in his view, had been given, or had simply taken, too much power in foreign affairs, and this had led to Vietnam and the erosion of American popularity around the world. While Church saw the presidency as too powerful, Ford came into the Oval Office determined to leave the presidency stronger than he found it. The occasion for the battle between Ford and Church was the CIA, but the real fight was over the respective power of the executive and legislative branches.

Otis Pike, who did not aspire to be president, similarly had an idealistic basis for his investigation of the CIA. Pike had flown an impressive 120 combat missions in the Pacific theater during World War II and had been an avid supporter of the Vietnam War until the last terrible years. To Pike, this investigation was about the Constitution as much as it was about the CIA. In some ways, Pike was even more aggressive than Church, often clearly driven and outraged both in writing and in conversation.

Cast off by the White House and convinced that Congress would get to the truth sooner or later, Colby made reasonable efforts to cooperate with the investigations. The White House, however, saw someone who was bending over backward to be helpful. "What I remember is that . . . poor Bill Colby, who I think was having serious psychological problems, just was dumping the files out of the CIA. . . . It was pretty wholesale," recalled Brent Scowcroft.[14] (Colby was certainly under stress, but whether he was having serious psychological problems is moot.) Meanwhile, as the congressional committees saw it, Colby wasn't giving up enough and the White House was blocking their requests. There was no way a DCI could win in a situation like this.

Colby developed several levels of secrecy to deal with the requests of Congress, and each level had its own rules for how the documents would be handled. Interestingly, the documents that were given the highest level of secrecy, which the investigators could not see at all, were those that contained "sensitive matters where Executive Branch prerogatives are involved."[15] Under this scheme, Congress could see many CIA in-house histories, which are often very critical of the CIA, but not those items that would have made it possible for the CIA to point the finger at a past president. Even after the CIA's people had classified and prepared the documents for Congress, the material was first sent to the White House for review. So Colby was taking steps to protect the presidency, even giving that institution higher priority than the Agency.

As the investigations were going on, Colby became increasingly pliable when it came to the CIA's intelligence estimates. The NSC had asked for unclassified reports on Soviet aid to North Vietnam in March 1975 to back up requests by Ford for aid to South Vietnam. The reports did not show an increase in aid by the USSR—in fact North Vietnam was receiving much less aid than South Vietnam. The NSC staff inserted language into the report to make it look like the opposite was true, and Colby went along. There were only so many fronts on which he could fight.

But by early April, Colby had reversed an earlier position on the resiliency of South Vietnam. By now the South's situation was nearly hopeless. At one meeting, he asked for permission to state his views on policy—which DCIs aren't supposed to do—and asked for evacuation efforts to focus on getting two million South Vietnamese people out of the country before it was taken over by the North Vietnamese. It was a heartfelt plea from a man who had lived among the Vietnamese and really believed the United States was fighting to save them. The following day, Ford gave a speech in which he said that there was little that America could do for South Vietnam. The United States was out by April 29.

American prestige around the world received a one-two punch from the fall of South Vietnam and the revelations coming out of Congress. Then, one May morning, Scowcroft woke Ford. The Cambodian navy had seized the American merchant ship *Mayaguez* and had taken its crew prisoner. "So I called for a meeting of the Intelligence Community at 7 o'clock in the morning so I could get an update," Ford recalled. The incident, unfolding over the next two days, was a true test of the Intelligence Community's ability to get quick, coordinated information to the president. At several points he was disappointed. "I am very concerned about the delay in reports," he told Colby at one meeting. "We must have the information immediately. There must be the quickest possible communication to me." At another, he complained, "There should be a quicker way to let us know [that the ship had been seized]." And after one Colby briefing, he stated, "We have to be more factual or at least more precise in pointing out our degree of knowledge."[16]

The fact was, it was a fluid situation and there was little information to be had—specifically about the location of the crew. Ford was quite pleased when they managed to get the radio transmissions of a navy pilot, who thought he saw a group of white men on a Cambodian vessel, routed directly to the White House situation room. But fifteen Marines were killed during an ill-advised attack on an island where intelligence suggested the crew of the *Mayaguez* had been taken, whereas they were actually on the mainland. The entire episode did not raise the president's confidence in the Intelligence Community or his DCI.

Despite this, it was only a few months before Ford called for a covert action plan for Angola. Asking for and authorizing a new secret war right in the middle of a congressional investigation was incredibly risky. The CIA followed orders and offered up a plan while warning that there was really no hope of keeping the proposed actions secret for very long. Colby agreed, and told the president so. By this time, though, Ford already had a secret list of possible replacements for the embattled DCI. At the same time, Kissinger never stopped riding Colby. In fact, he often got personal, and in an unkind reference to Colby's devout Catholicism, once said, "Bill, you know what you do when you go up to the Hill? You go to confession."[17]

Bill Colby knew that each day he kept his job was a miracle. A dismissal was always looming. He had been in the CIA too long, and had seen too many DCIs dismissed, to think that his career could survive a year of intelligence investigations. The end came as a part of a Ford shake-up of his entire foreign policy team. Many observers saw chaos in the White House, with the Nixon holdovers forever fighting with the Ford newcomers. Schlesinger, the secretary of defense and former DCI, had to go because he contradicted Kissinger too often. Kissinger had to give up the assistant for national security hat and be secretary of state only, because his policies of détente made Ford vulnerable to attacks from the Republican far right. In the midst of this shake-up, who would pay much attention to the resignation of a DCI?

Scowcroft noted that Ford "fired him not because he thought Colby was incompetent but, because of all the scandals, he thought he just had to have a new DCI."[18] In fact, Ford privately said that he admired Colby's integrity and consistency, his courage and intelligence. He also remembered how gracefully Colby went out. "Colby understood it and didn't object to it, and so forth."[19] Colby accepted his fate and was out of the Oval Office in fifteen minutes.

Colby's CIA career was over, but he couldn't leave yet. Ford's hand-picked replacement, George H. W. Bush, was in China as ambassador. Congress was still demanding files and generally annoying the president. Both Ford and Colby made appeals to Senator Church not to go with the assassinations section of the report, the section that revealed an Eisenhower who wanted Lumumba dead and a Robert Kennedy who sent hit men out after Castro. Church went ahead anyway. Colby called a press conference at Langley headquarters. It was the CIA's second press conference—the first one had been an announcement that the Soviet economy was taking a serious downturn in the early sixties. At this one, Colby stated flatly that people would die because of the Church report. Terrorists would come after them. This same argument had already been put before Church, and most of the names in the report had been excised. Nevertheless, it was a pronouncement that got the attention of the press, and one that was recalled a month later when a terrorist group in Athens killed CIA officer Richard Welch. (By coincidence, at the time of Welch's murder in Athens, I was next door in Naples, Italy, as commander in chief of NATO's southern flank. When Mrs. Welch came through Naples on her way back to the United States, I met her and provided hospitality.)

It's hard to overstate how much this killing undermined the investigations. Welch's death put a human face on Colby's predictions—even though it has since been very well established that the killing and the investigations had nothing to do with each other. Even at the time, Colby suspected and feared it might be the start of a spy war with the KGB. But Ford had a real opportunity to take the teeth out of the investigations, and so for the first time, an American president greeted and saluted the remains of a slain CIA officer in a public show of support for the Agency. Probably not coincidentally, Congress voted *not* to release the Pike report (which was later leaked to the *Village Voice*).

In the end, the Rockefeller Commission's report was too watered down to amount to much. The Church report recommended new charters for the Defense Department's agency for coordinating intelligence, the Defense Intelligence Agency (DIA); the CIA; and the NSA; but these were not written. The Pike report wanted the DIA abolished, criticized the NSC oversight mechanism, and called for increased congressional oversight, but had a rather small impact. It also recommended a ban on assassinations, which was implemented.

Before these investigations, no one really thought about an American president's ordering an assassination—it's far too unpleasant a proposition. Since then, we've grown accustomed to the fact that there is a ban on the practice, though we have directed military attacks specifically on Muammar Qaddafi and Osama bin Laden. But at the time, this unpleasant issue was a question of presidential authority and a flashpoint in the power struggle between the White House and Congress.

When Colby returned from testifying on assassinations before the Church Committee and reported to the White House, he recalled being treated like a "prisoner in the dock." He had explained to the committee that the CIA had standing orders prohibiting assassination. And then, he recalled, "Church ended by saying that is not enough. That, to be certain, we need more than orders. We need to have a law which prohibits assassination in time of peace." Kissinger snorted. "It is an act of insanity and national humiliation to have a law prohibiting the President from ordering assassination."[20] By the time the reports were out, it looked like a law against assassination would pass Congress if it were proposed, but in the end, the idea of having Congress tie the hands of the president was more galling than the idea of not being able to assassinate people. "We had agreed with the committee of the House and the Senate committee," recalled Scowcroft, "that in order to avoid them trying to legislate, that we would incorporate directives directly on assassination and all that stuff."[21]

Ford feels now that it was a good idea. "I have not seen any instances [where] my executive order or the ban on assassinations has crippled our foreign policy." Still, the former president believes that the order may need to be revisited to meet the problems of today, though he cautions about moving too fast.[22] Unlike a law passed by Congress, any president at any time could remove the ban on assassinations with the stroke of a pen, in total secrecy.

Colby's replacement as DCI had presidential ambitions himself. George H. W. Bush came to the job with a more political career than any other DCI. In fact, many think it was politics that got him the job. There are variations on the story, but some believe that Donald Rumsfeld, who was Ford's chief of staff, saw Bush as a rival for either the Republican nomination for the vice presidency or the presidency. By convincing Ford that Bush should be DCI, he got him out of the way. Or so the story goes. Ford says he came up with the idea on his own.

Bush's stewardship of the CIA was brief—only ten months long. But it's been remembered fondly by the Agency as a respite from the body blows of 1975. Bush went easy on the Agency, where other appointees might have taken the opportunity to clean house and make it look like we were getting real reform in the wake of the investigations. Bush's main mission as DCI, it seems, was to raise morale, and he did that well.

Face-to-face interactions between the president and the DCI started up again. Also, recalled Scowcroft, "[Bush] used to come in from time to time and bring . . . a clandestine agent, or someone who had done something, to build morale."[23] But at the same time, he acquiesced to an experiment that Colby had opposed, one that would put the Agency's analysts under suspicion well into the Reagan years. A group of right-wing Republicans, neoconservatives including Albert Wohlstetter, Edward Teller, and Paul Wolfowitz, were not happy with the CIA's estimates of Soviet military strength and accused the analysts of softness and bias. After a time, they succeeded in getting an independent parallel analysis—what was known as the Team A/Team B approach. Both teams would look at the same material, and see if they drew different conclusions.

There's nothing wrong with independent analyses, of course. In practice, though, this experiment was not honest. Instead of doing a parallel paper, Team B provided a point-by-point critique of the CIA's position. Then Team B's information was leaked. The result was a more fearsome picture of Soviet strength than was warranted.

The long year of intelligence, 1975, in addition to being about CIA past misdeeds, had at its core the question of executive versus congressional power. It was an extension of Watergate and disgust over Vietnam. It was a reaction to Ford's attempts to restore and preserve the powers of the presidency. In Ford's view, "Colby, for a professional bureaucrat (because he was), was doing what he would normally do." And that was? "I think he bent over backwards to be cooperative with the Congress. It wasn't necessary, it was just his temperament."[24] Kissinger summed up the situation as a "runaway congress and a runaway CIA director."[25] Neither assessment is entirely fair to Colby, who often fought with Congress and never entirely appeased it.

CHAPTER EIGHT

JIMMY CARTER AND TURNER

*The DCI Empowered**

I n 1976, President Jimmy Carter was elected in some measure as a result of the public and congressional uproar and discontent over Watergate, the loss of public trust in the integrity of the White House, and the reports of domestic abuses by the CIA against U.S. citizens. President Carter had a mandate not only to clean house and raise public trust in national leadership but also to get the country's intelligence apparatus under control. As a former naval officer who had served in the Navy's nuclear power program

*In this chapter I am a principal actor. The disadvantage of this, of course, is that it is difficult to be objective. I have attempted to be so, but whether I have or not the reader will have to judge. An advantage of having been a participant is that I am very familiar with what happened in this, a key chapter in the book. It is key because so much of how President Carter reshaped our intelligence process has either been reintroduced in the wake of 9/11 or is under consideration.

under Admiral Hyman Rickover, he knew the importance of intelligence
to national security. It needed to be fixed, not degraded, but first it had to be
brought under control, the president's control. However, he was not off to a
good start. His first nominee for DCI was Theodore Sorenson, who had
been John F. Kennedy's speechwriter. Subsequently Sorenson had become a
vocal critic of our involvement in Vietnam. As he prepared for his confirmation hearings for DCI before the Senate Select Committee on Intelligence, it became apparent that there would be questions as to whether
some of those statements were unduly critical, perhaps unpatriotic. Faced
with this unpleasant, and perhaps unwinnable, situation, Sorenson withdrew his name from consideration.

Two weeks after Sorenson's withdrawal, on February 8, 1977, I went
into the Oval Office for the first time. As I went through the door, President Carter was standing in front of a fireplace beneath a portrait of
George Washington. I did not notice anyone else in the room, although it
turned out the vice president, Walter Mondale, was there, and a photographer who caught my handshake with the president. The president suggested we go into his private office. We eased through a door on one side of
the oval and across a narrow passage into a cozy office that looked out on
the Rose Garden.* Jimmy Carter quickly dropped a bombshell on me:
"Stan," he started, "you are one of two candidates I am considering to be
Director of Central Intelligence."[1] I saw my career in the United States
Navy flash before my eyes. If he selected me for this position, one to which
I had not aspired, I could say good-bye to everything I had worked for in
the Navy. Jimmy Carter may have anticipated this. He immediately in-
formed me that being DCI wasn't just running the CIA, but much more.
And so began my education about what my predecessor, George H. W.
Bush, described to me a few weeks later as "the best job in Washington."[2]

---

*Today the office is infamous as the "Monica Lewinsky" room.

What struck me immediately was the amount of information about the role of the DCI the new president already had. It certainly could not have been acquired during his few short weeks in office. That Jimmy Carter had immersed himself so deeply in studying the role of the DCI showed me how important defining the authority of the DCI was to him. The DCI, he explained, was responsible for coordinating all of the agencies of the government involved in intelligence work—the Intelligence Community. As a military officer, I had been a consumer of intelligence for years, but I did not understand that the DCI's reach went well beyond the CIA, at least in theory. These days, whenever I make a speech or an appearance on TV, I'm consistently introduced as the former "director of the CIA." There was no such title then. It was "director of central intelligence," which covered not only the CIA, but what Jimmy Carter was telling me was to him the more important part of the job—management of the fifteen agencies that comprise the Intelligence Community. The CIA is just one of those fifteen. I can't really blame people for not knowing this if I, as a military professional, was not aware of it. When I've read about my predecessors and successors, I've discovered why I'd been so unaware. Despite the best efforts of a number of DCIs and presidents, no DCI has ever had sufficient authority to manage the Intelligence Community effectively.

After just a few minutes of discussion, the president told me he had settled on me as his DCI. Like a drowning man, I blurted out, "Mr. President, I do not think there is sufficient authority to coordinate the Intelligence Community as you have suggested."[3] I was relieved that President Carter did not ask me to be specific as to what additional authorities were needed; I had no idea. He responded, though, that we would look into it. It took almost a year, but in January 1978 he signed a presidential executive order that gave me, as DCI, more authority over the Intelligence Community of our country than any former DCI had had. Unfortunately, it was also more authority than any subsequent DCI has had. It was even more than the new director of national intelligence has today under the legislation passed in December 2004.

Over and above the specific authorities the Carter executive order gave me was the fact that this president clearly wanted his chief of intelligence to manage the Intelligence Community. For instance, just prior to my swearing in as DCI, the president met with me and the heads of the other fourteen agencies. We sat around a table in the DCI's conference room at CIA headquarters in Langley, Virginia. In the course of the conversation the head of the Defense Intelligence Agency referred to me as the "titular" head of the Intelligence Community. President Carter instantly rebuked him and said that I was *the* head of the Community. The president was, it seemed, willing to empower his DCI. Only the president can do this meaningfully. All the other agencies of the Intelligence Community are part of larger departments, like the Department of Defense or the Department of State. Their heads of intelligence can appeal to their cabinet secretary if they don't like what the DCI is doing. The DCI can hold his or her own in this arena only if the president is willing to back him or her up.

The most important, specific authority President Carter's executive order gave the DCI was "full and exclusive" responsibility for preparing the budgets for all of the fifteen agencies. It seemed to make a lot of sense to have one person who represented the interests of the entire Community balance the priorities of the fifteen agencies. At first this arrangement worked splendidly. With authority over the budgets, I could develop themes to address the nation's needs for intelligence—not just the immediate needs of a particular department, but long-range, strategic requirements. The military did not see it that way, however. Their first recourse was to persuade the president to make adjustments in the budgets I submitted. Each year the president met with the secretary of defense, the representatives of the other departments with intelligence bureaus, and me to review the budget I had proposed. On a number of occasions the president accepted their arguments and overruled one or more of my budget recommendations. That, of course, is just how the system should work. Clearly the DCI should not have the final say.

Where the system broke down, in my view, was when the military's arguments were based on parochial interests. For instance, it galled the military that our best photographic satellite, which was first launched in early 1977, had been invented by the CIA. It was, therefore, under my operational control in my second role as head of the CIA. It was a marvelous system, much like a TV in space that sent back pictures almost instantly. One shortcoming was that it could miss important targets if they were temporarily obscured by thick clouds or smoke as the satellite passed over them. In 1978, the CIA developed an ingenious solution to this problem. It combined a radar satellite with a photographic one. Thus, if a target were obscured temporarily, the satellite could switch quickly from optical pictures to radar ones and be sure of getting something. I had recommended we set aside funds in the next budget to procure this satellite. I discussed this with Secretary of Defense Harold Brown the day before we were scheduled to meet with President Carter on that year's intelligence budget.

Harold has one of the most incisive minds I have ever encountered. The speed with which he dissects problems and comes to conclusions is almost terrifying. In fact, it sometimes causes problems in group discussions. Someone would be making a point when Harold would interrupt. Anticipating what the speaker was about to conclude, he would offer his opinion before the speaker had actually made his case. In this instance, Harold immediately saw the benefits of this combined optical-radar satellite. He agreed that it should be in the budget as a CIA project. With his support, I had no reason to believe President Carter would overrule my recommendation.

What I did not foresee was the pressure that would beset Harold from below. The Department of Defense (DOD) had a radar-only satellite of its own on the drawing board. A number of people in the DOD wanted at least one space reconnaissance vehicle to be under the control of their department. Therefore, they preferred that there be two separate satellites, one optical managed by the CIA and one radar operated by the DOD. What that meant, however, was that if clouds, smoke, or something else did obscure a target as the optical satellite passed over, we would not be able to take a radar picture until the radar satellite happened to come along. In the interim, the consumer, perhaps a military commander engaged in battle, would have nothing to go on. Still, before our meeting with the president, Harold's staff persuaded him to change his mind.

I received a call the next morning saying I could no longer count on support on this issue from the secretary of defense. At the meeting with the president, Harold deftly out-argued me, refuting the points on which we had agreed just hours before. In the end, the United States got two types of satellites: one that took only optical pictures and one that took only radar images. The former was operated by the CIA, the latter by the DOD. Eventually the DOD virtually took over the CIA's optical version as well, even though satellite photographs have a much wider application than the needs of the military. It seemed obvious to me at the time, and still does, that the country lost imaging capability by having the two separate satellites rather than the two capabilities in one satellite.

Of course, we attempted to solve budget issues like this without recourse to the president if at all possible. I would first discuss them with the heads of the fourteen other intelligence agencies in a meeting of what was termed the National Foreign Intelligence Board (NFIB). This was a long-standing procedure. The difference now was that I had "full and exclusive" authority to make decisions, whereas previously it had been necessary to gain consensus. Making decisions by consensus or committee helps ensure that all points of view are considered. A consensus tends, however, to settle on least-common-denominator solutions rather than imaginative and decisive ones. It is just too easy for individuals to hold tenaciously to their positions, knowing that full or near full agreement is necessary. With my having the authority to decide without consensus, the others knew that being obdurate was not likely to pay off. There is no way to prove it, but I believe the process we employed resulted in decisions that were more in the national interest than departmental interests.

The second new authority given the DCI in the Carter executive order was to prioritize and direct the efforts of the agencies that collect intelligence. The key ones are the National Security Agency (NSA) for electronic intelligence, the National Geospatial-Intelligence Agency (NGA) for photographic intelligence, the National Reconnaissance Office (NRO) for operating satellites, and the CIA's Directorate of Operations (DO) for human intelligence. The new executive order created the National Intelligence Tasking Center (NITC), under the DCI's control, to coordinate these four principal collection agencies, plus other smaller collection efforts spread around the Intelligence Community. A new deputy DCI for collection tasking would meet with representatives of the collecting agencies whenever a need for some specific data arose. He would canvass the agencies to determine which could likely produce some or all of the data needed. He would then parcel out assignments. It seemed to make sense to have one individual orchestrating the overall collection effort. Often a clue from one collection system will give another system just what it needs to focus its efforts effectively.

A hypothetical example, but one not unlike an actual event, would be that satellite photographs discovered a manufacturing facility in a foreign country that appeared to be designed for enriching uranium. That could lead to an attempt to determine if there were radioactive emissions, perhaps by flying an aircraft into the area or by inserting a human agent. Communications from the facility might also be monitored to determine if it was in contact with other nuclear facilities or bureaus. It would take good coordination to ensure this kind of teamwork. That was what the NITC was designed to produce.

This promising system did not survive very long. The military was genuinely concerned that the director of the NITC would not accord sufficient priority to the needs of our military for tactical battlefield information. After all, for all the years of the Cold War, military concerns took priority in most decisions on national security. This included the intelligence needed to get the military's job done. It was, then, understandable to me that the military wanted to control such intelligence operations as photographic satellites. It is not necessarily the case, though, that a DCI would neglect the military's interests when adjudicating priorities for the use of satellites, electronic listening systems, or other devices for collecting information. And, of course, military control of collection systems can lead to neglect of nonmilitary priorities.

An actual instance of this occurred in 1998. We did not detect India's preparations for reopening its testing of nuclear weapons, something that should have been discernible from satellite photography. The reason was that the photographic satellites were all focused on Iraq. There, well before our invasion in March 2003, our military had imposed no-fly zones. It was important to the military to keep close track of Iraq's antiair defenses, which might attack our aircraft on patrol in the no-fly zones. It was, though, unlikely that this coverage had to be so intense that an occasional check on India and other nations in the region could not have been managed. In this case, military dominance in the use of satellites hurt the larger national interest. In short, untrammeled military control is not necessarily always desirable.

At an annual budget meeting with the president in late 1978, Harold Brown made the case that because a particular electronic satellite was employed predominantly for tactical military purposes it should be shifted out of the DCI's budget and into that of the DOD. The president agreed. The next year Harold successfully argued that the information gathered by a type of spy plane skirting the borders of the Soviet Union and China should also be taken out of my budget. With systems such as these with multimission capabilities, there was no right or wrong answer. Each was a judgment call by the president on whether the military could rely on the DCI to give its interests adequate priority, or vice versa. Presidents are in a difficult predicament here, because politically the military has a much larger constituency behind it than does the Intelligence Community. It is an uneven playing field. What these adjustments meant, of course, was that when the systems were transferred to the DOD's budget, not only did I, as DCI, no longer prepare the budget for them, but the NITC no longer managed their operations. This whittling away at the DCI's authorities continued after President Carter left office and has reached the point that 80 percent of the money being spent on intelligence is controlled by DOD.

Still another authority given the DCI by the Carter executive order was to establish priorities for the efforts of the various analytic agencies across the Intelligence Community. It seemed to make sense to have someone ensure that all topics on which we needed to be informed were being studied. Authority over analysis, though, needs to be exercised judiciously so as to ensure that no one is directing the analysts as to what conclusions to reach. We created the National Foreign Assessment Center (NFAC) to apportion out the analytic tasks. The concept was to assign two or more analytic agencies to each major problem so as to elicit contrary views if they existed. Again, though, the military did not want even such limited interference by the DCI. Here, I am afraid, pure self-interest of the military set in. The intelligence agencies in the DOD are all subject to pressures not to produce intelligence that undercuts policies the DOD is pursuing. Thus these agencies would prefer that they do all the analysis on subjects relevant to the military and not risk having a DCI air contrary views.

Typical of the problem the military was seeking to avoid was a major difference between the military and the CIA over an annual estimate of the strategic nuclear forces of the Soviet Union. In the spring of 1977, shortly after I took office as DCI, I made my first presentation to Congress on these forces. A congressman asked me what it meant when I told them that the Soviets had X number of this kind of missile and Y of that, and so forth. How could he place that information into a context for making decisions? To attempt to answer this criticism, the next year we developed measures for what kind and amount of damage X and Y numbers of Soviet missiles could theoretically do to the United States; for example, how many of our ICBMs could they destroy, or how much urban area could they level? These statistics gave a more graphic picture than just numbers and types of missiles did, but were still a bit abstract for congressional decision-making.

Considering the number of our ICBMs we might lose to a Soviet attack, though, raised an interesting issue: How many of our missiles would survive if—in the worst possible case scenario—the Soviets were to attack us first with all of the nuclear weapons they had? At that time our policies on nuclear weapons assumed that such a Soviet first strike could completely disarm our nuclear retaliatory forces. An intelligence evaluation as to whether that was really a danger was something Congress, the president, and others could readily utilize. Thus, I directed the CIA's analysts to simulate an all-out Soviet attack on the United States and then calculate how much, if any, of our nuclear retaliatory forces would survive. The result was that our surviving retaliatory force could level all of the urban areas of the Soviet Union at least once! A rational Soviet first strike was simply out of the question because our retaliation would be so great.

The reaction from the military to this analysis was violent. Their strategic nuclear force structure and appropriations from Congress for it were based on the assumption that the Soviets could conduct a first strike. They argued that what we in the CIA had done as an intelligence analysis was the equivalent of a war game and that war-gaming was neither our expertise nor our business. From one perspective they had a point; from another they did not. On the military's side, the fact that we described the potential lethality of the Soviet forces in terms of U.S. forces destroyed did involve us in where those forces were located and how they would respond under attack. The CIA, quite properly, is not privy to or concerned with military war plans. And the first DCI, Sidney Souers, had voluntarily forsaken the CIA's right even to have access to U.S. military capabilities.

On the other side, this analysis added qualitative character to what was otherwise a purely quantitative estimate of Soviet forces that had left people like the congressman numb. It was not purporting to forecast what would actually happen in war, as would a war game. It was only describing the maximum lethal potential of the Soviet Union's nuclear forces. I attempted for more than a year to accommodate the military's concerns on this without success before I sent the study to the president. By then, however, he had been defeated for reelection and it had little impact.

Another closely related problem I had with the DOD concerned the Soviets' ability to detect U.S. submarines. We were able to watch as Soviet antisubmarine aircraft searched for our submarines off Soviet coastlines. What we did not know was whether they were actually finding our subs. Clearly it would have helped the CIA immeasurably in estimating Soviet antisubmarine capabilities to know whether there actually were U.S. submarines where the Soviets were looking. But there was no way short of going to the president that I could get the Navy to provide that information to the CIA. The Navy people were, quite naturally, concerned that the CIA analysts might not have the expertise to interpret the data correctly. If they did misconstrue the data and Congress believed the CIA, the Navy's appropriations for submarines might be slashed. On the other side, what this meant was that only the Navy was able to assess the vulnerability of its submarines. Yet our national military policy for deterring an attack on the United States with nuclear weapons depends largely on the invulnerability of our ballistic missile submarines. Having the Navy be the only judge of that invulnerability was unwise. I chose, however, not to appeal to the president.

This issue over submarines illustrates, again, the recurring conflict in the world of intelligence. Most intelligence agencies belong to a department that makes policy, like the DOD. They generally have the best expertise in the government in their areas of concern. That should enable them to interpret the intelligence data best. Yet these intelligence agencies are inevitably under pressure not to reach conclusions that could jeopardize the policies of that department. Equally likely, the analysts in policy-making departments may have such ingrained views about their department's area of expertise that they overlook new developments or new ways of seeing the same situation. The CIA, on the other hand, is the one intelligence agency that by its charter does not make or recommend policy. This is a wise proscription, as it attempts to ensure that the CIA does not inadvertently develop a bias about what it collects and analyzes. It has, as they say, no horse in the race. It may or may not, though, have equivalent expertise for interpreting the data collected.

Still another CIA analysis that caused a furor early in my days as DCI was that of an impending drop in Soviet oil production. Since the Soviets exported oil, even at concessionary prices to their eastern European satellite countries, this discovery had wide-ranging implications. It was not only, or even primarily, the DOD that objected to this information, but also the Department of Energy, the State Department, and the oil industry. The CIA had detected that the Soviets were extracting oil from many of their wells by a technique of injecting water to force the oil out of the ground. This did the job, all right, and was quicker and easier than refurbishing the wells. The problem was that it left a good amount of non-recoverable oil in the ground. Since the Soviets have very large reserves of oil, this should not have made a big difference, but without more new drilling than they were doing, those reserves could not be tapped. There was great gnashing of teeth on the Washington scene for a couple of months about this analysis. Even then there was no widespread agreement. As it turned out, our intelligence estimate, which we published openly, alerted the Soviets to the problem in their own backyard. They improved their extraction procedures, got more oil out of each well, and kept production levels up for several years. Their long-standing neglect eventually caught up with them, however, and their production did drop off.

Unfortunately, conflicts of interest between the CIA and, mainly, the DOD on budgets, collection, and analytic conclusions has led to unhealthy competition, even jealousy, between the military and the CIA. It works in both directions. The CIA's people, feeling elite and superior and suspecting that the DOD's desire to support policy skews intelligence analyses, tend to discount any analyses done by DOD agencies. On the other side, the DOD mistrusts CIA analyses on the grounds that the CIA lacks the DOD's specialized expertise.

There was one period during Jimmy Carter's tenure when cooperation between the CIA and the military was particularly needed. We managed to get just enough of it, but not without considerable mistrust and unease on the military's part. This was the 444 days that began on November 4, 1979, when a group of Iranian "students" captured the U.S. embassy in Tehran and took sixty-six Americans hostage. In a way this crisis actually began on Valentine's Day 1979, when I had been awakened at 5:30 A.M. by a phone call from the CIA duty officer. His message was startling and totally unexpected: "Our embassy in Tehran has been overrun and we have lost all communications with it."[4] By the time I reached the war room at CIA headquarters, the crisis was over. The brand-new Iranian government of Ayatollah Khomeini had intervened, forced the "students" out of the embassy, and returned it to our control. Thus, on November 4, when I received an identical phone call in the middle of the night, I was certain I was dreaming.

It was Sunday, but I was surprised when there was no meeting of the national security team. I can only deduce that we all assumed this problem would be resolved as the one on Valentine's Day had been. It was not. Monday morning the national security team assembled in the situation room in the basement of the White House. We met for at least three hours. We were to do that almost every day, Sundays included, for the next three months before the pace slackened some. At each meeting I was asked for an intelligence update. Each time there was little I could say. The "students" had just appeared from nowhere in February. There were small indications that this group in November was of a different ilk, but our intelligence team inside Iran was very limited. After all, the shah was our trusted friend and you are careful about spying on friends, so before his fall we had few assets in place—and not much chance of acquiring them once his regime crumbled. And now, with Khomeini's religious fanaticism driving the government, it was very risky for the CIA officers we did send into Iran. These officers did a superb job of preparing for the military rescue attempt the following April. They scouted the embassy to determine where and how well it was guarded. They purchased trucks to transport the rescue force into and around Tehran. They rented a warehouse in which to store the trucks. What they could not do was determine who was who within the Khomeini-dominated government. Hence, in my briefings I was unable to help much in forecasting how the government in Tehran would respond to various initiatives we were considering.

National security meetings would inevitably turn to what we could do to pressure the Iranians to release the hostages. It is difficult to imagine the number of options we considered. It is difficult to imagine how a small group of people could develop such different views as to what could and should be done. Should we, for instance:

- Send emissaries to negotiate? If so, who? Different people backed different individuals.

- Freeze Iranian assets in U.S. banks, even in their overseas branches, where it was probably illegal to do so?

- Conduct punitive military attacks? Perhaps on an oil refinery?

- Enlist friendly countries to weigh in with Tehran? Which ones? Communists?

- Ask the United Nations for a condemnatory resolution or for economic sanctions? But would even our friends give up their lucrative contracts with Iran in order to help?

- Advise President Carter to stay in the Rose Garden as a sign of dedication to solving the problem or go out and campaign for reelection?

- Lay naval mines in Iranian harbors to close off their commerce? I favored this, but most others wanted to avoid any military action.

- Suggest that the president meet with the families of the hostages? Or not risk becoming too emotionally involved?

- Stop purchasing Iranian oil before they stopped shipping it?

- Move military forces into the area even in the face of Iranian threats to harm the hostages if we used force?

- And many more.

From time to time the president would join us in these meetings. It was not long, however, before he expressed frustration that almost every recommendation that came to him was countered with strong reservations on the part of one member of the national security team or another. This was especially the case when it came to military options. Secretary of State Cyrus Vance was particularly opposed to military action. President Carter made it clear that while he would consider using the military, he strongly favored securing the release of the hostages through negotiations—only thus could we ensure the safe return of all of them.

Clearly, though, he needed at least a backup military rescue option in case the Iranians began harming our hostages. We took the threat of harm to the hostages seriously enough that we did not dispatch an aircraft carrier that was already in the Indian Ocean to the Persian Gulf. Additionally, we took great precautions to ensure that the fact that military planning was going on did not leak to the media.

One result of the extreme to which we went in that direction was that I was initially left out of the planning for a rescue mission, which I realized on the seventh day of the crisis. I noted that when our daily meeting in the White House situation room ended, all those who might be involved in military planning gravitated upstairs to the office of Zbigniew Brzezinski, the president's assistant for national security, instead of heading for their cars or offices. Back in my office, I placed a call to Brzezinski. I told him it was obvious that rescue planning was going on and I was incensed at not being included. Where, I asked, were they going to get the intelligence to do the operation? He replied that the Defense Intelligence Agency would provide that. I pointed out that we had created the position of director of central intelligence to bring all intelligence clues together in one place. On top of that, it was foolish to have only a military intelligence agency provide support for a military operation, as it would be subject to pressure from the military's operational people. I was then admitted to this tight-knit rescue-planning group and met with it regularly thereafter. Again, this demonstrates the jealousy and mistrust between military intelligence and the CIA. The need for secrecy in this circumstance cannot be denied, though. If the Iranians had word just minutes before a rescue force arrived, they could quickly kill the hostages or, at the very least, move them to a different location. This kind of trade-off between secrecy and expertise dogged us all the way to the military operation itself.

For instance, Texas tycoon Ross Perot came on the scene and almost gave us away. I knew Ross slightly, and he had phoned me a few days after the hostages were taken. The previous February, at about the time we were having problems in Tehran, two of his employees had been arrested and jailed there. He had pulled off a rescue of them very nicely. He now wondered if he could be of help to us. I asked him to come to Washington to discuss the situation with us, but to be very discreet about why he was coming. He came immediately and even used an alias when he checked into his hotel. His advice was to infiltrate a rescue force through the commercial airport, rather than by a military assault of some sort, which is what his people had done. In our case, though, instead of having two people to spirit out of the country, we had sixty-six. Perot had no formula for dealing with that. His two hostages and their rescuers had driven out of the country, bribing guards at the Turkish border. Unfortunately, despite Ross's personal precautions, we began to hear rumors that Perot was helping us plan something in connection with the hostages. We had to break off all contact.

Still, Perot's advice was useful with a second problem we had, that of six previously unaccounted-for Americans. Five of these six had managed to slip out a back gate of the embassy compound while the takeover was happening, and one was in an outlying office. They wended their way to refuge with the Canadians. Two were housed in the ambassador's residence and four in the residence of the Canadian deputy chief of mission. When the Canadians informed us of this, we were relieved to know the six people had escaped and to know where they were. Some media people had deduced that the embassy staff had been larger than sixty-six and that something was amiss. The president himself, as well as Cy Vance, phoned the media outlets involved and requested that they not alert the Iranians by publishing stories about the missing six. These entreaties persuaded them to withhold speculation. They understood that there was more at stake than just a story.

Recognizing that rescuing six was a distinctly different matter than sixty-six, the president turned to me at a meeting of the NSC in mid-November and said, "Stan, the CIA is to take charge of planning a way to secure the release of the six Americans hiding out with the Canadians in Tehran."[5] I was gratified with the president's confidence in the CIA in turning this task over to us. In two short months the CIA not only developed a plan but pulled off the escape of the "Canadian Six," albeit with some close calls.

For instance, there was this conversation between an Iranian immigration official at the Tehran airport on January 25, 1980, and a CIA undercover operative:

"Your passport shows a middle initial of 'H.' German passports always spell out the middle name."

"Yes, I am ashamed of my middle name. I was born in 1935—it is Hitler."[6]

The situation—with this fortunately quick-witted response—involved two CIA operatives who went into Tehran to train the six for an escape right through the international airport. The success of the operation, though, must be attributed to painstaking planning back at the CIA headquarters in Langley, Virginia, and the Canadian foreign office in Ottawa. Each of the six individuals had to be given a new identity. Each needed an ostensible reason for being in Iran. Passports had to be forged with numerous entry and exit stamps, including one showing entry into Iran.

The CIA's masters of disguise created a Hollywood film company, Studio Six Productions, as a cover for who these people were and why they were in Iran. A business office was created for Studio Six in Hollywood. It responded to anyone who phoned in. The company placed full-page ads in *Variety* and *The Hollywood Reporter*. Steven Spielberg even responded by sending in a script. The script that was chosen was called *Argo*, a sci-fi tale. A team of eight Studio Six personnel was supposedly traveling around the world looking for a filming site for *Argo*. It was not at all unusual for a film company to do such a search. There was a production manager, a cameraman, an art director, a transportation manager, a script consultant, an associate producer, a business manager, and a director. Each of the eight, the six internees and the two CIA operations officers who joined them, needed to be ready to pretend to hold one of those positions. Each also required a new driver's license, business cards, and various "pocket litter" that we all carry and that identifies us. It was a massive job of disguise and deception, one that required us to consider every possible problem.

Just before the attempted escape, I briefed the president on our plan for getting the six hostages out. I told him that we were going to let the hostages themselves make the decision about whether they went through the airport as a group or individually. He said he thought we should not place that burden on the hostages but make it for them. We did, and they went as a group.

Finally the day came for their departure, January 28, 1980. The two CIA operatives left their hotel in time to reach the Tehran airport by 5:00 A.M. and do a quick reconnaissance of the scene. Everything looked normal. Half an hour later the six arrived at the terminal in a van from the Canadian embassy. They were booked on a 7:30 A.M. Swissair flight to Zurich. Everything went smoothly and they reached the gate apparently without arousing any suspicion. Hearts plunged into stomachs, however, as Swissair announced a delay in departure due to mechanical problems. The eight of them were sure they were to be reinspected. But it was not so. After an hour's delay, as their bus approached the aircraft they were to board, they saw that the name painted on the plane's nose was "Argau," a Swiss canton!

When they arrived in Zurich, several of them kissed the tarmac. I experienced a heartwarming American response a few weeks later after the story had leaked out (and the Canadians had vacated their embassy in Tehran). I was at the annual press correspondents' white-tie "Gridiron" dinner in Washington. As part of the ceremonies, the toastmaster introduced the ambassadors at the head table. There was polite applause for each. Just as the applause was dying down for the ambassador from Canada, the audience rose to its feet and changed it into a mass ovation.

John Kennedy had entrusted his reputation to the CIA at the Bay of Pigs and been let down. Jimmy Carter did the same with the Canadian Six. The Agency came through for him.

While we were plotting this Canadian Six escape, I was also pushing the president to let the CIA contribute to solving the larger problem of the hostages being held in the embassy compound. In mid-November the number was reduced to fifty-three by the Iranians' voluntary release of thirteen African Americans and women. Apparently the Iranians expected that their doing so would somehow cause divisiveness within the American public. Fifty of the remaining hostages were being held inside the embassy compound; and three, including the chargé d'affaires, L. Bruce Laingen, were trapped in the Iranian Ministry of Foreign Affairs, where they had been when the embassy was stormed.

The rescue-planning group was focused on two key problems. The first was how to get a rescue force to the embassy in Tehran without first being detected. The second was how to extricate both the hostages and the force from Iran after rescuing the hostages. Because it was deemed too risky to send an aircraft carrier into the Persian Gulf, within a couple hundred miles of Tehran, we had to work from a carrier just outside the eastern end of the Strait of Hormuz in the Gulf of Oman—some 680 miles from Tehran. The helicopters that would transport the rescue force to Tehran would have to be refueled, somewhere, somehow.

In early January, I reviewed the plan the military had developed for refueling. It involved capturing a remote Iranian air force base, refueling the helicopters, and then holding the base until the helicopters reached Tehran and the hostages were released, a period of about twenty-four hours. I judged it to be far too high a risk, because the probability of the Iranians detecting that we had been on their air force base was too great.

I went to the CIA special operations people and asked them to look at the problem of trying to rescue the hostages at such an extreme (from the point of view of helicopter capabilities) distance. Within a few days, after studying the topography of the desert between Hormuz—the starting point for the helos—and Tehran, they concluded that we could land refueling aircraft on the desert floor in a remote sector well outside of any population centers, bring in the helos, top them off, and send them on their way to Tehran. What's more, they were prepared to fly a light aircraft to the desert spot they had selected, land by the light of the full moon, and take core samples of the ground to determine for certain whether it would bear the weight of heavy refueling aircraft. They believed they could fly in and out at night undetected.

This was far better than what the military was planning. I rushed down to the White House with this proposal. It was critical that we get a decision early enough to take advantage of the late January full moon. To my distress, the answer was that negotiations for the release of the hostages were going nicely and we did not want to risk upsetting things. I received the same response in February. But in March, the answer changed to "yes." The negotiations had broken down or, perhaps more accurately, the Iranians had not ever been serious. If we moved quickly, we could take advantage of a full moon in early April.

I had already positioned the small aircraft forward, fearing that if I did not receive permission until the last minute we would not be able to get it there in time. In the category of believe it or not, just before that aircraft left the United States, the planners at the Agency informed me that the pilot had an artificial leg. "But," they assured me, "he is by far our best pilot!" What next? A blind pathfinder? Anyway, I authorized this man to risk landing in a desert at night, not really knowing if the sand would hold his little plane, or indeed, if he could orient himself adequately should there be sand whipping up as he landed. There would be two motorbikes in the plane just in case they had to "walk out"! They were taking a third person, though, and there was no room for a third bike. The third man was an Air Force officer, to make the Air Force comfortable that the core sampling would be done correctly—another indication of a lack of trust in the CIA. The military, incidentally, also insisted on sending a small team of officers into Tehran to check on the preparations that CIA operatives had made there to receive the rescue force. That team almost got caught, nearly blowing the operation.

The exploratory flight to the desert went smoothly, other than a big bounce on landing. It proved the viability of the CIA's concept, which the military then adopted. The president opted to send in the rescue force on that basis, staking his reputation on the CIA. It served him well again, as the CIA's initiative had finally made a rescue attempt feasible. The decision to undertake the rescue mission had to have been an excruciating one for Jimmy Carter, who had so wanted to solve this problem without bloodshed or loss of life. And up to the very last, his secretary of state, Cy Vance, remained opposed to the military mission, even signaling his intent to resign afterward.

The rescue mission itself unfortunately failed. This has been widely attributed to breakdowns in the helicopters. Anticipating this, the military had sent eight helos when only six were required. When the mission aborted, all eight were in flyable condition, albeit three of them had problems. Any of those three could have gone forward, though at some risk; and this was a combat operation where risks were not unusual, not a training exercise. In short, if any one of the three pilots had persevered, the mission would at least have gone to one more stage.

Both the release of the Canadian Six and the exploratory flight into the desert for the rescue operation were technically covert actions—that is, they were operations for purposes other than collecting intelligence—in which the CIA was involved. By law I was required to inform Congress in "a timely manner" of all covert actions. That posed a dilemma here. Either the rescue operation itself or the exploration of the desert site could have been thwarted if the Iranians had gotten wind of it beforehand. In the case of the rescue operation, the president was using a right he had under the War Powers Act not to inform Congress in advance. My informing Congress about the exploratory flight would have given away the fact that a military mission was coming. In both instances, I informed the intelligence committees as soon as I could afterward. They were not happy, but were understanding.

While I think we in the CIA served the president well in these two covert actions, we let him down badly with respect to our coverage of the Iranian scene. We had not appreciated how shaky the shah's political foundation was; did not know that the shah was terminally ill; did not understand who Khomeini was and the support his movement had; did not have a clue as to who the hostage-takers were or what their objective was; and could not pinpoint within the embassy where the hostages were being held and under what conditions.

As far as our failure to judge the shah's position more accurately, we were just plain asleep. In late December 1977, President Carter was in Tehran. He toasted the shah as being "an island of stability" in an unstable area. We in the CIA were not aware that this was anything but the case. Eight months later, after rioting had broken out in Tehran several times, I received a draft of a National Intelligence Estimate that said that the shah would survive another ten years. I sent it back, insisting that we at least acknowledge that the shah had problems, as indicated by the sporadic rioting against him. It was egregious, though, that I did not insist on a thorough review of where the shah stood. Almost all of us in the national security establishment had been to Iran under the shah. We had not noticed any instability, as we were treated royally, but limited in where we could go and what we could see. The Iranians we met were urbane and wonderfully hospitable. And the shah had become an essential underpinning of U.S. policy in the Persian Gulf region. Producing an intelligence estimate that the shah might not survive would have been seen as inviting that to happen.

Even so, we should have been far more objective. President Carter, Zbigniew Brzezinski, and the national security staff were more so than we at the CIA had been. In late 1978, while the shah was still in power, I received a memo of reprimand from the president complaining about the quality of the political intelligence he was receiving on Iran and the Middle East. This was a hard blow. I attempted to shield the CIA analysts from it by keeping the memo in my desk. True to Washington form, it was only a few days before it was leaked to the press.

As it turned out, the shah went downhill fast. He left Iran and went into exile just five months after the draft NIE had predicted he was good for ten years. No one remembered to point out in the NIE that he had deserted the country under similar pressure in 1953. We should have done a psychological profile that would have analyzed why a man with his formidable military and police powers would give up rather than use these powers. President Carter in particular would have found a psychological profile valuable, as such profiles were among his favorite intelligence reports. He has commented, "When I got ready to go to Camp David, I asked for a psychological profile on Begin and Sadat. That was one of the most valuable things I ever had. When I got to Camp David I knew all about them. It turned out that the analysis, which was absolutely accurate, was that Begin under pressure would resort to minutiae and semantics. He would escape from having to make a decision by starting to worry about the definition of words, and that sort of thing. And Sadat, on the other hand, under pressure would resort to generalities. He would talk about global issues and a panoply of inner relationships among nations in the Mideast. So I used that difference. Also Sadat was impervious to pressure back home, whereas Begin was deeply obligated to his party. So those kinds of data paid rich dividends to me."[7]

Jimmy Carter, despite having no experience in government at the federal level, knew from the very beginning of his presidency that he wanted that kind of support from the Intelligence Community. I could have anticipated that from an experience I had with him a little over two years before. I had called on then-governor Jimmy Carter in Atlanta. He was my Naval Academy classmate and had invited me to stop by if I was ever in Atlanta. I will never forget that what I thought was going to be just a friendly, social meeting took quite a different turn. We talked about old times, but for only about two minutes. During the rest of our half hour together, Jimmy Carter grilled me about the state of our military. Was our equipment appropriate? What were our plans for dealing with the Soviet submarine fleet in a war with the Soviet Union? How was personnel retention? And on and on. I was a vice admiral and a fleet commander. I thought of myself as having a broad grasp of my profession, yet I could not respond to my own satisfaction to many of his questions. I ended up researching a number of them and sending him my answers in writing.

As he showed me to the door at the exact end of the scheduled thirty minutes, he told me that in two days he would announce that he was running for the presidency. Clearly he was a candidate who was diligently studying up. I said, "Good luck, Jimmy," never thinking he would actually make it. That, though, would be the last time I ever called him "Jimmy." From his inauguration on January 20, 1977, I have, of course, addressed him as "Mr. President."

In addition to targets of opportunity like myself, Governor Jimmy Carter informed himself about military and intelligence issues in a number of ways. He was one of two governors who served on the Trilateral Commission, which studied issues of foreign policy. On that commission he met and was tutored by Zbigniew Brzezinski, who would later be his assistant for national security. He read the report of the Church Committee of the Senate and he met with Senator Church, whom he considered for his vice presidential running mate. The running mate he selected, Walter Mondale, also had been on the Church Committee and had strong feelings about reforming intelligence. And, between being elected and inaugurated, President Carter met for a long session with my predecessor, George H. W. Bush. Bush wanted to stay on as DCI, but he carried too much political baggage and Carter needed to send a message that he was cleaning house.

Jimmy Carter had studied sufficiently to have a good idea of what he wanted from the intelligence apparatus: "I learned from different sources that the intelligence agencies were highly fragmented and non-communicating with each other. I had assumed as governor that the CIA was it. That is all I ever heard about. I didn't know about the DCI, I didn't even know about the State Department's intelligence, I didn't know about other agencies. So, I could see that there needed to be some single person who would perform two generic jobs. One was to coordinate the different agencies so there would be a team, so they would know what each other was doing. And, secondly, so that the president would have a respected and honest force of integrity who could bring their collective message on controversial issues to the White House. So my concept would have one person who would understand the complexity of that group of agencies, which I didn't know, and didn't want to know."[8]

This kind of presidential thinking dominated the debates on how to reshape our intelligence in ways to give the DCI the additional authority that I thought was necessary and that the president had said he would consider. The secretary of defense, Harold Brown; the national security advisor, Zbigniew Brzezinski; and I negotiated for almost a year. Actually, the key person in it all was Brzezinski's deputy, David Aaron. David had been on the staff of the Church Committee and clearly came away from that experience with a conviction that a stronger DCI was needed. What is significant, in my view, is that the president did not dictate that we should increase the authority of the DCI. He dictated only the result he wanted, one person to coordinate the intelligence activities and sort out for him what he needed to know from the myriad of intelligence agencies. The logic of getting to where President Carter wanted to go, however, took us into new territories of authority for the DCI.

How well did the Carter system work? It would be presumptuous for me to claim that it worked better than some other process would have. It is logical, though, that decisions on budgets, collection, and analysis are likely to be directed more toward the national interest if made by a single person with the national interest in mind than by compromise in a committee in which each member has to be concerned about parochial interests.

As noted earlier, there were strong differences between the secretary of defense and myself, such as when he appealed the budget decision I had made to procure a combined radar–visual imaging satellite in lieu of one of each type.

There were also differences on what to collect and how. There were no major disagreements here that reached the presidential level during my time as DCI, however.

As far as analysis goes, there has been a long-standing tradition of incorporating footnotes to express dissenting views. The military had lots of these. Toward the end of my tenure as DCI, I encountered an extreme case. As also mentioned earlier, at my direction in 1979 the CIA conducted an analysis of how much damage a Soviet nuclear first strike could do to our nuclear retaliatory forces. Footnotes galore came in. I then found that my own analysts in the CIA who had done the work viewed it as an inappropriate study for an intelligence agency to have done. Still, I chose to stick to my guns, but let the CIA analysts submit a dissenting note of their own. The president clearly knew that the opinion expressed in the NIE was that of his intelligence advisor, and me alone. I was following in the footsteps of Beetle Smith, not Allen Dulles, in claiming that intelligence estimates voiced the views of the DCI.

With these various checks and balances, I thought the Carter system of managing intelligence worked quite well. In looking back on our common experience with it, Harold Brown agreed: "There was a lot of conflict, but I think in the end it came out all right. I think if you look at how the programs went at that time, I think they went better than they have gone since."[9]

The core problem here is that it is unprecedented for an outsider, such as the DCI, to control the budgets and operations of components of departments like Defense, State, Justice, Treasury, and, more recently, Homeland Security. There is a clear potential for conflict between what the departmental secretaries believe their needs are for intelligence and what the DCI believes. The departments may well have special requirements the DCI does not recognize or understand. On the other hand, the DCI may know there is a high national priority for some information a department can best obtain. Still, having an outsider tell any department how to operate one of its arms is bound to lead to concern. That is especially the case with the Department of Defense, where success in battle can depend on good intelligence being passed quickly to the battlefield.

Overall, President Carter tipped the management of intelligence decidedly toward centralization under the DCI. This was the direction in which the country had been moving since the time of Franklin Roosevelt's appointment of Bill Donovan as Coordinator of Information in 1941. In addition, Carter gave me, as DCI, all the support any DCI could expect from a president: ample time on his calendar, including regular briefings, sometimes three times a week; a willingness to read intelligence reports; a real interest in those reports, including asking follow-up questions; a strong aversion to leaks of secret intelligence data; and a willingness to authorize considerable risks in the collection of intelligence.

In one instance, however, I pushed him further than I should have, stirring up a prolonged spate of adverse publicity about how I was managing the CIA. When I took over the Agency, there were two serious problems in the Directorate of Operations branch of the Agency.

The first was to avoid any repetition of questionable or illegal activities the Church Committee had uncovered from the past: for example, administering drugs to unwitting Americans; virtually torturing a Soviet defector, Yuri Nosenko, for more than three years (from April 1964 to

September 1967) through solitary incarceration, isolation, and harassment; plotting assassinations; opening U.S. mail illegally; and building files on American citizens opposed to the war in Vietnam.

Second, it did not take a management expert to detect that the DO was overstaffed after a large buildup for Vietnam. The DO itself had conducted a study of its staffing seven months before I arrived. It concluded that there were 1,325 more positions in the DO than were needed as the war in Vietnam closed down and normal personnel needs again prevailed. I noted, for instance, that an OSS-CIA legend who was at the top of the seniority scale, Cord Meyer, was a special assistant for miscellaneous projects to my deputy, a job someone of much lesser qualifications could easily do. Cord, though a wonderful man with a legendary reputation who had been an incredibly valuable asset to the Agency, was now in excess of our needs. Retaining men like him in such jobs was insulting to them and a disservice to the younger officers of the Agency whose advancement was blocked by these old-timers sitting in place.

To deal with the first problem I established various thresholds where I would make the decisions; for example, when we would pay an agent more than a certain amount of money and when we would recruit an agent in the cabinet of a major country. These control points were resented, as the DO was not anxious to accept outside direction, particularly from someone with no experience in espionage. There was, however, no way I could not attempt to ensure that excesses like virtual torture did not reoccur. The long-term health of the CIA depended, I felt, on not repeating the mistakes of the past.

Challenging the autonomy of the DO, though, was not a trivial matter. A small, but typical, example was when I asked each branch of the CIA to provide me with the names of their most promising personnel. I wanted to monitor those people and be sure their assignments nurtured their capabilities. The leaders of the DO dragged their feet for half a year because, in their view, this simply was not my province.

In grappling with the second problem, overstaffing, I opted to reduce only 820 positions, rather than the 1,325 recommended in the DO report. These were to take place over two years to minimize personnel turbulence. One stipulation was that all the positions had to be in the headquarters at Langley, none overseas where actual espionage was conducted. Additionally, they were to come from the bottom 5 percent of their evaluation group over the previous three years. The people filling the positions that were eliminated either retired or transferred to another position. We worked very hard to find positions for them in the Agency or in other departments of the government. Unfortunately, at the end of the three years there were seventeen individuals who could neither retire nor move to another position.

The DO people seized on the reduction of 820 positions as an opportunity to attempt to get me fired. They launched a disinformation campaign (one of their basic skills). One morning I read in the *Washington Post* that President Carter had forced Frank Carlucci on me as my deputy. The theory was that Carter did not want to fire me, but that he was dissatisfied with me and was going to have Carlucci actually take over. It happened that it was I who came up with the idea of having Carlucci as the deputy and had pleaded with the president to release him from being ambassador to Portugal.[10]

Still, the flood of disparaging stories in the media had to be of concern to the president. One day he pulled me aside after a cabinet meeting and said he was asking former governor of Pennsylvania William Scranton to look the situation over. In a few weeks Governor Scranton reported the facts back to the president and concluded that I was doing a good job. The president stood by me until the end of his term in office.

The point is that only with presidential support can a DCI survive and prosper.

In retrospect, I probably should not have effected the reduction of 820 positions at all, and certainly not the last 17. My predecessor, George H. W. Bush, was DCI when the study recommending the reductions was completed. He simply let it sit, which was far more politically astute than my action. I was probably driven, though, by my military training of being concerned for morale all up and down the line. In this case the junior people were suffering from too much direction from the unneeded numbers of senior people above them. It was, though, an interesting example of how strongly the DO can resist control from outside its ranks.

Jimmy Carter had as little background for assuming presidential responsibilities for our national intelligence activities as any president since World War II. He had not been a senator or congressman or a general. Only his fellow governors Ronald Reagan and George W. Bush lacked experience in the federal government, where politicians are bound to receive intelligence briefings, pass on intelligence appropriations, or interact with the Intelligence Community in other ways. Yet Jimmy Carter pushed the envelope of DCI authorities further than any other president. In part I attribute that to his thirst for being well informed, and, in part, to the logic of where he was taking the Intelligence Community: to have the operations of a diverse collection of agencies coordinated by one manager who would, at the very least, eliminate duplication of effort and questionable use of assets, and report directly to the president. As we shall see, much of the debate today on how to transform our intelligence apparatus to meet the demands of defeating terrorists centers on the model Jimmy Carter established.

CHAPTER NINE

RONALD REAGAN, CASEY, AND WEBSTER

The Resurrection of "Wild Bill"

As the 1980 presidential campaign started to turn in Ronald Reagan's favor, the future president turned to his loyal friend and campaign manager, Bill Casey, and asked him what he would like in return for all his rainmaking and stumping on behalf of the Reagan campaign. Casey already knew—he wanted to be secretary of state or, if he had to settle for less, director of central intelligence.

Fast forward to election night, 1980. As one state after another fell into Reagan's column, he turned to Bill Casey and asked him, "Are you ready to be director of central intelligence?" Had Reagan forgotten what Casey really wanted? Or was he trying to tell his friend he was not going to get the more exalted position? "If I can't be Secretary of State," Casey answered.[1] Shortly after the election, in a meeting with Richard Allen, who was to become the next national security advisor, Casey played coy, claiming he wasn't even sure if he wanted a job in the administration. Finally, under questioning by Allen, he gave his best aw-shucks response: "Oh, well—I'd take State." Allen told him plainly that it wasn't in the cards, while thinking (but not saying), "Bill Casey, you don't look like a secretary of state. You don't talk like a secretary of state. You only think like one."[2]

Casey's most direct approach was to Reagan on November 21 in a letter that made a pitch for Secretary of State Casey by advocating "a tougher minded focus on American interests rather than the needs and demands of other countries." It did not work. A few days later I was briefing President-Elect Reagan on world affairs in Blair House, across the street from the White House. At the conclusion of the briefing, Reagan took me aside and informed me that I would be leaving and Bill Casey would be replacing me.

When Casey became DCI, not secretary of state, he utterly failed to do what DCIs before him had been expected to do, even those with political aspirations. He refused to divorce himself from politics and to give up advocating policy. If he wasn't going to get the office in Foggy Bottom, he was willing to settle for being a shadow secretary of state in Langley. This set the stage for a fierce rivalry with Reagan's secretaries of state.

There was never any chance that Casey would become secretary of state. There were too many other more qualified people and the stakes were too high. But DCI was a natural fit for Casey; in a way it was like coming home. He had worked under Bill Donovan in the OSS and admired Donovan to the point of idolatry. Both were lawyers. Both were wildly ambitious. Both were eager to be close to the president and were not shy about putting forth policy ideas. But 1980 was not 1940, the USSR was not Nazi Germany, and the CIA was not the OSS. Casey was a throwback to the past in an organization that badly needed to look forward. But for Reagan, he was a natural choice.

"You're the expert, Bill," Reagan told Casey shortly after hiring him as campaign manager. "Just point me in the right direction and I'll go."[3] Reagan's legendary warmth and accessibility worked like a charm on Casey. That special quality of Reagan's—his innate ability to create loyalty and faith—was compounded in the case of Bill Casey by the fact that they were both about the same age, had strongly similar convictions, and wanted more than anything to see communism wiped off the face of the earth. So, even though Casey and Reagan grew distant due to the demands of their jobs, there was always a warmth and loyalty between them.

This president also had a need for one of his DCI's services for a more political purpose than most of his predecessors. Reagan had come to power pushing his conservative creed and lambasting the détente of Kissinger and Nixon. He couldn't carry on normal diplomacy with the Russians. Yet, because of the thousands of nuclear-tipped warheads each side had pointed at the other, he couldn't take them on militarily. One thing he could do, though, was work to undermine the USSR through covert actions. With his only experience in intelligence being with "Wild Bill" Donovan, Casey was ready and willing to unleash his shadow warriors, believing he could actually win the Cold War through covert actions. So Casey would cook up covert actions, and Reagan would quickly approve them. "Reagan is the Will Rogers of intelligence," one CIA insider told Bob Woodward, "he never met a covert operation he didn't like."[4]

Before Casey took over at the CIA, the president-elect sent in his transition team, a group of former CIA officers and right-wing Senate staffers from the intelligence committee who had been seething about the Agency for years. Their actions at the CIA soon caused them to be intensely disliked, which was truly surprising. During the presidential election campaign, the hope that Reagan would win was palpable in the corridors at Langley. What they did not expect was that the Reagan team would come with a prejudice against them. Reagan's people who came out to Langley labeled the CIA staff "elitist," "leftist-orientated," and blamed them for "consistent gross misstatement of Soviet global objectives."[5] Their main complaint was that the NIEs kept saying that the Russians, while being a serious threat, were not as dangerous, as well armed, or even as well fed as Americans. In dealing with this team during the transition period, I tried to be as helpful as I could, even giving them a list of the CIA people I felt had the most potential for the future. It soon came back to me that the team members were saying that if Turner liked these people, they should be tagged for dismissal. Overall, I found this transition group to be as unbalanced, opinionated, and unwilling to listen as any group I have ever encountered. They came to their task with their minds made up, and no facts were going to change their conclusions.

They wanted to beef up the covert action section and to fire essentially every single senior officer who had been involved in estimates on the Soviet Union. Even Soviet analyst and future DCI Robert Gates, who said he believed that "under Nixon, Ford, and Carter, I had been regarded as something of a hard-liner toward the Soviets," thought that his head would roll.[6] Still, there was an expectation that the CIA would be elevated to a new level of trust and activity, and would receive budget increases. At least that's what Reagan's campaign rhetoric had led them to believe.

They would, however, get Casey. As Gates wrote: "Without parallel in the history of postwar American intelligence, Bill Casey as DCI had his own foreign policy agenda. . . ."[7] That agenda had been shaped by years of alternating business and politics. In World War II, Casey served with the OSS in London and was chief of the special intelligence branch for the European theater of operations—a plum as well as an important assignment. Casey claimed that during this time he personally looked at "the structure of the British and European intelligence services for Donovan's initial paper urging President Roosevelt and the Joint Chiefs of Staff to develop a peacetime central intelligence agency."[8]

After the war, Casey made a series of smart investments that netted him millions. He worked on Republican campaigns beginning in 1940. From 1971 to 1973, he was a controversial chairman of the Securities and Exchange Commission. He followed this up by becoming equally controversial as undersecretary of state for economic affairs, until he was chased out by Kissinger. He served as president of the U.S. Export-Import Bank under Ford, and, during Ford's last year in office, was a member of the President's Foreign Intelligence Advisory Board (PFIAB). In 1977, I inadvertently had a hand in ending his service on that board. When the Carter administration came into office, we agonized over what to do with the PFIAB. It was so loaded with right-wing ideologues, like Casey, that we would have wanted to change the membership substantially to give it more balance. But would it be worthwhile to do that? After several discussions on this, President Carter said that the decision was in my hands. If I wanted the board to continue we would keep it, but if not we would wrap it up. I reasoned that Congress had just formed two committees for oversight of intelligence and that those would serve most of the purposes of PFIAB. I opted to terminate it and with it Bill Casey, whom I did not know.

Despite the fact that he had authored two dozen books on investing and on law, and was working on a history of the OSS when he met Reagan, Casey said his hobby was "not writing books." He would gather the materials, read widely in his chosen subject, and then let it go. "Most of the fun is doing the research and thinking about it, and I decide to spare myself the pain of writing."[9] CIA colleagues witnessed this same intellectual curiosity and reading habits. "Casey liked big briefing books for all of his meetings and appointments—whether he needed them or not," recalled James McCullough, director of Casey's executive staff.[10] Casey would meet with anyone and read anything. "The guys who put this out are crazy," he once wrote in a note to his deputy Robert Gates, attached to Lyndon LaRouche's *Executive Intelligence Review*, "but the [article on] Qaddafi and Khomeini . . . is interesting."[11]

This wide-ranging intellect, combined with his careless, disheveled physical appearance (he was bald with wisps of white hair, wore expensive but crumpled clothes, and had an ambling gait), all came together to give him the look of a college professor with his head in the clouds, earning him nicknames like "Spacey." The other moniker whispered behind his back, "Mumbles," was due to his consistent failure to speak loudly and clearly during meetings. Some wit at the CIA joked that his speech patterns obviated the need for telephone scramblers. During Senate and House Intelligence Committee hearings, this mumbling soon cleared the room of senators and representatives who could not understand what he was saying.

He also had real problems keeping secret papers secure. Sometimes they would turn up at his home after a search by his security officers. And he had some terribly unattractive nervous tics. "Sitting at his desk," Gates said, "Casey was nearly always in motion. He constantly fidgeted with paper clips, bending and unbending them, picking his teeth with them. Disconcertingly, he would often chew on the end of his necktie."[12]

Reagan's campaign team courted Casey in 1980. His political and business connections were openings to the all-important financial support of New York City's power centers. Casey rejected Reagan's first overtures to join the campaign, but he later agreed to a meeting at the Colony Hill Hotel, near Casey's Long Island estate. It went well, and Reagan's people started to get excited. "Well, what did you think?" Owen Smith, a Casey confidant, asked in the lobby after the meeting. Casey played it cool. "He could be president," he said with a shrug.[13]

Looking more closely, Casey saw a campaign in disorder, rife with fac-

body told me?" he asked at a White House correspondents' dinner. "Well, I know this: I've laid down the law . . . from now on . . . no matter what time it is, wake me, even if it's in the middle of a Cabinet meeting." He did not refer to the mining.[34]

Casey's machinations in Central America were covert actions only by definition. That is, they were actions by an intelligence organization to make things happen, not to collect intelligence, but the fact that the United States was attempting to change the political scene in Central America was not covert at all. The United States was using covert action overtly. This had not happened in quite the same way ever before. In Guatemala, Iran, Cuba, Chile, Angola, and other Cold War battlefields, Eisenhower, Kennedy, and Nixon had wanted to hide CIA involvement, at least while the action was going on. The Reagan team made no such attempt. This the Intelligence Oversight committees of Congress termed "overt" covert actions. So it was not *what* we were doing that was secret— it was *how*. The details of the operations were to be kept hidden, even if the fact that we were conducting operations was not.

Casey was thrilled with the whole Iran-contra conspiracy, calling it "the ultimate covert action."[35] As the layers of secrecy came off, he departed for a Donovan-style trip to the front lines in Central America to visit the contras. When he returned, the director of his executive staff remembered him as "a tired, suddenly older man more than a little bewildered by the situation to which he had returned." One of his first responses to the brewing scandal was to dash off a memo to the president, recommending that Reagan fire George Shultz. Maybe Casey thought he could take his place and avoid the coming storm. During his congressional testimony, even his supporters thought he looked "visibly exhausted and at times incoherent."[36]

On the morning of December 15, 1986, a CIA doctor was in the

DCI's office conducting a routine checkup of the DCI. Casey was complaining about his blood pressure medicine, which he'd stopped taking because of the side effects. Without it, he said, "I'm already feeling—" and suddenly stopped. He couldn't speak. His right leg and arm began jerking violently.[37] They didn't know what was happening until Casey arrived at Georgetown University Hospital. A brain tumor had caused the seizure. When the seizure passed, Casey was able to agree to surgery, and got a request back to Langley: He wanted his work at the hospital by the time he got out of surgery. McCullough remembered, "I could scarcely believe my ears. He was facing brain surgery, but he was treating it like he was at the dentist for a tooth extraction!"[38]

The surgeons were able to remove most of the tumor, but Casey was left paralyzed on his right side and could not speak. Meanwhile, at the White House, Reagan reluctantly agreed to abandon his DCI. White House staff member Don Regan showed up at the hospital to do the deed, only to be blocked by Casey's wife, Sophia. "If the President has something to say to Bill, he can come over here himself. He's Bill's boss."[39] Gates had more luck. By that time, Sophia had gathered from her husband, through a yes-or-no interview and his head gestures, that he was ready to step down. Although he tried, he was unable to sign the letter Gates brought for him, which read, "Dear Mr. President, I hereby submit my resignation as Director of Central Intelligence effective this date, January 29, 1987. It has been a great honor serving you."[40] Sophia signed on his behalf. Casey died on May 6.

Senator Daniel Inouye, chair of the Senate Intelligence Committee, would call Iran-contra, the final chapter of Casey's life, "a story of deceit and duplicity and the arrogant disregard of the rule of law. It is an elitist vision of government that trusts no one—not the people, not the Congress and not the cabinet. It is a vision of government operated by persons convinced they have a monopoly on truth."[41] To express its deep concern for this "deceit and duplicity," Congress enacted legislation that created an independent inspector general for the CIA.

In my view, the greatest harm Casey did was to sow the seeds of distrust that led Congress to pass such legislation. It is not that having an independent inspector general is a bad thing. It is that Congress felt compelled to have one because it did not trust the DCI. This was a blow to morale at the CIA, already sagging under the weight of investigations of Iran-contra, including the indictment of several senior CIA officers.

And all this turmoil came at a very bad time. It distracted Casey and his successors from the worst case of spying against the CIA in its history: the traitor Aldrich Ames. In a September 1994 report the CIA's new independent inspector general, Frederick Hitz, traced Ames's spying back to 1985. It was clear to the CIA back then that it faced a major counterintelligence problem. A significant number of agents in the Soviet Union were compromised. Some were recalled to the Soviet Union from abroad. In many cases these agents were executed. It took the FBI and the CIA nine years to apprehend Ames despite the fact that he was unprofessional in his spying and left many, many footprints. Hitz's report was scathing in its accusations that the intelligence losses from 1985 to 1994 were not pursued to the fullest extent of the capabilities of the CIA.

On December 18, 1986, Reagan appointed Gates acting DCI, and all concerned thought he would be the next permanent DCI. But during the five months he was acting, it became apparent that he would become the new lightning rod for the Iran-contra investigation. He either knew where the bodies were buried, or, at worst, he was complicit. He was savaged by Congress and the press, and, according to Gates, "the White House was nowhere to be seen."[42] Gates decided ultimately to ask that his nomination be withdrawn.

Enter William Webster. "[He] was a godsend to the Agency and to me," Gates recalled. "He had a huge reputation for integrity, honesty, and fidelity to the Constitution."[43] Webster had served in World War II and Korea as a naval officer, and spent almost twenty years as a lawyer in private practice before becoming a U.S. district court judge for Missouri's eastern district. From 1973 to 1978 he was an Eighth Circuit Court of Appeals judge, and then the director of the FBI from 1978 to 1987.[44] He was just about to slip into retirement when he was called on to lend his integrity to the CIA.

Webster's appointment was something new. The CIA had had its share of lawyers, but never before a judge. It had had a number of run-ins with the FBI, but never had it been run by a former FBI director. Webster had a clear directive—restore trust in the CIA. His job was made easier by his nonpartisan nature and good relations with Congress, but also by the fact that by 1987 the Soviet Union was clearly in decline. There was no longer a sense of alarm or calls to "unleash" the CIA. What the president needed now was a CIA that could provide clear information on a world that was becoming less polarized and on new arms control agreements that required objective analysis, not politically slanted intelligence. Webster was a far more hands-off director than Casey. He had enough to do in managing the relationship with Congress and dealing with the Intelligence Community at large. He left Gates in charge of the CIA.

With Mikhail Gorbachev instituting real reform in the Soviet Union, it was time to take a fresh look at the old problems. By and large, though, analysis remained stagnant, never clearly stating what the analysts seemed to know—that the old Soviet order was collapsing. There was a growing awareness that the USSR was on its last legs, and the CIA dutifully reported the numbers that suggested this to be true. But it failed to tell the story behind those numbers and failed to shake the assumptions of the policy-makers. Unfortunately, the Agency still felt as though it were on thin ice from Iran-contra and was avoiding controversy until it weathered the storm. As the Cold War, which had been its main raison d'être, drew to a close, then, the CIA was essentially sidelined by the machinations of Bill Casey, its most politically oriented DCI. Any bureaucracy that has been chastised, like the CIA was at this time, is not usually ready to put its neck out again soon and take additional risks.

CHAPTER TEN

GEORGE H. W. BUSH, WEBSTER, AND GATES

Confusion and Compromise at the Cold War's End

Anyone paying attention could almost hear the CIA rooting for George H. W. Bush during his campaign against Michael Dukakis. It went beyond politics. The CIA claimed Bush as one of its own, even though he had served as DCI for only ten months. During that short tenure, he had restored morale at a time when such a thing seemed impossible. As the CIA briefed candidate Bush, he made promises of how he would handle things for the CIA if he were president. This made quite an impression on Robert Gates and others.

Once elected, Bush started telling his briefers from the CIA about his preferences even before he moved into the Oval Office, signaling a presidential appreciation of the Agency and its product that it had not enjoyed

since the days of Kennedy. Bush wanted daily briefings. But when someone recommended that the DCI do the briefings himself, Bush reacted
immediately. He preferred "working-level officers"[1] have direct contact
with him. Back when Bush was DCI, he often took officers with him to
brief President Ford. Doing so built morale at the CIA and gave the president a chance to talk directly with possibly the most knowledgeable
source on the subject. It also fit with one of the most admirable qualities
of his personality. "He treated everyone alike," remembered Gates, "gar-
deners, the staff in the residence, the Secret Service, clerks, and Cabinet
officers—in an open, friendly, and dignified manner . . . and none of it
was artificial or insincere."[2]

This had a powerful effect on the Agency. One can imagine the reaction of a working-level analyst who is invited to brief the president as the
first thing in his day. As Bush recalled, "The PDB—the President's Daily
Brief—was the first order of business on my calendar. I made it a point
from day one to read the PDB in the presence of a CIA officer and either
Brent [Scowcroft, assistant for national security] or his deputy. This way I
could ask the briefers for more information on matters of critical interest,
and consult with Brent on matters affecting policy."[3] The groups were almost always small. "Having too many people around creates a problem,"
Bush recalled. "I held it to the National Security Adviser and sometimes
the Chief of Staff. If the group grows, pretty soon word gets out that he's
considering bombing Bosnia or whatever."[4]

While the group may have been small, the topics were of great consequence. For instance, the early-morning hour allowed Bush—eventually
dubbed the "mad dialer" for his habit of conducting business by phone—
to call on European leaders in the middle of their working day. Thus, the
briefer was still in the room, ready to amplify on the topic at hand if necessary. Such briefers would return to Langley on a real high. They had ac-

tually seen and contributed to the gears of Bush's international workings. They saw firsthand that their work was appreciated and that it had a real, immediate impact on foreign policy.

Bush had kept such a low profile during his years as vice president to Reagan that most expected him to simply carry out "Reagan's third term." Instead, Bush released hundreds of Reagan appointees. In the State Department, the new secretary, James Baker, told his aides, "Remember, this is not a friendly takeover."[5] One of the biggest differences that Bush wanted to see was an end to the palace politics of the Reagan era, wherein factions fought factions. At the same time, Bush's former government service had taught him to value secrecy, which sometimes does promote factionalism. For instance, when Bush approached Gorbachev for the first time, neither his DCI nor his secretary of defense knew about it. And while he ordered his subordinates to follow procedure, he often reached down a few layers in the bureaucracy to find fresh opinions. Insisting on a working-level CIA briefer is one example, but he did the same at the Department of Defense and the NSC, giving people like Paul Wolfowitz and Condoleezza Rice a voice in his decision-making.

But one of the biggest departures Bush made from the Reagan era was in his relationship with his DCI. "Casey was an inappropriate choice," he once stated bluntly. "We would be having a Cabinet discussion of agriculture and there would be Casey. That shouldn't be—the DCI should not enter into policy discussions."[6] Similar reasoning kept Casey's successor, William Webster, in office, even though he was long since ready to retire after almost eleven years in the FBI and CIA combined. "Bush apparently wanted to try to reestablish the apolitical nature of the DCI's job and demonstrate that it would not necessarily turn over with a change of Presidents," according to Bob Gates.[7] It also benefited Bush, who carried a taint from Iran-contra, to keep Judge Webster, with his reputation for integrity.

Webster told former Senate Select Committee on Intelligence (SSCI) staffer Loch Johnson during an interview, "I probably have more access to the President of the United States than any of the previous thirteen directors." Given Bush's fondness for the CIA, this may well have been the case. However, "that does not mean that I have a major role in policymaking. I don't. In fact, it was my understanding from the beginning that the CIA has to maintain its objectivity."[8] During his confirmation hearing, Webster rejected the notion of the DCI's being a Cabinet-level position, understanding that it could result in accusations of politicization of intelligence.

Webster inherited one issue that involved the CIA considerably in covert actions. This was what to do about Panama's military strongman, Manuel Noriega. Interestingly, Noriega was also one of the first political issues I had had to deal with as DCI back in 1977. I found that George H. W. Bush, as my predecessor, had met with Noriega in Washington about a month before leaving office as DCI. Noriega had been receiving a stipend from the CIA at that time, purportedly to provide intelligence on Central and South America. The Carter administration, though, adopted a hands-off policy on Noriega. We took him off the payroll and shunned him. But by 1985, under Reagan, Noriega was back on the CIA's payroll. This series of mixed messages likely convinced Noriega that the United States would leave him alone. Instead, in 1988, Reagan ordered three different covert actions against him. The first two are still secret, but evidently were ineffective. The third never got off the ground. The CIA briefed the SSCI about the operation, and the *Washington Post* ran a headline the next day: "Covert Action on Noriega Is Cleared." The White House accused the SSCI of leaking the story, and the SSCI returned the favor by claiming it was actually the White House that leaked it to make the SSCI look bad. One way or another, this ended the covert action.

Such was the United States' policy on Panama as Bush faced the debates of the 1988 presidential campaign. His opponent, Michael Dukakis, claimed that Bush had been "dealing with a drug-running Panamanian dictator."[9] Bush took a hard line on illegal drugs during the campaign. After the election, he took a stand: "There must be no misunderstanding about our policy . . . Noriega must go."[10]

Soon a new $10 million covert action was on the way. It funded opposition groups, bought ads in the media, and purchased radio time. The CIA hoped to sway the May 1989 election in Panama. International monitoring organizations watched the Panamanian election closely, and reported widespread fraud. Noriega reacted by nullifying the results and appointing his own man president. His thugs roamed the streets, and the opposition candidate was brutally beaten. Bush's reaction was a mix of economic sanctions and military posturing, plus calling on the Panamanian people to rise up. "They ought to do everything they can to get Noriega out of there," he said.[11] Soon, a coup was in the offing. The U.S. military, already positioned in the Canal Zone, helped block key roads and were given permission to arrest Noriega. He slipped through their fingers as the roadblocks were easily circumvented. The coup leader was caught, tortured, and killed by Noriega's people. Even fellow conservatives roasted Bush. "A bunch of Keystone Kops," pronounced Jesse Helms.[12] "An unserious presidency," wrote George Will.[13]

Bush said he was "frustrated," but still felt military action was "not prudent."[14] Instead he approved another, much more robust covert action that included permission to use force. Some in the CIA protested. With the ban on assassination in place, they feared they could be prosecuted if someone were killed. Scowcroft was indignant: "The CIA just sat on their hands, because . . . they were afraid someone was going to get killed. . . . There was absolutely no help from the station chief down there."[15] Bush assured the officers they would be protected if there was an "accident," but nothing came of the operation. It, too, was exposed by a leak to the media.

So instead of the quick and tidy covert operation that everyone wanted, Bush unleashed a sizable military operation that cost the lives of twenty-three Americans and hundreds of Panamanians. A number of administration figures, including Scowcroft, felt that the ban on assassinations got in the way of the low-cost solution.

Bill Webster also had to provide the intelligence support for another major foreign policy initiative of the Bush administration. This was our response to the invasion of Kuwait by Iraq in August 1990. The Intelligence Community certainly must have seen the buildup of Iraqi forces on the Iraqi border with Kuwait in July. What it did not do was predict the invasion. In fact on the day before Iraq invaded, the CIA sent an assessment to the president predicting that Iraq would not invade. The next day, the CIA scurried to the White House to pull it back. It must not have had sources that could distinguish between preparations for an invasion and a threatening bluff.

The CIA's biggest gaffe after the invasion, however, was an assessment that the Iraqis would withdraw from Kuwait before a deadline set by Bush. The CIA wasn't alone in this. Prince Bandar of Saudi Arabia, the long-time Saudi ambassador to the United States, agreed, and Bush himself told a reporter, "My gut says he will get out of there." Only the Defense Intelligence Agency predicted it would come down to a fight.[16]

It is interesting to note that while the subsequent military operation was explicitly for the liberation of Kuwait, Bush had authorized covert operations expressly for the purpose of regime change in Iraq. When those operations failed and military action started, the CIA had a large role in providing intelligence to the forces in the field. It was not given high marks for this by the commander of Desert Storm, General Norman

Schwarzkopf. "Stormin'" Norman was, of course, looking for tactical intelligence upon which to base immediate operational decisions. And, as was his style, he wanted crisp, clear statements as to where his opposition was and what it was doing. Much of what the CIA was feeding him, however, had to come from satellite photography. That photography almost always required interpretation. CIA interpreters, who were most accustomed to dealing in broad, strategic issues, tended to do just what Schwarzkopf accused them of—introducing caveats and footnotes. From the general's point of view, what he was receiving was useless.

A dozen years before I had encouraged the military to work with the CIA to get these kinks out of the system, but to no avail. If they did not fully control the intelligence-gathering satellites, the military did not want anything to do with them. Our failure to iron out procedures for getting tactical intelligence from national satellites led to the acrimonious recriminations from Schwarzkopf. Where he was more justified in complaining was when the CIA apparently failed to disclose to our troops that it knew there were chemical weapons in certain Iraqi weapons depots that those troops blew up. "If I was still in office," thundered Colin Powell years later when this came to light, "I would be raping and pillaging throughout the intelligence and operational community to get to the bottom of this."[17]

When it came time for Webster to leave, his successor, Robert Gates, came from the inside. On December 15, 1988, Gates got a call from Brent Scowcroft, now Bush's assistant for national security. Would he leave the CIA and come work as Scowcroft's deputy inside the White House? As Scowcroft recalled, "I think Bush always admired the way Gates had withdrawn his nomination during the Reagan administration so he wouldn't create political problems for Reagan." Gates was loyal, and was even ready to sacrifice his own career for the president. Scowcroft explained to Gates that he shouldn't think of working in a policy job as leaving the CIA. "I said, 'Bob, look, I know you are out there at the CIA, you are deputy and so on, but the best thing for you if you want to be DCI is to get out of there for a while. Come down here, when the time comes I promise I will support you.' "[18]

While on the NSC staff, Bob Gates built a strong relationship with George H. W. Bush. Gates was a short man, with boyish looks that left one observer with "the impression of a well-behaved and precocious youngster."[19] But his evident intelligence ensured that Bush and others would always take him seriously. Gates had joined the CIA in 1966; worked on loan on the NSC staff under Nixon, Ford, and Carter; and returned to the CIA in 1979. From then until January 1981 he was my executive assistant. He was particularly helpful to me because he knew the operations of the NSC staff so well and could help avoid misunderstandings. After I left, he worked closely with Casey as director of his executive staff, and then he was deputy director for intelligence from 1982 to 1986, when he became Casey's second in command.

As Scowcroft's deputy, Gates spent many hours a day at President Bush's side. When he wasn't working with Bush, he was working with Scowcroft, who also enjoyed a strong relationship with the president. By the time Gates left the White House to become DCI, he says, "I considered Brent Scowcroft my closest friend in the world."[20] For President Bush, Gates had nothing but praise—"immensely well-versed in foreign affairs," "eager learner"—and if he had any faults, it was that he was too loyal to some people who didn't deserve it.[21]

"It helped that Gates had been a professional [in the CIA]," President Bush told an interviewer, "but I picked him [for DCI] because he did such a good job sitting right here [next to Bush on the deck at Kennebunkport]."[22] On May 8, 1991, Gates joined Bush in his cabin on Air Force One. Gates was not surprised when Bush asked him to replace Bill Webster as DCI, and he accepted without missing a beat. "I had been certain in

1987 when I withdrew my nomination that the opportunity to be Director would never come again. To have the brass ring come around a second
time for that position was the sort of thing that just didn't happen in
Washington." On the other hand, Gates wrote, "Being at the right hand
of the President—of this President—was about as gratifying as it could
get. I would be giving up [by becoming DCI] that constant contact, and
the great fun we all had besides, even in the tough times."[23]

Gates expected more tough times ahead at the confirmation, and he
was right. He had several powerful supporters, but memories of Iran-
contra were still fresh. In addition, an astounding number of former CIA
people testified against Gates in closed sessions. The nomination reached
the Senate on June 24, 1991. Hearings were scheduled for mid-July 1991.
But because, in a separate hearing, former CIA official Alan Fiers pleaded
guilty to two misdemeanors involving the withholding of information
from Congress, the hearings were delayed. Fiers had admitted greater
knowledge of the Iran-contra affair than had been previously known. The
committee first wanted to investigate whether Gates had knowledge of
what Fiers had disclosed. It even had the FBI conduct an investigation on
Gates, and then did not start hearings until September 16. They continued
until October 18, 1991, at which time the SSCI voted 11–4 to recommend
Gates to the full Senate.

According to an SSCI report, the Gates nomination was the "most
thorough and comprehensive of any nomination ever received by the
Committee. Thousands of documents were reviewed; hundreds of wit-
nesses were interviewed."[24] Gates testified for four full days in open and
closed sessions and responded to almost one thousand questions; he wrote
nearly one hundred post-hearing written responses.

During his testimony, he evoked Bush: "I can pull [the CIA] through
because of my relationship with the president."[25] To some, this sounded
perfect. To others, it reminded them that Gates was repeatedly accused of

helping politicize intelligence under Casey. But Gates's relationship with
Bush did more good than harm as far as Congress was concerned. It especially meant a lot to those who were concerned about the Intelligence
Community. A DCI with a close relationship to the president would presumably have more latitude for managing the Intelligence Community,
not just the CIA, than a DCI with a distant relationship. Important members of the SSCI sent a clear message to Gates during the confirmation
hearings that they expected him to manage the Community. "The alternative was clear enough," remembered one staffer. Congress would take matters into its own hands if real Community coordination wasn't achieved.[26]
Gates remembers using this to his advantage as DCI. "I was able to go
back to these people in the Community and say, 'You've got two choices:
you can do it my way, in which you have a part and a say; or they [Con-
gress] are going to tell you how to do it.' . . . So I used the Hill against the
Community, and that worked pretty well."[27] That Gates had to resort to
this sort of leverage was in part because the presidential executive order
under which he was operating, one issued originally by Ronald Reagan,
weakened the DCI's authorities over the Community from the orders of
Jimmy Carter. After a long and contentious confirmation process, Gates
was confirmed by the Senate by a vote of 64-31 and sworn in as DCI on
November 6, 1991, some six months after accepting the offer from President Bush.

Gates was the first career CIA person to rise to the top of the CIA
from the analytic side rather than from the espionage and covert-action
side. He was also the first Soviet specialist to become DCI. For years the
CIA had valued generalists, even though the majority of the CIA's efforts
were directed at the Soviet Union. Ironically, Gates rose to the top levels
just as the Soviet Union was passing into history and the CIA was being
lambasted for not having predicted the Soviet Union's demise.

In Scowcroft's view, "I don't fault them for not predicting the fall of the Soviet Union."[28] But others felt quite differently. Colin Powell wrote that the CIA didn't "anticipate events much better than a layman watching television." George Shultz felt the Agency gave "bum dope" to the president, and let its analyses be "distorted by strong views about policy," and was "unable to perceive that change was coming to the Soviet Union."[29] Senator Daniel Patrick Moynihan lashed out: "For a quarter-century the CIA has been repeatedly wrong about the major political and economic questions entrusted to its analysis."[30]

In contrast, a number of CIA officers believed that they either did get close to predicting the fall of the USSR, or that they predicted it outright. These, however, were lower-level analysts who believed Gorbachev was a real reformer; it was the skepticism of higher-level officers that went forward to the policy-makers. For instance, in 1988, Gates, who was then in the number-two position of deputy director of central intelligence, claimed that "a long, competitive struggle with the Soviet Union still lies before us." And later that year, he pronounced, "The dictatorship of the Communist party remains untouched and untouchable."[31]

The tone of these estimates changed in 1989, however. The hard facts were the same—the Soviet economy was imploding—but the focus of the predictions was on a possible political breakdown. In one case the deputy director for analysis even appended his own dissent to a National Intelligence Estimate, stating that Gorbachev would lose control of events.[32] Gates took the most alarmist nuggets from these estimates and wrote to Bush: "The odds are growing that in the next year or two, there will be popular unrest, political turmoil, and/or official violence [that may add up to] significant political instability." Bush told Gates and Scowcroft to start drawing up contingency plans.[33]

Bush reminded his aides that Gorbachev was "still a Russian and a Communist, which counts for more in the final analysis" than any overtures or partial reforms. And Gates believed, and told Bush, "Gorbachev might be succeeded by not another Gorbachev, but by another Stalin," so open support of Gorbachev was ill-advised. Gates's skepticism was so well known that when he met Gorbachev for the first time, the Russian told him, "I understand that the White House has a special cell assigned the task of discrediting Gorbachev. And I've heard that you are in charge, Mr. Gates." He then looked to the secretary of state, James Baker. "Perhaps if we are able to work out our problems, Mr. Gates will be out of a job."[34]

Gates did not lose his job. Rather, his, and the CIA's, predictions grew increasingly dire for the Soviet Union. Gates told the House Armed Services Committee in December 1991, "The disintegration of the armed forces and ongoing ethnic conflict will combine this winter to produce the most significant civil disorder in the former USSR since [1917]."[35] And the forecast in a classified NIE issued in June went beyond disorder: "In any event, we believe that the USSR in its present form will not exist five years from now."[36]

"I'm sorry we didn't say it more strongly," Deputy Director for Analysis Douglas MacEachin reflected.[37] But what was really missed was the rise of Boris Yeltsin as a popular alternative to Gorbachev. Yeltsin came in from left field. Journalist and CIA historian Thomas Powers had an interesting take on the widespread resistance to the idea that the Cold War was about to end. In his view, all believed deep down that the only way out of this East-West rivalry was a war, but "because such a war was anathema to most people, psychologically we had a very deep investment in believing that nothing was going to happen—forever."[38]

We can see this in the story former DCI William Colby told of when he really knew that the Cold War was over. Not long after Gorbachev fell, Colby was in Moscow as a private citizen. Even though it was December, he took a walk after dinner and wandered onto Red Square, past the

Kremlin. He said he was sure that he was not being followed: "I'm professional enough to know." That made this moment in history finally settle
in: "I had no fear and for someone with my background to be able to walk
in that holy of holies alone and without an escort—if that isn't victory, I
want to know what is."[39]

Gates remembered well the moment he realized what the end of the
USSR would mean to the CIA. When Armenia and Azerbaijan went to
war over the treatment of a pocket of Armenians in Nagorno-Karabakh
and the waning Soviet state sent in troops, the CIA got most of its information from CNN. "Our efforts had long been focused on events in
Moscow, and we were only beginning to realize how small and inadequate
were our collection capabilities and expertise on the non-Russian re-
publics and ethnic groups." It took weeks to even get newspapers from the
region, and the satellite photos did nothing but tell them where the troops
were. Gates was faced with the realization that in this case CNN was doing a better job: "They could comfortably go openly where we could not.
And we hadn't even gone there secretly."[40] Then again, even in places
where the CIA had gone secretly, CNN was sometimes doing a better job.
The president first heard about the coup against Gorbachev from Scowcroft, who heard it on CNN, not from his DCI.

What Gates was confronted with, then, was where to refocus the CIA
now that its primary target, the USSR, was gone. In November 1991,
Bush ordered twenty policy agencies and departments to identify their intelligence needs through the year 2005. Terrorism came out high on the list,
but it was focused on state-sponsored terrorism, not the al Qaeda,
nongovernmental, type.[41] But it was a move in the right direction. The
administration also demanded more intelligence on nuclear proliferation—
attempts by countries or groups to steal or develop nuclear weapons. The
CIA previously focused on large-scale weapons and their delivery

programs, like China's and India's. But with the breakup of the Soviet Union and the subsequent scattering of its scientists, as well as uncertainty about the security of its warheads, potentially many countries now could be only a few years away from being nuclear capable.

Bush became particularly interested in the proliferation of weapons of mass destruction during Operation Desert Shield versus Iraq in 1990. Any proof of an Iraqi nuclear program, which Iraq was suspected of having, would help his attempts to create and hold together an anti-Iraq coalition. The CIA reported that all indicators pointed to Iraq's having such a weapons program. But the Intelligence Community discovered how close Iraq had been only when inspectors were allowed into the country after the Gulf War. At that time, the CIA sent five agents in with a UN inspection team. The agents were "unmasked" and expelled. Scowcroft recalled, "It was a good idea [sending in agents undercover as inspectors] and it was authorized."[42] The problem, of course, was that the discovery of CIA agents among the inspectors gave Saddam Hussein the perfect pretext for blocking further inspections, setting the stage for Gulf War II.

During the Bush administration the CIA appropriately started examining other nuclear programs. In 1992, it reported that the North Koreans were only two years away from having a weapon. The Agency's people also helped prevent Iran from acquiring enriched uranium from a plant in Kazakhstan. By 1992, Washington was comfortable with the idea that the demise of the USSR permitted nonproliferation to be the number-one topic of intelligence interest. Consequently, no one blinked an eye when Gates revealed to Congress that the CIA was sharing intelligence with the Russians to gain their help in preventing the flow of weapons and matériel out of that country—one of the most profound signs that the Cold War was over.

But nuclear proliferation was just one area where the CIA planned to give new emphasis. The Agency had to transform from what DCI Bedell Smith had called a "Cold War Department" into a truly central and genuinely diverse intelligence organization. But this responsibility would pass to a president who was much more distant from the intelligence process and to a new DCI.

CHAPTER ELEVEN

BILL CLINTON, WOOLSEY, DEUTCH, AND TENET

The CIA Without the Cold War

Wiilliam Casey's resignation in January 1987 set the revolving door of the DCI's office in motion again. He had been DCI for six years. Over the next ten years the Intelligence Community would have four different directors before George Tenet arrived and settled in for a seven-year tenure (the second longest, behind Allen Dulles).

Like Jimmy Carter, Bill Clinton inherited a DCI who carried the taint of a close association with a Republican administration. Bob Gates was strongly associated with Reagan, Bush, and Republican foreign policy. He was not acceptable to the new administration.

Clinton left his replacement DCI and each of two successors largely alone. There were no close political associations, as with Reagan and Casey, and no close working relationships, as with Bush and Gates. Clinton's appointees as DCI were largely apolitical. This is somewhat surprising since Clinton is so political a person. But because Clinton had so little to do with them, the DCIs would be largely free from political influences and considerations.

Clinton's first DCI, R. James Woolsey, was definitely not from the CIA club. Even worse in the eyes of some people in the Intelligence Community, he was a former military official who had been walking the halls of the Pentagon. Earlier in his career he had been on Nixon's National Security Council staff, and had been on several arms control negotiating teams. From this perspective, he was potentially a good choice, as the CIA was shifting to arms control monitoring as a key mission.

From another perspective, Woolsey's having been in the Reagan and Bush administrations would keep Clinton from appearing soft in the foreign policy arena. But from a career perspective, moving to the CIA was a real change in trajectory. Woolsey had been moving on a path that led to secretary of defense. The CIA was a diversion for someone whose service as undersecretary of the navy could be seen as a stepping-stone to secretary of defense.[1] He found himself meeting President Clinton in Little Rock sometime past midnight on December 21, 1992. They had a vague conversation about world events but did not directly discuss whether Woolsey would be offered the DCI slot. Based on this meeting, Clinton felt that "Woolsey was clearly intelligent and interested in the job."[2] The next day, Woolsey, at Clinton's request, went to see Wes Hubbell at the Rose Law Firm and answered questions about possible conflicts of interest. Still no job offer. Woolsey later found out from the secretary of state designee, Warren Christopher, that Clinton had tapped him for DCI.

He was informed of his nomination when Christopher gave him what amounted to a polite order to attend a press conference at which the nomination would be announced. But first, Woolsey reported to future press secretary Dee Dee Myers and to Clinton advisor George Stephanopoulos for a spin session. There was some concern on Myers's part that a reporter might try to paint Clinton's appointments as "a bunch of Carter administration retreads." Woolsey pointed out that he had also served in the Bush administration with ambassadorial rank. Myers was surprised: "Admiral Woolsey, I didn't know you served in the Bush administration." Woolsey replied, "I'm afraid I'm not an admiral, Ms. Myers. I never rose above the rank of captain in the army." Myers was glad they'd had this little talk. "In that case," she said, "I better take the word 'admiral' out of the press release."[3]

It seems that Woolsey's most attractive feature, as far as the Clinton team was concerned, was the fact that he was known on Capitol Hill as "the Republicans' favorite Democrat," a man with solid credentials and conservative leanings where defense was concerned.[4] Having a DCI candidate who wouldn't come under fire during confirmation was more important to Clinton than picking someone with whom he knew he could work. Clinton didn't really plan on a close relationship with his DCI.

This lack of a strong relationship between Woolsey and Clinton must count as a missed opportunity during the interlude between the end of the Cold War and the 9/11 attacks. The CIA was an organization crying out for new direction. No one discussed doing away with the military, the NSA, or the NRO, but some, like Senator Daniel Patrick Moynihan, wondered if we needed a CIA. Only a solid presidential partnership with a forward-thinking DCI could have defined a new mission for the CIA in the dramatically and rapidly changing world environment.

Clinton was not as concerned with what the intelligence establishment did as he was with fulfilling his campaign promise to cut out $7.5 billion, or about a quarter of the intelligence budget. As many in the Agency saw it, an organization that could legitimately claim a major contribution to victory in the Cold War was to be rewarded by being decimated. However, it was by no means intelligence alone that was being cut at this time. Congress was focused on a "peace dividend"—money that could be diverted from spending on national security to domestic programs.

It also became quickly apparent that Clinton would keep his DCI at more than arm's length, further dampening CIA morale. There was the bizarre incident when a small private plane nearly crashed into the White House but landed short on the lawn. It wasn't long before the joke was making the Washington rounds that it was Woolsey trying to get some face time with Clinton. Woolsey seemed to be the only major player on the national security team to be accorded this arm's length treatment. The NSC staff "regularly interacted with the Chief Executive," recalled counterterrorism expert Richard Clarke.[5] Still, Clinton did not ignore the CIA's product. He read it just like he read and retained every piece of information with which he came in contact. "Every morning I start my day with an intelligence report. The intelligence I receive informs just about every foreign policy decision we make," he claimed.[6] But he did not want to be briefed, probably because the CIA's briefers and procedures were too formal for him.

The Clinton administration's primary focus was its domestic agenda. Clinton believed it was his mandate. The common wisdom was that Bush had lost the election because he focused too much on foreign affairs. Even covert action, relished by most presidents from Truman to Bush, suffered. The first casualty was the termination of Bush's covert funding of the Iraqi National Congress, a collection of Iraqi expatriates. According to one CIA insider, during the presidency of George H. W. Bush, "the question we kept getting from the White House was 'How much do you need?' After Clinton and [Assistant for National Security Anthony] Lake came in, it changed to 'How much can you get along on?'"[7]

When Woolsey took office, he almost immediately started lobbying against the cuts that Clinton had proposed during the campaign. If the cuts went ahead, Woolsey argued, we'd miss out on acquiring a new generation of satellites. Clinton backed down, but left Woolsey to convince Congress on his own. Woolsey didn't help his own case, however. At his first closed-door session with the SSCI he came on a bit strong. Thus began what one reporter called "one of Washington's great Hatfield-McCoy disputes" between Woolsey and SSCI chairman Dennis DeConcini, "a highly personal, two-year fight."[8] Said DeConcini, "Woolsey felt like he knew best, and nobody could tell him otherwise."[9]

In the absence of cover from the president, Woolsey was at the mercy of Congress. He was called to testify in open hearings eight times in 1993. The members of the committee were well aware of the distant relationship between Woolsey and Clinton. Democratic Representative Dan Glickman, chairman of the House Intelligence Committee, noted that "there is a serious distance between the White House and the CIA."[10] Several senators went so far as to secretly discuss going to the White House to demand that Woolsey be fired.

As much as he wanted to focus on the domestic agenda and shift resources to deficit reduction and domestic programs, Clinton found after entering office that he had been left holding the bag in Somalia. The CIA said Somalia was an untenable situation. They had good intelligence on Somalia thanks to agents developed when the Horn of Africa was a Cold War hot spot. Bush's national security team had been unanimous in supporting a humanitarian mission and in 1992 had opted to send in U.S. troops to head up a multinational force. The mission was limited in scope—to just keeping the peace in the area surrounding Mogadishu. Then, in mid-mission, the United States went through a change of president, a change of DCI, and a change in the UN's mission.

The UN assembly decided to restore a central government to Somalia. This sparked a war against the foreign peacekeepers by the forces of the rebel Mohammed Farah Aidid. The CIA's initial predictions for a successful operation now clouded. Two hundred thousand people had loyalties to

Aidid. A limited war against this warlord was not possible. Despite an impressive intelligence network in the region, U.S. and UN forces were never able to nail down Aidid. When the CIA finally did get a human asset in his inner circle, that source of information was eliminated when a U.S. Black Hawk helicopter, responding to military intelligence, opened fire on a building where the CIA's asset and Aidid supporters were holding a meeting. Everyone inside was killed.

One plan that succeeded was the capture of Aidid's financial backer, Osman Ato. The CIA's Directorate of Science and Technology had managed to plant a homing transmitter in Ato's vicinity. A dramatic scene unfolded in north Mogadishu. With a helicopter tracking Ato from afar, a man on the ground confirmed Ato was in the suspect car when it stopped for gas. A helicopter full of Delta Force troops descended, and a sniper immobilized the car with a bullet through the engine block. Troops swarmed the car and arrested Ato. But lieutenants would never substitute for Aidid. A quick capture of Aidid would have spared the Clinton administration the embarrassment of bringing the troops home from a mission still unaccomplished. A disastrous raid on October 3, 1993, by troops from Delta Force and Army Rangers and targeted on two of Aidid's lieutenants, cost the joint force eighteen dead and seventy-three wounded, and led to the administration's deciding to withdraw our forces from Somalia.

Whereas in Somalia the CIA appeared unable to serve policy, in Haiti it appeared to work directly against policy. During the Cold War, the Agency had become cozy with the Haitian military, just as it did throughout Central America—as long as the generals weren't Communists. In Haiti, their most prominent asset was Lt. General Raoul Cedras, who appeared to support Haiti's elections and transition to democratic rule. But even when Cedras turned on Haiti's elected president, Jean-Bertrand

Aristide, by joining a coup that sent Aristide into exile, the Agency wouldn't drop him from the CIA payroll.

This crisis of leadership in Haiti was already full blown when Clinton entered office. Driven by fear of armed gangs, thousands of Haitians were making dangerous voyages on improvised boats in attempts to reach Florida. President Bush ordered them returned to Haiti. Candidate Clinton promised a more humanitarian treatment. During the transition period, the CIA showed him overhead photos demonstrating that his promises had spurred an increase in boat building. They forecast two hundred thousand new refugees as a direct result of his promises. Clinton had to pull back quickly from his position of permitting Haitians to apply for asylum.

However, Clinton was clear on his foreign-policy objectives: "I want to emphasize how important it is to me personally to restore the democratic government to Haiti and how important it is to the United States that we return President Aristide to power."[11] In October 1993, he ordered thirteen hundred marines to the island with food and supplies on a humanitarian mission. At the dock in Port-au-Prince, an angry mob shouting anti-American slogans and "Somalia!" made it impossible for them to leave their ship. It took a much larger force and more concerted effort to get aid to Haiti and to restore democratic rule.

And then it emerged that there had been an intelligence relationship between the CIA and the military junta all along. Emmanuel Constant, an admitted CIA asset and leader of a brutal paramilitary arm of the junta, had organized the mob on the docks. The Agency had courted the worst elements in the junta, as it often has had to deal with similar people throughout the world. However, as the *New York Times* noted in an editorial, in the case of Haiti the CIA had lost sight of providing intelligence and was interfering with policy.[12]

Somalia and Haiti reinforced whatever reasons President Clinton had for keeping his distance from the CIA. Then Aldrich Ames provided another. As noted earlier, Ames was an officer in the Directorate of Operations and revealed to have been a spy for the Soviet Union from 1985 to 1994. He had enough security clearances to compromise more than one hundred operations and was responsible for the executions of at least ten Soviets who were spying for the United States. In the CIA, he acted almost as though he wanted to get caught. He was often drunk, careless, slothful, and ignored rules and procedures. His behavior should have raised serious questions at the CIA long before he was finally found out.

Woolsey's response to the Ames scandal was roundly criticized. A reporter for *Time* wrote that he "acted more like a lawyer defending a client rather than a director intent on cleaning up the worst spy scandal in the agency's history."[13] He was characterized as waiting for an investigation instead of acting, and of merely scolding, in writing, eleven officers (some retired) who had been negligent. Unfortunately for Woolsey, his hands were, essentially, tied. He acknowledged that four of the officers did deserve more than a written reprimand.[14] Three of them, however, had already retired and were beyond punishment. The remaining officer was scheduled to retire imminently. Nonetheless, the CIA rank and file felt a series of reprimands was inadequate punishment for one of the most serious breaches of security in the CIA's history. The congressional committees on intelligence were equally upset and wanted heads to roll for the Agency's having taken nine years to identify Ames.

With the White House keeping its distance from the scandal, Woolsey was never more alone. Representative Dan Glickman remarked, "The magnitude of the losses cried out for more active White House participation." But, he continued, "Woolsey did it all by himself, which minimized its qualitative and quantitative importance."[15] Only after the dust had settled did Clinton decide, under pressure from his former secretary of defense, his vice president, and his assistant for national security, that it was time for an overhaul of the Intelligence Community.

The first step (this being Washington) was to form a commission. At this point Congress inserted itself into the process, demanding a congressional panel rather than an executive commission. What came out was a joint effort, with former Defense Secretary Les Aspin leading a group of six members of the President's Foreign Intelligence Advisory Board and ten members appointed by Congress, including two senators and two representatives. (Aspin died in May 1995, three months into the process. Clinton replaced him with Carter's secretary of defense, Harold Brown.) Senator John Warner, one of the two senators on the commission, and a supporter of Jim Woolsey,[16] sponsored the legislation creating the commission. Warner was concerned that Woolsey was being unfairly treated and also thought that a commission would help the battered Agency.

This was the largest and most inclusive review of the Intelligence Community since 1975, and is notable for the fact that none of its major recommendations have been implemented. The review suggested a six-year term for the DCI (hoping to place him beyond a single four-year administration, and thus above politics); a smaller and more focused Community; public disclosure of the Intelligence Community budget; and more openness, accountability, and oversight. Surprisingly, it recommended against the creation of a director of national intelligence over the entire Intelligence Community, separate from the CIA.

The ideas of separating the roles of DCI and head of the CIA and enhancing the authorities of the DCI over the Intelligence Community are recurring themes that go well back in the Community's history. In July 1961, the President's Foreign Intelligence Advisory Board had proposed to President Kennedy that the two jobs be separated. While Kennedy did not endorse the recommendation, in January 1962, as noted earlier, he directed DCI John McCone to leave the day-to-day operations of the CIA to his deputy and "to carry out your primary task as DCI."[17] In 1976, the Church Committee of the Senate recommended that the president consider separating the DCI from the CIA and that the authorities of the DCI over the Intelligence Community be enhanced. In response, President Ford issued a written directive encouraging his DCI to delegate management of the CIA to his deputy. In 1977, President Carter gave me oral instructions to focus on managing the Intelligence Community. In 1987, Senator Arlen Specter, then a member of the SSCI, introduced legislation to create a director of national intelligence, separate from the head of the CIA, but nothing came of it. It took the intelligence failure associated with 9/11 to galvanize the Congress into legislating the separation of the two jobs.

Beyond Ames, another problem that had been festering for decades and that erupted on Woolsey's watch was the complaint of hundreds of women in the CIA about sexual harassment and a glass ceiling. A shocking 45 percent of the Agency's female officers complained of harassment. The conventional wisdom was that the Directorate of Operations was the worst offender. Not surprisingly, the nature of espionage requires CIA case officers overseas to work at all hours, day and night. They are often required to meet their contacts in sleazy environments, and work with unsavory people who offer sexual inducements. In such circumstances, CIA women overseas are particularly vulnerable to harassment from agents or even their own colleagues. In one instance during my tenure as DCI, I had to discipline a very senior male officer for using a CIA "safe house" (a place to rendezvous with agents) for an affair with his mistress. Woolsey was sympathetic to the women's complaints. He characterized the Directorate of Operations as "a fraternity . . . a white male one."[18] The CIA eventually settled most of the lawsuits, paying out almost a million dollars in back pay.

In dealing with Congress over the budget, Woolsey found himself taking the heat for the fact that the National Reconnaissance Office (which manages spy satellites) had gone $159 million over budget. Congress was understandably annoyed at having to discover this on its own. It looked as though Woolsey had been trying to hide the information. Once again, Woolsey didn't get a lifeline or even a gesture of support from the White House, which had by that time decided, in the words of one senior official, "Woolsey has been miscast."[19]

This lack of support, plus the lack of face time with the president, had to be wearing on Woolsey. On Christmas Day 1994, he asked his wife and three teenage sons to vote on whether he should continue as DCI. He said he would abstain from the vote. The tally came out four for resigning. The next day, Woolsey called Clinton to tell him he was on his way out, wrote his letter of resignation, recorded a video communication for the CIA workers he was leaving behind, and flew to the Caribbean.[20] "Mr. Woolsey's greater failing was that he settled for tinkering with an intelligence system that needs a complete overhaul and a fresh look at its annual $28 billion budget," the New York Times opined.[21] Woolsey saw the problem as rooted in a lack of presidential support. In 1996, he endorsed Bob Dole for president.

The search for a new DCI appears to have centered on candidates with backgrounds in the military or in civilian oversight of the military. John Deutch, deputy secretary of defense, and Admiral William Crowe (retired), former chairman of the Joint Chiefs of Staff and then ambassador to the United Kingdom, both received offers and both declined. Retired Air Force General Michael Carns accepted. At first, he looked like the perfect candidate to gain approval of the Senate—no one had heard of him. A closer look revealed someone truly respected and qualified. He had a Harvard business degree, had flown two hundred combat missions during Vietnam, had been vice chief of staff of the Air Force, and enjoyed support from Colin Powell and Robert Gates. "I think it's a first-rate appointment," Gates told a reporter. "While he has not been in the business, he understands intelligence."[22] I was impressed and flattered when Carns contacted me and said he would like to get together and ask my advice. One would think that someone who had held the number of sensitive jobs Carns had would have been through a thorough background check. In the course of the investigation for DCI, however, the FBI found irregularities in the hiring of, payments to, and efforts on behalf of foreign-born domestic help. Carns withdrew his nomination before he appeared before the Senate.

So the offer went back to Deutch and with it a lot of pressure from Clinton. I was present at one instance of this pressure. The president had invited a group of retired military officers who had supported him in the election campaign to lunch at the White House. Deutch was also there, and in his remarks to us the president said that he was hoping Deutch would accept his offer of becoming DCI. Deutch finally relented and became the first foreign-born DCI, having been born in Brussels in 1938 and naturalized in 1945. There was no question as to his intelligence and governmental experience. He'd been a professor of chemistry, chairman of the chemistry department, dean of science, and provost at MIT. He'd served as director of energy research, acting assistant secretary for energy technology, and undersecretary at the U.S. Department of Energy. At the Department of Defense, he was a systems analyst when I first met him,[23] then became undersecretary for acquisition and technology, and was serving as deputy secretary when he was tapped for DCI.

Deutch's confirmation sailed through the Senate with a unanimous vote. His promise to start reform at the CIA was a problem from the CIA's perspective, but not as much as the fact that it was clear that what Deutch really wanted was to be secretary of defense. The only person who'd pulled off such a move was James Schlesinger.

Deutch helped implement one of the biggest downsizings in CIA history, from around twenty-two thousand employees during the Reagan era to about sixteen thousand in 1998. The actual numbers are classified. This was twice the reduction recommended by Al Gore's National Performance Review. Earning even more animosity from all levels of the CIA, Deutch also brought in some new people. One of them was George Tenet, who Deutch did not know well but who came with the experience of having been majority staff director at the SSCI from 1988 to 1993 and in charge of intelligence on the NSC staff from 1993 to 1995.

Some of the first CIA professionals to go were the chief of the Latin American Division and the station chief in Guatemala. Deutch had walked into an unfolding scandal regarding Guatemala. Back in 1990, an American innkeeper, Michael DeVine, had been tortured and killed in a remote section of Guatemala. The CIA soon found out that one of its own Guatemalan assets, an army colonel, had been responsible. The colonel was a brutal figure in a dirty war against Guatemala's indigenous population that had claimed two hundred thousand lives. But by killing an American, had he gone too far? While it did inform the Justice Department, the CIA neglected to tell either the State Department or Congress. It did not cut off ties to the colonel. In fact, he received an additional $44,000 of U.S. taxpayer money. Nor was he held accountable for the similar torture-murder of Efrain Bamaca Velasquez, a Guatemalan who was married to an American lawyer.

Clinton was assured that the cooperation between the CIA and the Guatemalan army intelligence death squads was over. As details of the DeVine and Bamaca Velasquez killings surfaced, Secretary of State Warren Christopher said on *Face the Nation*, "I'm satisfied there's no money going down there now." He was wrong. There was money going down there, and neither he nor the president knew about it. It was money to support what the CIA called a "liaison relationship." According to a White House official, this was "not something that rose to the president's level."[24] When he learned of it, Clinton ordered all funding cut immediately and later had the Intelligence Oversight Board investigate.

"In the course of our review," the panel wrote, "we found that several CIA assets were credibly alleged to have ordered, planned or participated in serious human rights violations such as assassination, extrajudicial execution, torture or kidnapping. These actions were while they were assets—and the CIA's Directorate of Operations headquarters was aware at the time of the allegations."[25] Clinton has been quite often blamed for not getting more involved in the CIA, and rightly so. But with these scandals and that of Haiti all rooted in events that predated his presidency, it is understandable that he would not want to get too close. In the case of Guatemala, Clinton decided in 1999 to apologize on behalf of the nation, infuriating conservatives and the CIA's old guard: "For the United States it is important that I state clearly that support for military forces and intelligence units which engaged in violence and widespread repression was wrong, and the United States must not repeat that mistake."[26]

Another early hot issue for Deutch was the morass in the former Yugoslavia. CIA analysts had concluded back in 1990 that the country would cease to function in 1991 and would break up by 1992. Clinton ordered U-2 flights over Bosnia not long after taking office, but it took pressure from the UN ambassador, Madeleine Albright, to get agents on the ground in Bosnia to interview former prisoners. Albright, one of the few true hawks on Bosnia, presented a pair of U-2 photographs to the UN in August 1995. The scene was Srebrenica, and the first photo showed an empty field. The second one showed a series of freshly covered mass graves. It took a special appeal from Albright to make use of these photos. They'd been taken for tactical military reasons, not for the reasons she wanted to show them. "I alternate between being impressed with what intelligence can do and depressed at how slow it can be in making it all happen," she told a reporter.[27]

In neither covert action nor reporting did the CIA leave a very strong impression by its performance during the Yugoslavian crises in Bosnia and then Kosovo. A proposed covert training program was outrageously expensive, a coup plot against Yugoslavian leader Slobodan Milosevic never got off the ground, and faulty CIA targeting led to a precision-guided bomb utterly destroying the Chinese embassy and killing five. The CIA's DO was at a low point. It had been unable to capture a warlord in a primitive African country or to dispatch a petty Yugoslav dictator.

Nor could the CIA deal with that thorn in the side of U.S. foreign policy, Saddam Hussein. In the 1980s, we supported Saddam Hussein because he was engaged in a war with Iran, which had become our nemesis in the Middle East. The CIA even supplied satellite photography to the Iraqis. By Clinton's time we were working against both regimes. In an effort to overthrow Saddam Hussein, Woolsey had continued funding of the Iraqi National Congress that began under George H. W. Bush. Deutch thought he would have better luck with the Iraqi National Accord (INA), which had Saudi backing and was full of former military officers who believed they could erode support for Hussein with their broadcast network and their high-level contacts. Clinton approved $6 million for the INA's efforts, which were eagerly backed by Deutch and the Saudis, with the caveat that the coup would not put the Shiites in power. Everyone involved underestimated the powerful grip Hussein had on his military. He effortlessly penetrated the INA, gathered the necessary counterintelligence, and in June 1996 had about one hundred plotters rounded up and quickly executed. He then turned to take his frustrations out, once again, on the Kurds in the north, known allies of the CIA.

Things were not working out well for DCI Deutch. The newly elected Republican Congress had a different agenda for the Intelligence Community. SSCI chairman Arlen Specter told Deutch that the committee would function as his "board of directors."[28] Meanwhile, the staff director of the

House Permanent Select Committee on Intelligence (HPSCI) stated that "the three worst Directors of Central Intelligence ever were John Deutch, John Deutch, and John Deutch."[29] This was not going to be a cozy relationship. Congress could assert itself so aggressively because Clinton, even though he was becoming more interested in foreign affairs and, by extension, the CIA, was still a distant manager.

Both Clinton and Deutch believed that the 1990s presented an opportunity to fashion a more open and accountable CIA. Clinton ordered the largest declassification project ever—fifty million pages of official records dating back to before World War II and up to the Vietnam era. But he, like most presidents, also had a secret side when it came to his own administration. There were sixty thousand more documents classified in 1993 than in the previous year under George H. W. Bush. And Bush is the one with the reputation for secrecy. Deutch, for his part, said he was "in favor of as much declassification and as much openness as possible."[30] (I found this approach both amusing and satisfying. One of the hallmarks of my administration as DCI was openness. This was, however, absolutely anathema to the CIA professionals in the late 1970s. I reasoned that the Church Committee had raked the Agency over the coals and that only by publicizing whatever we could of CIA accomplishments could we retain public support. The Agency's public affairs officer, Herb Hetu, whom I brought in with me, came to me one day and said, "Stan, do whatever you want to on openness, but don't use that term—it drives the CIA pros right up the wall."[31]) In late 1996, Deutch got his taste of what an open and accountable DCI would have to face.

The *San Jose Mercury News* had published an article about the "Dark Alliance" between the CIA and known drug smugglers during the contra wars in Central America. It accused the Agency and its assets of introducing crack cocaine to Los Angeles. Deutch did something admirable but ultimately fruitless. He flew to Los Angeles to face an angry crowd in South Central that had been stoked by Congresswoman Maxine Waters. Here, he faced blame from concerned citizens and conspiracy theorists alike for actions taken long before he was DCI. The investigation, completed long after he left the position of DCI, concluded that, indeed, as the CIA inspector general told Congress, "There are instances where the CIA did not, in an expeditious or consistent fashion, cut off relationships with individuals supporting the Contra program alleged to have engaged in drug trafficking activity, or try to resolve the allegations."[32] Nonetheless, the SSCI's investigation in 1996 did not find information to support the allegation of CIA involvement in U.S. drug sales to finance the contras.

Understandably, Deutch was fed up and exhausted. When the position of secretary of defense went to William Cohen, Deutch resigned and went back to MIT. Clinton now joined Truman and Nixon in a three-way tie for the record of burning out DCIs. "I hated to lose John Deutch at the CIA," Clinton wrote. "He had done a fine job as deputy secretary of defense, then had stepped into the tough CIA job after Jim Woolsey's brief tenure."[33] Plus, now Clinton had to find a new DCI and get him confirmed.

Finding a nominee proved not to be so difficult. Anthony Lake had served well as assistant for national security. Perhaps Clinton would finally have a good working relationship with his DCI. The problem was that now he had to contend with a Republican Congress. Once again, an ethics problem turned up. It could have been viewed either as an innocent oversight—Lake had failed to divest stocks in a timely manner—or a willful conflict of interest. Congress was also upset over revelations that the Clinton team had either turned a blind eye to or encouraged Iran to send weapons to the beleaguered Bosnians—a "green light" they called it. Either way, they railed on Lake for not informing them as assistant for national security. The confirmation hearings dragged on for four months, becoming, according to Lake, "nasty and brutish without being short."[34]

Lake held on until March 17, 1997, when he told Clinton he wanted out. "If it had been up to me," Clinton recalled, "I would have carried on the fight for a year if that's what it took to get a vote. But I could see Tony had had enough."[35] "It was a case of character assassination," asserted Senate Minority Leader Tom Daschle. "The intelligence committee has become an extension of the Republican Senate Campaign Committee."[36]

Clinton nominated George Tenet on March 19, 1997. Lake, after some thirty years of public service, became a historical footnote. Tenet was Deutch's deputy director from July 1995 through the remainder of Deutch's tenure—December 15, 1996—and was currently acting director. Adding in his time on the staffs of the SSCI and the NSC, he had spent virtually ten years in intelligence. Like Deutch before him, he had no problem with confirmation. Unlike Deutch, he worked to remain in Congress's good graces. He seemed to realize that with the president studiously avoiding the CIA, he needed to work closely with Congress. Tenet did "tremendously effective feeding and caring on Capitol Hill. His congressional affairs shop is very slick, and I admire them for that," recalled a former CIA analyst.[37]

The operations side of the CIA was where Tenet focused his attention. The epic slide in personnel was over, and it was now time to rebuild and recruit. Tenet saw a "global role" for the CIA and reversed the tendencies of his two predecessors toward more technical collection. The CIA would have to "rebuild our field strength," he claimed, if it "wanted to stay in the intelligence business."[38] In this, he was supported closely by, almost in partnership with, Representative Porter Goss from Florida, a former CIA agent and a future DCI. "This is going to be a long-term rebuild," Goss claimed.[39] Goss thought that "the cupboard is nearly bare in the area of human intelligence." And he wanted "more arrows in the quiver" for covert action, namely "cyberspace" and "mind management."[40]

The president was being routinely lambasted for letting the CIA's network of agents deteriorate.

There were other ways Tenet wanted to take the CIA back in time so as to take it forward: reversing the trend toward openness was one of them. He released the Intelligence Community budget in 1997, because of an FOIA lawsuit, and did so again the following year, but in 1999 refused. His predecessor had promised to declassify files on eleven major covert operations. Tenet stopped it at two (Guatemala and the Bay of Pigs), claiming that the CIA didn't have the manpower to vet the rest.

Clinton actually appeared a little more involved once Tenet was DCI, but not consistently enough and not in the way Tenet really needed. Clinton wanted to enhance Tenet's role in coordinating the Intelligence Community, but he didn't provide the follow-up support that a DCI needs. "Every time you try to give me more authority," Tenet told Clinton, "you get me in a fight with a building much bigger than mine [that is, the Pentagon]."[41] But Clinton very actively engaged Tenet and the CIA in a new and nontraditional direction—a peace effort in the Middle East. Tenet reportedly resisted, but in the end he dutifully followed orders.

In mid-October 1998 at the Wye River plantation in eastern Maryland, the Israelis and the Palestinians sat down to peace talks. Israeli prime minister Benjamin Netanyahu felt he could accept the Palestinian Authority's having a more heavily armed police force only if there were an assured way to monitor it. Clinton called in the CIA as an "honest broker" of information between the Israelis and the Palestinians. A lot of CIA employees saw this as dangerous, because it carried the Agency close to having an investment in the success of a policy. Others saw it in line with activities such as verification of arms control treaties, which the CIA had carried on for years. Tenet claimed, "The CIA is not making policy, but helping carry it out. This is consistent with the agency's history of fighting terrorism and helping friends and allies in the region live together peacefully and safely."[42] Former DCI Woolsey worried that the DCI might be turning into a negotiator. One would hope that the CIA used this opportunity to develop more knowledge about and assets within the world of Islamic terrorism, which, by this time, was high on everyone's list of concerns.

The CIA publishes a classified in-house magazine, *Studies in Intelligence*, which can offer fascinating insights into the thinking of the analysts, managers, and case officers who run the CIA. In 1997, it published an article subtitled "The Coming Intelligence Failure." At a time when efforts to beef up the CIA were focused on collection, the article predicted, "The year is 2001. . . . At a time when the interrelationship among political, economic, military, social, and cultural factors had become increasingly complex, no agency was postured to conduct truly integrated analysis. From the vantage point of 2001, intelligence failure is inevitable."[43]

As the second Clinton term wound down, Porter Goss claimed that the administration had "crippled our intelligence capabilities. . . . In every single management area of foreign policy that affects national security we aren't very good under the Clinton Administration. There are no successes that I can think of that are particularly grand." Goss gave his colleagues (and himself) credit for what progress had been made: "The Hill has filled the vacuum on championing the cause of intelligence. We did not get a lot of support from the Administration. I don't think they use intelligence well."[44] It was around this time that Goss made it known that he was ready and willing to serve as DCI. But he specifically wanted to do so under a Republican president. The notion of a politically neutral DCI seemed to have been lost.

CHAPTER TWELVE

GEORGE W. BUSH, TENET, 9/11, AND BEYOND

Quo Vadis?

W hen he became president, George W. Bush inherited George
Tenet as his DCI. He opted to try him out even though Tenet
came with a long history of association with Democrats. There is no hard
evidence to confirm it, but it is easy to speculate that the new president's
father may have influenced him to give Tenet a try in the name of reduc-
ing turnover in the job of DCI and of keeping the position apolitical.
How well Tenet performed and how well he was supported by George W.
Bush are questions it is too early to attempt to answer fairly. What we can
do, though, is look at how they dealt with intelligence and consider what
additional lessons their experiences give us for shaping American intelligence for the future.

In May 2001, Bush appointed Brent Scowcroft to head a commission to review the state of our intelligence. The commission produced a study the following December. It reportedly recommended both separating the DCI from the CIA and transferring three collection agencies housed in the DOD to the management control of the DCI (NSA for electronic spying, NGA for photographic spying, and NRO for the operation of spying satellites). This was the most radical solution yet proposed for empowering the DCI. For some reason the study remains classified and is inaccessible. It seems likely that the solution proposed by the commission was not supported by the Bush administration, particularly Secretary of Defense Donald Rumsfeld, the then and still "owner" of those three agencies. In his view, "There may be ways we can strengthen intelligence, but centralization is not one."[1] From remarks George Tenet has made on intelligence reform, it seems likely he would have been in opposition as well.[2] His view is, "I don't think you should separate the leader of this country's intelligence from a line agency."[3] In short, the report was dead on arrival.

On August 6, 2001, Tenet submitted to the president a President's Daily Brief with an article titled "Bin Laden Determined to Strike in U.S."[4] From what we can learn, the president must have assumed that his departmental and agency heads would do what they should to anticipate and blunt such a strike and did not pursue it further. From August 6 until September 11, though, Tenet continued to sound a shrill alarm, even antagonizing some people by his persistence. He told the Intelligence Community, "We are at war."[5] The Community paid so little attention to the DCI that some intelligence agency heads never even saw Tenet's warning and none took any direct or specific action. This clearly demonstrates the indifference of those agency heads to direction from the DCI. It also bespeaks Tenet's lack of interest in the activities of the Community in that he did not seek to find out what they were doing in response to his warning. Overall he is reported to have given Community matters very little attention.

When the attacks of 9/11 occurred, Tenet was the first member of the Bush national security team to respond with a plan of action. It was not a Community plan. Rather, Tenet proposed using CIA operatives to guide the military into Afghanistan. Within the CIA he had worked to get the espionage and covert action people ready for such an eventuality. They were ready and performed superbly in helping guide the military to a quick victory over the Taliban. His performance with this aggressive, action-oriented plan must have appealed to the president and confirmed the wisdom of keeping Tenet on.

The Taliban had not yet been driven out of Afghanistan when the administration began considering an invasion of Iraq. According to Bob Woodward, on December 21, 2002, the president questioned Tenet about whether the intelligence indicating that Iraq had weapons of mass destruction (WMD) was solid enough. Tenet's reply was that it was a "slam dunk."[6] It is difficult to guess what drove him to this unequivocal response, because the estimates of his and other agencies following the problem were hardly that clear. Was this because he is a decisive person? Was it because he wanted to please Bush? Was it because he was listening to those in the CIA who believed Iraq had WMD and discounting the naysayers? Was it because he ignored what other agencies were saying, particularly the State Department's Bureau of Intelligence and Research?

Beyond Tenet's personal role, it is clear that something was terribly amiss within the CIA's analytic branch if it let the DCI get that far off track. The Agency reportedly acknowledged in a classified report in late 2004 that its estimate of chemical weapons in Iraq before our invasion was wide of the mark. This, if true, would be an unprecedented move of acknowledgment that a major estimate was in serious error. Surely Agency people have found over the years that some of their products missed the mark. Here, they apparently felt they were so far off the mark as to require a confession. It is reported that there will be further, similar retractions on biological and nuclear weapons. It is likely that the "slam dunk" blunder (assuming Tenet said it, and that seems likely since he has not publicly refuted Woodward) was a very large factor leading to Tenet's resignation. Whether he was eased out by the president or had just had enough we may never know. He left on July 11, 2004. He will be remembered as the DCI who brought stability to the CIA after the turnover of three DCIs between late 1991 and his arrival in 1997; and who improved the morale of an organization battered by public and congressional scrutiny since 1986.

However, Tenet and most of the Intelligence Community failed to recognize that Saddam Hussein or the United Nations had in one way or another disposed of Iraq's chemical and biological weapons and its program for developing nuclear weapons. It took a long time to establish authoritatively that there had been no WMD in Iraq at the time of our invasion. In the meantime, national attention shifted back to the intelligence failure of 9/11. On November 27, 2002, Congress created the National Commission on Terrorist Attacks upon the United States, known as the 9/11 Commission. It was composed of ten members, half appointed by the president and half by Congress, with equal representation by each political party. The commission released its public report on July 22, 2004. When it was published by the Government Printing Office (as well as in an authorized paperback edition from W. W. Norton & Company), it instantly became a best-seller. This is rather unusual for a government document, but it reflects an intense national interest. One finding of this report was that there were "pervasive problems of managing and sharing information across a large and unwieldy government that had been built in a different era to confront different dangers."[7]

Congress used the commission's report as a basis for drafting a statute on intelligence reform. On December 17, 2004, the president signed the Intelligence Reform and Terrorism Prevention Act into law. There had been intense debate over just how much added authority should be given the DCI in this legislation. The Senate wanted a strong leadership role. The House, influenced by pressure from the DOD, favored a much lesser one. The end result was, of course, a series of compromises. Where genuine compromise was not possible, there is ambiguity. On balance the law provides for a leader for the Intelligence Community who is weaker than what was recommended by the 9/11 Commission. One still unanswered question is whether the Intelligence Reform and Terrorism Prevention Act of 2004 prepares us to deal more confidently and effectively with terrorism. Another and even more important unanswered question is whether we could and should be doing even more and, if so, what?

In my judgment the answer to the first question is a qualified "yes." Depending on just how the ambiguities in the legislation are resolved, we are probably going to be better prepared. My answer to the second question is that we definitely can, and must, do more because these congressional changes to our intelligence organization are only halfway measures. Congress needs to remove some of the ambiguities in the Intelligence Reform Act. Alternatively, the president could supplement the law through an executive order or by instructions to his national security team for dealing with those ambiguities. Either of these solutions would not, of course, be as permanent or as binding as a change in the law.

The new law made one highly significant change that went beyond what was possible with presidential prerogatives alone: to separate the role of DCI from that of head of the CIA. As we have seen, several presidents have suggested that DCIs delegate responsibility for managing the CIA to their deputies, but now there actually is a divorce. Beyond that, though, the law confuses what should be done as a matter of management by the executive and what needs to be enshrined in statute. For instance, with whom and how much the new director of national intelligence (DNI) should consult when preparing budgets is normally a matter of executive choice and style. Prescribing it in law, as the Intelligence Reform Act does, was just an attempt to give the DOD more say. Also, the requirement of the law that money appropriated by Congress must pass through the DOD en route to the individual DOD intelligence agencies dilutes the budgeting authority that the act gives the DNI. These are the kinds of issues that make the Intelligence Reform Act less than clear-cut.

The big question, then, is whether President Bush will line up with the presidents since FDR who have favored giving more authority to the DCI or whether he will give in to the DOD's persistent efforts to keep the DCI's authority limited. For instance, whenever you create a new bureaucratic entity, as the 1947 National Security Act did with the DCI, whatever authorities the new position is assigned, unless they are completely new, must be taken from other entities that already have them. In the case of the 1947 act, those transferred authorities were primarily from the bureaus of intelligence of the Army, Navy, and State Departments. Even though those departments themselves were willing in 1947 to have a centralized intelligence organization in addition to their own intelligence bureaus, they were not willing to relinquish control over any of their intelligence activities. The most powerful writ the new DCI received in the 1947 act was "to make recommendations to the NSC for the coordination of . . . intelligence activities."[8] In short, it was a coordinator that was created, not someone with the authority to exercise real control over our intelligence apparatus.

Beyond entrenched parochialism, I surmise that much of the resistance to empowering a DCI to control all intelligence activities of the government comes from a concern that a powerful secret organization could be a danger to our democracy. This may have been a factor with both FDR and Harry Truman, who lived through the era of such a muscular, and ultimately destructive, organization as the Gestapo. We saw how FDR, in a desire to have more centralized intelligence, first created the Coordinator of Information and later the OSS, but never gave either access to one of the most valuable sources of intelligence: signals intercepts. Donovan complained about this enough that it could not have been an oversight. What we do not know is why Roosevelt was consciously and deliberately keeping his intelligence coordinator weak.

Truman was even more apprehensive. He wanted to know what his "spooks" were doing. In the first month after World War II ended, he wrapped up the OSS. Yet over time, the responsibilities of the new global position of the United States forced him to support the National Security Act of 1947, which created a DCI. Later he even agreed to expand the DCI's authorities into espionage and covert action, as well as into analysis. So it is very hard to draw lines when assigning responsibilities in tasking intelligence agencies. Giving too much authority to any one agency risks creating a monster; too little and you risk having a toothless, ineffective organization.

When Eisenhower became president, a great opportunity to strengthen the role of the DCI was missed. Ike understood the military's needs for intelligence as well as anyone. He saw an overriding need for greater central control. He wrote, "I concur in the need for strong centralized direction of the intelligence effort of the United States through the NSC and the DCI."[9] In fact, though, there was no significant strengthening of the DCI during Eisenhower's tenure simply because Ike's DCI, Allen Dulles, was not interested in managing the Intelligence Community. The irony here is that Truman, perforce, left the position of the director of central intelligence stronger than when he took office, even though he did not want a strong DCI; but Ike, who wanted a strong DCI, was thwarted in that desire by the indifference of his DCI to the larger Community dimensions of his job.

John Kennedy, despite being burned at the Bay of Pigs by the CIA's

ineptness, moved further toward empowering the DCI than had his predecessors. A year after taking office, he became the first president to endorse in a written directive the concept of separating the roles of DCI and
head of the CIA. He clearly signaled that being DCI was the primary
duty: "As head of the CIA, while you will continue to have over-all responsibility for the Agency, I shall expect you to delegate to your principal
deputy, as you may deem necessary, so much of the direction of the detailed operation of the Agency [CIA] as may be required to permit you to
carry out your primary task as DCI."[10] At the same time, Kennedy did not
ask Congress to change that portion of the National Security Act that required the same person to be both DCI and head of the CIA.

Lyndon Johnson was so suspicious of and indifferent to his intelligence apparatus that he drove John McCone to resign. While Johnson
worked better with Richard Helms as DCI, the position itself was not
changed significantly during his tenure.

Richard Nixon was even more mistrusting of the CIA. He did,
though, commission James Schlesinger to review the state of our intelligence. When Schlesinger reported that the DCI lacked authority, Nixon
gave that office more control over the preparation of the intelligence
budget.

Gerald Ford's perspective on empowering the DCI was shaped by a
concern that Congress not use the Church Committee report as a way of
hobbling the CIA. To preempt Congress, he issued the first presidential
executive order on intelligence. It emphasized what should not be done
more than what should, constraining the DCI rather than empowering
him or her.

Jimmy Carter sympathized with Ford's constraints and even added a
few of his own. The logic, though, of his wanting a single person to be responsible for getting the intelligence he needed to him led to the greatest
strengthening of the DCI ever. This included both "full and exclusive"

responsibility for submitting the budget for all intelligence agencies and for control of collection operations. But resistance from the military to the DCI's having these authorities was growing well before Carter left office.

That led to Ronald Reagan's reissuing the presidential executive order on intelligence in a weaker form than Carter's, despite his having campaigned on a pledge to revitalize the CIA. For example, rather than giving the DCI "full and exclusive" responsibility for the intelligence budget, the DCI was to do this "with the advice of the program managers and departments and agencies concerned."[11] This Reagan order persisted through the presidency of George H. W. Bush. That is surprising to me, since, as a former DCI, George H. W. Bush might well have had ideas of his own on the best role for the DCI. The Reagan executive order also remained in force during the presidency of Bill Clinton, whose indifference on intelligence meant that there were few changes in authorities during his tenure.

Under George W. Bush, the ink was hardly dry on the Intelligence Reform and Terrorism Prevention Act of 2004 before there was talk about the need to amend it because of the number of compromises in the new DNI's authorities. Still, I believe a key portion of the Intelligence Reform Act, the separation of the jobs of managing the Intelligence Community and running the CIA, is highly desirable. In my experience, the two jobs were just too much for one person to do well on top of being the president's intelligence advisor. As a result, most DCIs have neglected their responsibility to manage the Intelligence Community, even when they have been given sufficient support from presidents to exercise effective management.

Additionally, the two positions inherently conflict. The more attention a DCI pays to running the CIA, the more he is suspect by the Community of favoring the CIA above the other intelligence agencies. And, indeed, DCIs have almost always found that the CIA provided them, by far, the best finished intelligence, and so it was natural to lean on the CIA more than on the others. Over the years, this has resulted in an unhealthy jealousy of the CIA, especially among the intelligence agencies housed in DOD, and this mitigates significantly against true interagency cooperation and sharing. On the other side of that coin, the more time the DCI spends as Intelligence Community director, the less the CIA people see him as looking out for their interests. So the DCI has to walk a tightrope, which prevents his being a forceful advocate for either the Community or the CIA.

Most people in the DOD have opposed the creation of a DNI out of concern that the DNI's powers might intrude into the military's role in intelligence. Yet the actual authorities established for the DNI in the Intelligence Reform Act are less than those that President Carter gave me in his executive order on intelligence and are considerably less than those Brent Scowcroft's commission reportedly recommended.

CIA people have opposed the separation of the head of the Agency and the DCI, I believe, because it demotes the head of their agency down from being someone who reports directly to the president to someone on the second tier.

Opponents from both the DOD and CIA regularly adduce the oversimplistic argument that creating a DNI would simply be adding another layer of bureaucracy. This is nothing more than pandering to the pejorative connotation of "bureaucracy." All bureaucracies are not bad. We need to judge each proposal to add to existing bureaucracies by whether the functions to be performed are sufficiently important to warrant emplacing more bureaucrats. In this instance, the void in what needs to be done to coordinate budgets, collection, and analysis calls for some corrective action, I believe. In addition, a sizable bureaucracy for coordination already exists in the DCI's Community staff and may not have to be enlarged very much.

The debate on a DNI, then, has been not only intense, but often misleading. For instance, the chairman of the House Armed Services Committee warned that a DNI might not invest in new technical systems

needed for collecting military intelligence, and that a DNI might somehow interfere with the flow of intelligence within the military's chain of
command. Both assertions were based on questionable assumptions: one,
that a DNI would necessarily neglect the military's interests, and two, that
military interests always come before any others.

Another is that of the chairman of the Joint Chiefs of Staff. During
the debate on the Intelligence Reform Act, he wrote a letter to a congressman insisting that the money for all intelligence agencies under military
control had to flow from the Office of Management and Budget to those
agencies through the DOD, not directly from the DNI; and that the agencies' recommendations for what they needed in their budgets had to pass to
the DNI through the DOD. In short, the DOD would always be astride
the flow of dollars between the DNI and the agencies. The power the DNI
would get from holding the purse strings would be considerably diminished. As noted earlier, the chairman's proviso was written into the Intelligence Reform Act, giving the DOD a more influential position in the
budget process than any of the other departments; that is, State, Homeland Security, Justice, Treasury, and Energy. In this age of combating terrorism by many means other than military power, that may not be desirable.

The question, then, is will insertions like the chairman's proviso, and
how it is interpreted and put into action, leave the new DNI with adequate authority? Or will he or she be only a figurehead—another drug czar
giving speeches? Historically, despite the exhortations of a number of
presidents, DCIs have lacked authority over the disparate elements of the
Community. Still, with the CIA as a base of power, DCIs have always had
CIA people moving about within the Intelligence Community, keeping
them informed about what was going on. And, being head of the CIA
gave the DCI leverage within the Community. For instance, let's assume
the DCI wanted an estimate written on some topic that the military considered sensitive, because it might affect their appropriations from Con-

gress. The DCI would try to persuade the Defense Intelligence Agency to participate in the project. The DIA might resist, though it could do so only up to a point. That would be when the DCI, playing his role as head of the CIA, would direct the CIA to do the study on its own. The DIA could protect its interests only by joining in. Today, the new DNI might or might not be able to persuade the CIA to do that study on its own. The CIA director's loyalty might be more with his peer in the DIA than with his superior, the DNI. The DNI's hand, then, is weaker than was the DCI's. That, ironically, is the result of legislation that came from the 9/11 Commission's report that recommended empowering the new DNI. This should not be surprising, though. Throughout this book we have repeatedly seen failed attempts to empower a centralized head of intelligence, going all the way back to Franklin Roosevelt, who established the COI/OSS, but did not give it access to signals intercepts.

Today we have the same result from still another commission investigating the state of our intelligence. This one was cochaired by a senior judge, Laurence H. Silberman, and a former U.S. senator, Charles S. Robb. President Bush tasked it in February 2004 to study our intelligence as it related to weapons of mass destruction. It reported out on March 31, 2005, and its conclusions are harshly critical of our intelligence process as presently constituted. It describes the Intelligence Community as "fragmented, loosely managed, and poorly coordinated" and as being in "a closed world."[12]

The report's primary conclusion is that we need "an empowered DNI."[13] Beyond that it also concludes that the Intelligence Community has "an almost perfect record of resisting external recommendations."[14] The report then goes on to enumerate seventy-four specific recommendations. The irony is that these neither "empower" the DNI any more than does the existing law of December 17, 2004, nor do they suggest ways to overcome the Intelligence Community's inherent resistance to change the report as described. These recommendations, though, have considerable merit. Some suggest ways to organize the Intelligence Community better: for example, by mission rather than function, and with "a management structure that allows him [the DNI] to see deep into the Intelligence Community's component agencies."[15] The recommendations also suggest a number of improvements in operational procedures, such as more outside oversight and more innovative human intelligence techniques.

What the report does not suggest is how the new DNI should go about imposing such organizational and procedural changes on the Intelligence Community's fifteen agencies, those with the "almost perfect record of resisting external recommendations." It specifically notes that the law of December 2004 gives the new DNI powers that are only somewhat broader than before. It appears that the commission expected the DNI to be sufficiently persuasive to convince the agencies to reach agreement by consensus. I do not understand why the commission did not recommend empowering the DNI more when its report includes the statement, "They [the intelligence agencies] are some of the government's most headstrong agencies. Sooner or later, they will try to run around—or over—the DNI."[16]

The resistance to change we are seeing in this latest report, and what we have seen in the history of U.S. intelligence since FDR, is the product of two factors. The first is that the secrecy that is so essential to good intelligence makes the intelligence professionals feel that outsiders just cannot fully understand their work. They discount criticism as uninformed, as much of it is. They sincerely believe that outsiders simply cannot be well enough informed to be able to criticize meaningfully.

The second factor leading to resistance to change is that our present system of intelligence is a heritage of the Cold War. Back then, our security depended on being able to deter or defeat a military assault from the Soviet Union or its proxies. Under that circumstance, military needs for intelligence received number-one priority. That was particularly the case when the military was in combat, as with the conflicts in Korea and Vietnam. The military also played a dominant role in intelligence during the Cold War because the DOD has always had a huge budget—today, it's more than $400 billion a year. Consequently, it has been by far the most powerful bureaucracy in the government, readily garnering allies from industry and within Congress—the military-industrial-congressional complex. With the amounts of money and the number of jobs involved, the wishes of this group, each member of which has a separate agenda, cannot be disregarded by either Congress or the president. But should such a group have as dominant an influence on intelligence today when the threat to the country is terrorism, not war, and the military is not the dominant player in our response to terrorism?

I can imagine cases in which even the intelligence normally required for full military combat might have to take second place to the kinds of intelligence-gathering necessary to prevent another 9/11 or to uncover the proliferation of WMD. I cannot imagine someone in the DOD voluntarily putting military intelligence needs behind such requirements. It might even be unfair to ask them to do so. When I discuss such possibilities with military colleagues, they simply cannot overcome their conviction that the intelligence needed on the battlefield must always have number-one priority. This stems from their core belief that not just lives but the fate of our very society might be at stake in war. Yet 9/11 severely impacted our society and cost nearly three thousand lives. A nuclear 9/11 would make September 2001 seem like child's play. Decisions on how to employ our intelligence assets must, in my view, rest in the hands of someone who can make balanced judgments about what comes first for the nation.

There has not been much public discussion of the possibility that under some circumstances nonmilitary requirements for intelligence might take priority over military. That, though, must be a good part of what the

9/11 and Scowcroft Commissions had in mind when attempting to promote a stronger role for the leader of the Intelligence Community. With the Scowcroft report sidelined and the 9/11 Commission report's key recommendations not fully implemented, there is not much hope today, in my view, that even the most urgent nonmilitary requirements could take precedence over military ones. The case cited earlier of our failure to detect the 1998 Indian nuclear tests in advance shows that always according top priority to the military can be costly to the country. The Intelligence Reform Act makes several attempts to strengthen the hand of the DNI for such exigencies. One way is to give him or her veto power over any of the secretary of defense's nominees for head of NRO, NSA, or NGA. While this is an improvement over the past situation, it does not go far enough. The loyalty of the heads of those agencies will always be with the secretary of defense, who nominates, feeds, and promotes them, not with the DNI simply because he or she did not veto them.

What would it take to have a DNI with the authority to assign and enforce priorities for national needs over the military's requirements? It would be (1) "full and exclusive" responsibility for preparing the consolidated intelligence budget—in other words, the final say before the budgets are sent to the president, and (2) transfer of management control of NSA, NRO, and NGA from the secretary of defense to the DNI, as reportedly recommended by the Scowcroft report. This second point goes further than Carter's executive order by assigning NSA, NRO, and NGA to the DNI for management, as well as operations. I had only operational control. Because I did not have management control—for example, pay, assignments, and promotions—how effectively I could exercise operational control depended very much on personalities and my ability to elicit their cooperation. Some were extremely responsive. Some were extremely resistant.

Under the Scowcroft concept of having the three technical collection agencies, NSA, NRO and NGA, managed by the DNI, it would be logical and efficient to co-locate the CIA's human intelligence branch, the Directorate of Operations, with them. That would bring all forms of collection together under one coordinator. It would allow the DNI to orchestrate intelligence collection based on the needs of the country at that time; and to ensure that the development of new collection capabilities was done in a balanced and reinforcing way. However, it would also mean breaking up the CIA.

If the DO migrated to a new organization for all collection under the DNI's direct control, so should another branch of the CIA, the Directorate of Science and Technology, which provides technical support to collection operations. The analytic branch, the Directorate of Intelligence, would be all that was left of the CIA. Can we afford to break up this venerable institution that has, indeed, done much to keep our country secure? My opinion is that there would be much more gained than lost from doing so. It would be better not only for the nation but for the professionals in the CIA as well.

To begin with, the CIA's reputation in the country is at a nadir today. For its first twenty-nine years, the Agency was a mysterious government entity shrouded in secrecy, but presumed by the public to be doing something very good for the security of the country. Then came the Church Committee report of 1976, which exposed a number of improprieties and illegalities in the CIA's past. This drove the Agency's reputation way down. During my tenure as DCI, the national media were persistently criticizing the Agency for misdeeds of the past, and few colleges permitted CIA recruiters on their campuses. The CIA had been dragged out from under its cloak of secrecy, and in a very unpleasant way. From then until now, the Agency's standing with the public has waxed and waned with events. When I was DCI, our failure to understand Islamic fundamentalism sufficiently to anticipate the fall of the shah of Iran hurt the CIA's reputation badly. In later years, the Agency was battered by a failure to forecast the collapse of the Soviet Union very far in advance and by several almost inexcusable lapses of internal security such that it had Soviet spies in its midst.

The point is that the CIA today is an institution about which the public is reasonably informed. The recent failures over 9/11 and WMD in Iraq have once again seriously eroded the CIA's standing. The various commissions that have studied these failures, especially that of Silberman-Robb, have focused public attention on CIA shortcomings. It is going to be difficult to restore both the standing of the CIA with the public and the morale of its people. Splitting the CIA into organizationally separate bureaus of collection and analysis would allow each, in a sense, to start over. The new managers of each entity could define their new missions and begin to establish their own reputations without carrying as much liability from the past. Additionally, the managers of the new entities would have a better opportunity to break with unhealthy habits and procedures of the past, such as the fierce resistance to change that the Silberman-Robb report identified. Interestingly, one of the great icons of the CIA's DO, Ted Shackley, wrote in his memoir just prior to his death in 2002, that the appointment of a DNI "would be a good time to get rid of a set of initials that are carrying a heavy load of opprobrium and suspicion, however unjustified." And that then "the CIA would in effect disappear."[17]

Shackley, unfortunately, was right. The organizational name CIA has become more of a liability than an asset. The dissolution of the CIA would especially reduce the unhealthy rivalry between that Agency and the DOD intelligence elements. That has been, and is, one of the greatest weaknesses with our intelligence system.

What we could have, then, would be a deputy to the DNI for collection who would have full management control of the CIA's Directorate of Operations, the NSA, the NRO, and the NGA; and a second deputy to the DNI who would have authority to coordinate what was the CIA's analytic arm, plus similar elements throughout the Intelligence Community, but not dictate the results of their analyses. There are those who would, quite reasonably, argue that there are advantages to keeping collectors and analysts close to one another, rather than under separate management structures. A past recurring problem has been the failure of collectors to appreciate just what the analysts needed to know. Some DCIs have even reorganized to bring the two elements closer. Such actions, however, have been only palliatives, not solutions, because while they have brought CIA analysts closer to CIA human intelligence operatives, they have not brought the CIA analysts closer to DOD's human and technical collectors nor DOD analysts closer to CIA human intelligence operators. What we need today is to organize in ways that will increase the amount of discourse between all collectors, human and technical, and all analysts wherever they are in the Community.

There would, of course, be risks of placing considerably greater authority in the hands of the new DNI. The primary one is that a single decision-maker can be too certain of himself or herself and head in a wrong direction. A few DCIs, in my opinion, have had rather narrow perspectives. Offsetting this risk is the existing diversity and independence among the fifteen intelligence agencies and the fact that there is always the resort of appealing to the president. Secretaries of state and defense are not usually bashful people.

Another risk is that if we remove NSA, NRO, and NGA from the DOD, the military will simply re-create their own versions of them based on the excuse that they need them for tactical intelligence. This, indeed, could happen. If it does, we would waste money duplicating such functions.

Finally, there are risks that any system wherein the DNI has meaningful control over the intelligence branches of major departments like Defense and State simply will not work because it requires crossing territorial boundaries. The departments concerned might just stymie the DNI one way or another, through bureaucratic inertia, for instance. That would be unfortunate, but would not place us in a significantly different position from the one we are in today.

Are the stakes high enough to warrant such a realignment? The undue weight of military influence over intelligence collection and analysis in an era when we are combating a global and amorphous enemy, terrorists, is just one factor. Another is that the present system of decision-making is one of consensus. With the right combination of highly cooperative personalities, decision-making by consensus can be fine. With the wrong combination it can be a disaster. Committees do tend to offer answers that represent the least common denominator. Much more important, though, are the risks that consensus will not come rapidly enough or be sufficiently decisive to deter terrorists. Our terrorist opponents are imaginative, resourceful, and decisive. We cannot afford to be less. We have been fortunate not to have had another 9/11. However, the unfortunate result of that is an unhealthy complacency has set in. This is reflected in solutions that satisfy most people, and sound good, but in reality are weak responses to the problem. A true transformation to meet the challenge of terrorism cannot be a series of half-measures, such as those in the Intelligence Reform Act.

Now that we have gone through a spirited debate on the Intelligence Reform Act, my two-part recommendation—including giving full budget authority and management control of NSA, NRO, and NGA to the DNI—may seem more idealistic than realistic. That it is. At the same time, I believe it is important that we think through what the ideal solution to our intelligence problem is. Without the high goal in mind we may miss it altogether. Moreover, if a president, some influential groups in Congress, or a vocal segment of the public understands where we should be going, we might find a way to move more dramatically and effectively than we have.

On balance, I believe government leaders owe it to all Americans to push forward a bold transformation in this vital area, rather than be cowed by turf barons, bureaucrats, or timid souls. We just cannot afford to wait to learn by more failures like 9/11 and going to war in Iraq on the flawed assumption that WMD were there. Congress has left us in the difficult position of having created a much needed CEO for our $40 billion intelligence apparatus, but not having given that CEO adequate authority to do the job. This could be the worst of all worlds; that is, a DNI without direct control of the CIA and not enough control of the Intelligence Community to compensate.

At the same time, although the military's role in national security is less critical than it was during World War II and the Cold War, it is still very important. Perhaps even more to the point, we cannot ignore the power of the military-industrial-congressional complex. We should explore such compromise solutions as:

- Providing that in time of war control of the collection and analytic systems would shift to the Department of Defense on order of the president; and that from time to time in peacetime we would actually do such a transfer every so often to ensure it will work smoothly.

- Recognizing that directing electronic intercept and photographic systems to military problems can occasionally be time-urgent, the secretary of defense could be given a trump card, which only he or she personally could play, to override the DNI in situations of urgent military concern. Each time this was done the secretary would be required to notify the president, together with making a recommendation as to whether it was appropriate to shift control of all collection to the secretary of defense.

- On less time-urgent decisions on collection, priorities for analysis, and budget line items, it should be adequate protection for the military if there are committees established to debate these issues, with ultimate resort to appeal to the president.

- On budget issues where the secretary of defense believes that the DNI is not allocating sufficient resources to some area, it should be permissible for the secretary to add to the DNI's allocation from other funds available to DOD. This would be applicable particularly to tactical intelligence.

Even with these concessions to the military, we could have a DNI who would be a much stronger CEO for the Intelligence Community than at present. We need to be wary, however, of several good-intentioned but faulty proposals to strengthen the DNI further. One is to give the position a fixed term in office; ten years is often suggested. The objective would be to reduce the concern of a DNI that he or she might be fired for not acceding to political pressures to slant the intelligence. Balanced against that is the possibility that a DNI who carried over from one president to the next—and that would be inevitable—would simply be incompatible with the new president. I cannot, for instance, imagine a Bill Casey and a Jimmy Carter being able to work together. DNIs are utterly dependent on support from the president to have a productive directorship. We have seen how the lack of rapport between Truman and Hillenkoetter, Johnson and McCone, Ford and Colby, and Clinton and Woolsey resulted in little being accomplished. Beyond that, a fixed term could be a disaster for the country if a president made a poor choice for DNI and the nation was saddled with that person for a set number of years.

Another faulty proposal is to give the DNI cabinet status. Casey and

Tenet are the only DCIs to have had it. It would be nice if the DNI could speak from the same level as the cabinet secretaries with whom he or she is dealing, but that is more a matter of pride than of effectiveness. The downside of cabinet status for the DNI is overriding: It gives the appearance of the DNI's being on the president's politically partisan team.

There is still one more faulty idea being discussed. That is that we should rely less on cooperation with foreign intelligence services. Surely there are hazards in foreign liaison. Many foreign intelligence services cannot keep secrets. Many have quite different agendas from ours. Yet for us to have our own agents in every remote area of the world where terrorists may plot and train is unrealistic. Moving into an antiterrorism mode has forced us to rely more, not less, on tapping into foreign intelligence networks.

Beyond proposals that would make life more difficult for a DNI, there are those who are opposed to empowering the DCI/DNI on the grounds that changes in organizational wiring diagrams and in bureaucratic alignments will not improve our intelligence. What is needed, they contend, is better analysis, collection, and information exchange. These skeptics are both right and wrong. Elevating and empowering the DNI will not in itself solve problems.

We need, though, to look at some of the ways an empowered DNI could ensure better performance. To start with analysis, the new DNI should be the chief analyst for the Intelligence Community. He or she should be the person who challenges the products of analysis, demanding justification for the deductions made and the conclusions reached. He or she is the best person to show the analysts what decision-makers like the president would want to know about a particular situation and to inject special insights from his or her contacts with the president, cabinet officers, and chiefs of foreign intelligence services. He or she needs to set standards as to how confident an intelligence estimate should sound, insisting on the use of probabilities to do so. What if the CIA's analysts had

been required to place a percentage on their confidence that Iraq had
WMD in 2003? Would they have called it 70 percent? 90 percent? or a
slam dunk? And the Intelligence Reform Act specifically requires that the
DNI ensure that there is competitive analysis among the various analytic
agencies. That would have meant that in 2003 the lesser probability assigned to WMD by the State Department's intelligence bureau would
have been given more weight than it was. Who but someone outside and
above the chiefs of the analytic bureaus, like a DNI, could require the use
of probabilities and insist on competition? The more clear it is that the
DNI truly is the CEO of the Intelligence Community, the more likely it
is that he or she will be able to guide analysis in such directions. Finally, as
chief analyst the DNI should present to the president orally or in writing
the President's Daily Brief, National Intelligence Estimates, and other significant intelligence products. The president needs to know where his
chief advisor on intelligence stands on all intelligence products that reach
him. Additionally, the DNI needs to know what comments, if any, the
president has on them.

Another area of analysis where an empowered DNI could play an important role is in personnel recruitment and training. The Bush administration is committed to a 50 percent increase in the number of analysts in the
CIA. Doing so in a way that will have an impact in the short term, as well
as the long, will be a challenge. It will mean recruiting academics, businesspeople, and retired military officers for mid-level to senior positions, as well
as bringing in lots of brand-new people at the bottom. The prestige and
broad perspective of the DNI could help a great deal in inducing more experienced people to shift careers or, at least, to take a sabbatical from their
normal work. Special incentive pay from Congress would also be a big help
in getting the personnel buildup rolling. A DNI speaking from the perspective of the Community as a whole would be much better positioned to
persuade Congress to do this than would individual agency heads.

It is also important that the Community not rely only on infusions of talent from outside to improve its analytic products. A DNI with real authority could mandate the temporary interchange of analysts between agencies as a way for the strongest in the Community to help the weakest. Even two highly capable analytic organizations could benefit from cross-fertilization. Again, it would take the authority of a DNI to effect such exchanges.

With regard to collection, the strong hand of a DNI is also badly needed today. The standard response to the clear shortcomings in information collection against terrorism is that there is too little human intelligence. The administration is committed to a 50 percent increase in the CIA's human intelligence operatives. The FBI and the DOD are also increasing emphasis on human intelligence. But contending that our problems with intelligence stem largely from insufficient human intelligence resources is a misleading and superficial diagnosis. It misses the point of how important it is to have balance and coordination between the various systems for collecting information. Whether human intelligence is underrepresented can be judged only by looking at the total picture. To begin with, are we doing the best possible with what we have? Are clues from one system of collection being passed to others to cue them onto targets? Is the information we most need likely to come from human sources, electronic, or photographic? And what are the chances of getting a human agent in the right place?

Terrorists are a difficult target for human intelligence. In August 1990, our intelligence failed to predict Iraq's forthcoming invasion of Kuwait, and the failure was quickly blamed on a lack of human intelligence. I asked a friend who was a retired CIA human intelligence operative what the chances were that the CIA could have inserted an agent close enough to Saddam Hussein to learn that he was contemplating an attack on Kuwait. My friend instantly formed a zero with his thumb and forefinger. I am sure he did not mean we should not have tried. He certainly knew that when we were both active in the CIA, the human intelligence team had been able to insert an agent into a Middle Eastern terrorist group, and doing so had saved a lot of lives. It is just not easy. For instance, we almost inserted a second agent into a second terrorist group when I was DCI. The last rite of passage, however, was that this agent had to assassinate a particular government official in order to prove his *bona fides*. When they asked whether I would authorize the assassination in the interest of saving more lives, I said no. This is not to say that I was right or wrong. It is just another example of the always challenging, and sometimes insuperable, problems involved in infiltrating human agents. It is especially difficult with terrorist groups that are small, closely knit, and rather homogeneous. In addition, our human intelligence operations have heretofore been targeted primarily against nations. And with nations a substantial amount of the CIA's success has been with "walk-ins" who volunteered to help us, not recruitments. Other, perhaps, than experience with attempts to penetrate drug rings, trying to get inside terrorist groups will take entirely new skills, techniques, and procedures. For instance, it appears from the outside that the Directorate of Operations still insists that its operatives must be U.S. citizens without close familial ties abroad. When we expected sources to come to us, that may have been acceptable. In recruiting a terrorist to play traitor to his group, though, it is making the task unnecessarily difficult.

The administration's recent decision to increase CIA human intelligence operatives by 50 percent will compound the learning problem. This is not to say we should not pay more attention to collection by human intelligence, but we should not be overly expectant, especially in the near term. What is truly needed most is to find just where each type of spying fits into our overall collection effort. Only someone looking at the entire picture, like a DNI, can do that objectively.

Further, there is the issue of inadequate exchange of information among intelligence agencies, something very evident in the failure to forecast the events of 9/11. A strong DNI could be effective here because the Intelligence Reform Act gives him or her a mandate to "establish uniform security standards and procedures."[18] Misuse of the security classification system has for decades been a principal device intelligence agencies have employed to keep some of their most sensitive information to themselves. Today, the head of any intelligence agency can create any number of "codewords." Access to such codeword information is limited to people that agency has approved. The purpose is noble—to limit the risk of leaks of highly sensitive information. The application is, however, often maliciously parochial. It gives that agency an advantageous position within the Community of knowing something others do not. Knowledge is often power. Now, under the Intelligence Reform Act, the DNI can take control of all codewords and supervise their use.

In sum, it is easy, but misleading, to say that changing the DNI's position on the wiring diagram and enhancing his or her authorities is not going to be productive. It is an unacceptably parochial argument to claim that a DNI will likely neglect the military's interests. It is being alarmist to say that a more powerful DNI may steer our intelligence in wrong directions. The contending interests of agencies in our intelligence system today have prevented real reform for fifty-eight years. Such resistance is not going to disappear overnight. A key point here is how much more important the position of DCI/DNI has become since 9/11. Intelligence is truly our first line of defense against terrorists. We do not want to have to pick up the pieces after another terrorist attack like 9/11, or worse. We must anticipate the terrorists and cut them off before they can act. President Bush has labeled terrorism the number-one threat we face. In that case, it would be irresponsible not to give the person who manages that first line of defense the tools to do it as well as possible.

It is important, as never before, that the American public, not just politicians and bureaucrats, understand the issues at stake in how we organize and operate our nation's intelligence activities. Each of us has an interest in whether our intelligence apparatus is operating on as sound a footing as possible. Determining that will not be a one-time event—for example, the passing of a law or the signing of a presidential executive order. We will be remiss as a nation if we, the public, do not constantly examine and reexamine whether we are doing everything we can to enable our intelligence system to provide us with the warning we need to forestall terrorists.

Finally, a strong DNI could be the needed focal point for liaison with foreign intelligence services. None of them want to deal with the CIA today, the DIA tomorrow, and so on. In addition, we need one U.S. authority to determine just what of our intelligence we are willing to share with other countries in exchange for their information. Liaison relationships have become of increasing importance as the priority for our intelligence has shifted from the Cold War to terrorism. We cannot hope to have sources in every backwater where terrorists may plot and train, as they have in places like Thailand, Indonesia, and Somalia. We need clues from local intelligence services. A good example of why such liaison can be important is the four bombings in London on July 7, 2005. This was a case in which British-born Muslims of Pakistani extraction went to Pakistan for education in madrassas. Had there been good intelligence liaison between Great Britain and Pakistan, the Pakistanis might have been alert to this and informed British intelligence about it. That in itself would not necessarily have prevented the bombings, but adding such a clue would have made it more likely.

It is a moment for the president, Congress, and we, the people, to stand up and say, "Yes, we really do want to make defeating terrorists the country's top priority, and empowering a strong director of national intelligence would be a big step in that direction."

AGENCIES THAT COMPRISE
THE INTELLIGENCE COMMUNITY

The U.S. Intelligence Community consists of fifteen federal agencies, offices, and bureaus within the executive branch that are responsible for the collection, analysis, and dissemination of foreign intelligence. They are as follows.

INDEPENDENT COMPONENT

THE CENTRAL INTELLIGENCE AGENCY (CIA) collects intelligence, principally through human sources, and provides all-source analysis. The CIA also conducts counterintelligence overseas and undertakes covert actions at the direction of the president.

DEPARTMENT OF DEFENSE COMPONENTS

THE DEFENSE INTELLIGENCE AGENCY (DIA) provides all-source analysis of foreign intelligence and collects intelligence, primarily from human sources.

THE NATIONAL SECURITY AGENCY (NSA) collects, decrypts, and processes foreign signals intelligence and protects critical U.S. information systems from compromise.

THE NATIONAL GEOSPATIAL-INTELLIGENCE AGENCY (NGA) analyzes imagery and other geospatial information.

THE NATIONAL RECONNAISSANCE OFFICE designs, builds, and operates reconnaissance satellites.

ARMY, NAVY, AIR FORCE, AND MARINE CORPS INTELLIGENCE OFFICES collect and process intelligence relevant to the needs of those services.

DEPARTMENT OF STATE COMPONENT

THE BUREAU OF INTELLIGENCE AND RESEARCH (INR) analyzes all-source intelligence, but especially that collected through the State Department's diplomatic posts.

DEPARTMENT OF JUSTICE COMPONENT

THE FEDERAL BUREAU OF INVESTIGATION is responsible for counterintelligence and for intelligence on terrorism, primarily within the United States.

DEPARTMENT OF HOMELAND SECURITY COMPONENTS

THE DIRECTORATE OF INFORMATION ANALYSIS AND INFRASTRUCTURE PROTECTION monitors, assesses, and coordinates indications of threats to the U.S. homeland; gathers terrorist-related information; and assesses the vulnerabilities of critical infrastructure.

THE U.S. COAST GUARD provides information related to threats to U.S. economic and security interests in any maritime region, including international waters and American coasts, ports, and inland waterways.

DEPARTMENT OF ENERGY COMPONENT

THE OFFICE OF INTELLIGENCE (IN) analyzes foreign nuclear weapons, nuclear nonproliferation, and energy-security related intelligence issues.

DEPARTMENT OF TREASURY COMPONENT

THE OFFICE OF TERRORISM AND FINANCIAL INTELLIGENCE (TFI) collects and processes information bearing on U.S. fiscal and monetary policy and threat to U.S. financial institutions.

LIST OF ACRONYMS

ABM	Antiballistic Missile
AID	Agency for International Development
ASA	Army Security Agency
CIA	Central Intelligence Agency
CIG	Central Intelligence Group
COI	Coordinator of Information
DCI	Director of Central Intelligence
DDCI	Deputy Director of Central Intelligence
DDO	Deputy Director for Operations (CIA)
DDP	Deputy Director for Plans (CIA)
DDS&T	Deputy Director for Science and Technology (CIA)
DDI	Deputy Director for Intelligence (CIA)
DIA	Defense Intelligence Agency
DNI	Director of National Intelligence

DDO	Deputy Director for Operations (CIA)
DOD	Department of Defense
DOE	Department of Energy
FBI	Federal Bureau of Investigation
HPSCI	House Permanent Select Committee on Intelligence
ICBM	Intercontinental Ballistic Missile
JCS	Joint Chiefs of Staff
MAGIC	System for intercepting and decrypting Japanese diplomatic messages
MIRV	Multiple Independently Targetable Reentry Vehicle
NATO	North Atlantic Treaty Organization
NFAC	National Foreign Assessment Center
NGA	National Geospatial-Intelligence Agency
NIA	National Intelligence Authority
NIE	National Intelligence Estimate
NITC	National Intelligence Tasking Center
NRO	National Reconnaissance Office
NSA	National Security Agency
NSC	National Security Council
NSCID	National Security Council Intelligence Directive
ONI	Office of Naval Intelligence
OPC	Office of Policy Coordinator (formerly OSP)
OSP	Office of Special Projects (renamed OPC)
OSS	Office of Strategic Services
PDB	President's Daily Brief
PFIAB	President's Foreign Intelligence Advisory Board
PURPLE	Japanese diplomatic code
R&A	Research and Analysis (Bureau of the OSS)
SALT	Strategic Arms Limitation Treaty
SecDef	Secretary of Defense
SSCI	Senate Select Committee on Intelligence
WMD	Weapons of Mass Destruction

NOTES

1. FRANKLIN D. ROOSEVELT AND "WILD BILL"

1. Interview with Ned Putzell, August 15, 2003.
2. Putzell interview.
3. William R. Corson, *The Armies of Ignorance: The Rise of the American Intelligence Empire* (New York: The Dial Press/James Wade, 1977), 89.
4. Joseph C. Grew, *Ten Years in Japan: A Contemporary Record Drawn from the Diaries and Private and Official Papers of Joseph G. Grew, United States Ambassador to Japan, 1932–1942* (New York: Simon and Schuster, 1944), 359.
5. Joseph E. Persico, *Roosevelt's Secret War: FDR and World War II Espionage*, 1st ed. (New York: Random House, 2001), 58.
6. Ibid., 445.
7. Frank Burt Freidel, *Franklin D. Roosevelt: A Rendezvous with Destiny*, 1st ed. (Boston: Little Brown, 1990), 271–72.

8. Anthony Cave Brown, *The Last Hero: Wild Bill Donovan* (New York: Times Books, 1982), 72, 82.

9. Thomas F. Troy, *Donovan and the CIA: A History of the Establishment of the Central Intelligence Agency* (Washington, D.C.: Central Intelligence Agency, Center for the Study of Intelligence, 1981), 29.

10. Putzell interview.

11. Interview with Fisher Howe, July 23, 2003.

12. Thomas F. Troy, *Wild Bill and Intrepid* (New Haven: Yale University Press, 1996), 129. Bradley F. Smith, *The Shadow Warriors: OSS and the Origins of the CIA* (New York: Basic Books, 1983), 18.

13. Putzell interview.

14. Howe interview.

15. Waldo H. Heinrichs, *American Ambassador: Joseph C. Grew and the Development of the United States Diplomatic Tradition* (New York: Oxford University Press, 1966), 233.

16. Smith, *The Shadow Warriors*, 90.

17. Putzell interview.

18. Ted Bridis (AP), "The CIA Dept. of Quirky Tricks," *Washington Post*, December 31, 2003, A17.

19. Troy, *Donovan and the CIA*, 420.

20. National Archives and Records Administration, Record Group (NARA, RG) 226, M1642, 43, 207.

21. NARA, RG 226, M1642, 43, 348, 350.

22. Persico, *Roosevelt's Secret War*, 163.

23. NARA, RG 226, entry 210, box 355, folder 1.

24. Smith, *The Shadow Warriors*, 77.

25. Troy, *Donovan and the CIA*, 115.

26. Christopher H. Andrew, *For the President's Eyes Only: Secret Intelligence and the American Presidency from Washington to Bush* (New York: Harper-Collins, 1995), 113.

27. Persico, *Roosevelt's Secret War*, 142.

28. Persico, *Roosevelt's Secret War*, 136–37; Freidel, *Franklin D. Roosevelt*, 405.

29. NARA, RG 226, M1642, roll 22, frame 667.

30. NARA, RG 226, M1642, roll 3, frames 849–851.

31. NARA, RG 226, M1642, roll 3, frame 870.

32. Troy, *Donovan and the CIA*, 118–19.

33. NARA, RG 226, M1642, roll 34, frame 174.

34. Persico, *Roosevelt's Secret War*, 182.

35. Persico, *Roosevelt's Secret War*, 186.

36. Howe interview.

37. Brown, *The Last Hero*, 342.

38. Persico, *Roosevelt's Secret War*, 353–54; Smith, *The Shadow Warriors*, 293–94.

39. Smith, *The Shadow Warriors*, 378.

40. Roger Hilsman, *Strategic Intelligence and National Decisions* (Glencoe, Ill.: Free Press, 1956), 7.

41. NARA, RG 226, entry 1, box 4, folder 3.

42. Barry M. Katz, *Foreign Intelligence: Research and Analysis in the Office of Strategic Services* (Cambridge, Mass.: Harvard University Press, 1989), 14.

43. Howe interview.

44. NARA, RG 226, entry 1, box 1, folder 4; and M1642, roll 81, frame 179.

45. NARA, RG 226, M1642, roll 3, frame 905.

46. NARA, RG 226, M1642, roll 3, frame 778.

47. Ibid.

48. NARA, RG 226, M1642, roll 3, frames 398–404.

49. Ibid.

50. Troy, *Donovan and the CIA*, 228.

51. NARA, RG 226, M1642, roll 3, frames 1297–1334.

52. Ibid.

53. Ibid.

54. Ibid.

55. Smith, *The Shadow Warriors*, 399.

56. Ibid.

57. NARA, RG 226, M1642, roll 3, frame 869; Brown, *The Last Hero*, 631.

58. Troy, *Donovan and the CIA*, 282; Persico, *Roosevelt's Secret War*, 394.

59. Brown, *The Last Hero*, 632–33.

60. NARA, RG 226, M1642, roll 3, frames 405–406.

61. NARA, RG 226, M1642, roll 3, frame 418.

62. Troy, *Donovan and the CIA*, 264–65.

63. Corson, *The Armies of Ignorance*, 186.

2. HARRY S TRUMAN, SOUERS, VANDENBERG, HILLENKOETTER, AND SMITH

1. Christopher M. Andrew, *For the President's Eyes Only: Secret Intelligence and the American Presidency from Washington to Bush*, 1st ed. (New York: HarperCollins, 1995), 156.

2. Thomas F. Troy, *Donovan and the CIA: A History of the Establishment of the Central Intelligence Agency* (Washington, D.C.: Central Intelligence Agency, Center for the Study of Intelligence, 1981), 270.

3. Ralph Edward Weber, *Spymasters: Ten CIA Officers in Their Own Words* (Wilmington, Del.: SR Books, 1999), 6.

4. Harry S. Truman Library, Institute for National and International Affairs, and Center for the Study of Intelligence, *The Origin and Development of the CIA in the Administration of Harry S. Truman: A Conference Report* (Washington, D.C.: Center for the Study of Intelligence, 1995), 19.

5. Troy, *Donovan and the CIA*, 302.

6. Sallie Pisani, *The CIA and the Marshall Plan* (Lawrence, Kans.: University Press of Kansas, 1991), 128.

7. Interview of Sidney Souers, NARA, RG 263, entry 16 (HRP 89-2/0286), box 1, folder 24.

8. Loch K. Johnson, *America's Secret Power: The CIA in a Democratic Society* (New York: Oxford University Press, 1989), 14.

9. Weber, *Spymasters*, 2.

10. Michael Warner, ed., *The CIA Under Harry Truman, CIA Cold War Records* (Washington, D.C.: History Staff Center for the Study of Intelligence, Central Intelligence Agency, 1994), 19.

11. Margaret Truman, *Harry S Truman* (New York: Morrow, 1973), 332.

12. *Public Papers of the Presidents*. Harry S. Truman, 1946, Number 21. The President's News Conference of January 24, 1946.

13. Andrew, *For the President's Eyes Only*, 165.

14. Harry S. Truman, *Memoirs of Harry S. Truman, Volume Two: Years of Trial and Hope* (New York: Da Capo Press, 1956), 58.

15. Arthur B. Darling, *The Central Intelligence Agency: An Instrument of Government to 1950, The DCI Historical Series; Hs 1* (Washington, D.C.: Historical Staff Central Intelligence Agency, 1989), 82.

16. Arthur B. Darling, "Central Intelligence under Souers," *Studies in Intelligence*, Winter (1968): 59.

17. NARA, RG 263, entry 16, box 1, folder 24.

18. Arthur B. Darling, "With Vandenberg as DCI: Part I," *Studies in Intelligence*, Summer (1968).

19. Ludwell Lee Montague, *General Walter Bedell Smith as Director of Central Intelligence, October 1950–February 1953* (University Park, Pa.: Pennsylvania State University Press, 1992), 29.

20. Elsey Oral History, April 9, 1970, Harry S. Truman Presidential Library; Warner, ed., *The CIA Under Harry S. Truman*, 543.

21. Arthur B. Darling and United States Central Intelligence Agency Historical Staff, *The Central Intelligence Agency: An Instrument of Government to 1950, The DCI Historical Series; Hs 1* (United States: Historical Staff Central Intelligence Agency, 1989), 130–31.

22. Warner, ed., *The CIA Under Harry Truman*, 69.

23. David E. Lilienthal, *Journals: II: The Atomic Energy Years* (New York: Harper & Row, 1964), 391.

24. NARA, RG 263, entry 35 (HRP 89-2/00443), box 20, folder 3.

25. Declassified Document System, CD-ROM 1978010100081. Fiche: 1978-20D.

26. Arthur Meier Schlesinger, *The Imperial Presidency* (Boston: Houghton Mifflin, 1989), 128.

27. Rhodri Jeffreys-Jones, "Why Was the CIA Established in 1947?" in *Eternal Vigilance? 50 Years of the CIA*, Rhodri Jeffreys-Jones and Christopher Andrew, eds. (London; Portland, Ore.: Frank Cass, 1997), 33.

28. Warner, ed., *The CIA Under Harry Truman*, 83.

29. George F. Kennan, *Memoirs* (Boston: Little, Brown, 1967), 327.

30. Arthur Darling interview of Hillenkoetter. NARA, RG 263, entry 35 (HRP 89-2/00443), box 12, folder 26.

31. As pointed out in Andrew, *For the President's Eyes Only*, 170.

32. Darling interview of Hillenkoetter.

33. Ibid.; NIA tenth meeting. NARA, RG 263, entry 35 (HRP 89-2/00443), box 20, folder 3.

34. NIA tenth meeting. NARA, RG 263, entry 35 (HRP 89-2/00443), box 20, folder 3.

35. John Prados, *Keepers of the Keys* (New York: William Morrow & Company, 1991), 30.

36. Warner, ed., *The CIA Under Harry Truman*, 213–15.

37. National Security Act of 1947, public law 253.

38. Warner, ed., *The CIA Under Harry Truman*, 203.

39. Ibid., 238.

40. Darling interview of Hillenkoetter.

41. Richard Neustadt, Harry S. Truman Library, Institute for National and International Affairs, and Center for the Study of Intelligence, *The Origin and Development of the CIA in the Administration of Harry S. Truman: A Conference Report* (Washington, D.C.: Center for the Study of Intelligence, 1995), 20.

42. Lilienthal, *Journals: II*, 376.

43. Ibid.

44. Warner, ed., *The CIA Under Harry Truman*, 319.

45. Andrew, *For the President's Eyes Only*, 181.

46. CIA Records Search Tool at the National Archives and Records Administration (CREST) CIA-RDP67-00059A000400070009-1.

47. Darling interview of Hillenkoetter.

48. McCullough, *Truman*, 603; William R. Corson, *The Armies of Ignorance: The Rise of the American Intelligence Empire* (New York: Dial, 1977), 302.

49. Office of Reports and Estimates (ORE) 22–48, ORE 58–48, ORE 22–48 Addendum, ORE 46–49 in Haines and Leggett, eds., *CIA's Analysis of the Soviet Union, 1947–1991.*

50. Warner, ed., *The CIA Under Harry Truman*, 268.

51. Ray S. Cline, *The CIA Under Reagan, Bush and Casey: The Evolution of the Agency from Roosevelt to Reagan* (Washington, D.C.: Acropolis Books, 1981), 129.

52. Truman, *Memoirs*, 331.

53. Harold P. Ford, *Estimative Intelligence: The Purposes and Problems of National Intelligence Estimating* (Lanham, Md.: University Press of America, 1993), 69.

54. Richard A. Mobley, "North Korea's Surprise Attack: Weak US Analysis?" *International Journal of Intelligence and Counterintelligence* 13, no. 4 (2000), 507.

55. Montague, *General Walter Bedell Smith as Director of Central Intelligence*, 55.

56. Ibid., 5–6.

57. Walter Bedell Smith, *My Three Years in Moscow* (Philadelphia and New York: J.B. Lippincott Company, 1950), 33.

58. Montague, *General Walter Bedell Smith as Director of Central Intelligence*, 8; Lyman Kirkpatrick Jr., *The Real CIA* (New York: Macmillan, 1968), 112.

59. Russell Jack Smith, *The Unknown CIA* (Washington, D.C.: Pergamon-Brassey, 1989), 49.

60. Interview with Fisher Howe, July 23, 2003.

61. Evan Thomas, *The Very Best Men: Four Who Dared: The Early Years of the CIA* (New York: Simon & Schuster, 1995), 65.

62. Smith, *The Unknown CIA*, 56.

63. McCullough, *Truman*, 802.

64. Willard C. Matthias, *America's Strategic Blunders* (University Park, Pa.: Pennsylvania State University Press, 2001), 82; Montague, *General Walter Bedell Smith as Director of Central Intelligence*, 65; Warner, ed., *The CIA Under Harry Truman*, 372.

65. Truman, *Memoirs*, 377.

66. "ORE's [Office of Reports and Estimates'] record with respect to warn-
    ing of the invasion and of the entrance of communist China into the
    war," NARA, RG 263, HRP 89-2/01034, box 4, folder 55.

67. Ibid.

68. CIA Daily Summary, 10 November 1950, in Kuhns, Woodrow J., ed., *As-
    sessing the Soviet Threat: The Early Cold War Years* (Langley, Va.: Central In-
    telligence Agency, 1997), 463.

69. Truman, *Memoirs*, 379.

70. McCullough, *Truman*, 823.

71. Montague, *General Walter Bedell Smith as Director of Central Intelligence*,
    163; Smith, *The Unknown CIA*, 54.

72. Report from U.S. embassy, Guatemala City, in "Office of Current Intelli-
    gence: Daily Digest of Significant Traffic," Declass, CD-ROM ID:
    1991050101234.

73. Warner, ed., *The CIA Under Harry Truman*, 451–53.

74. NARA, CREST CIA-RDP79S01057A000500040048-2.

75. Montague, *General Walter Bedell Smith as Director of Central Intelligence*,
    234-235.

76. Kent notes for speech in CIA's Office of Current Intelligence situation
    room, 21 March 1952, NARA, RG 263, entry 35 (HRP 89-2/00443),
    box 12, folder 22.

77. Montague, *General Walter Bedell Smith as Director of Central Intelli-
    gence*, 145.

78. Ibid., 232–33.

79. Michael R. Beschloss, *Mayday: Eisenhower, Khrushchev, and the U-2 Af-
    fair* (New York: Harper & Row, 1987), 77–78.

80. Curtis Peebles, *Shadow Flights: America's Secret Air War against the Soviet
    Union* (Novato, Calif.: Presidio Press, 2000), 33–38; William E. Burrows,
    By Any Means Necessary: America's Secret Air War in the Cold War (New
    York: Farrar, Straus and Giroux, 2001), 156–59.

81. Warner, ed., *The CIA Under Harry Truman*, 436, 470.

82. Montague, *General Walter Bedell Smith as Director of Central Intelligence*, 171.

83. Rhodri Jeffreys-Jones, *The CIA and American Democracy*, 2nd ed. (New Haven: Yale University Press, 1998), 68.

84. John L. Helgerson in The Center for the Study of Intelligence (U.S.), *Getting to Know the President: CIA Briefings of Presidential Candidates, 1952–1992* (Washington, D.C.: Central Intelligence Agency, 1996), 30.

85. Montague, *General Walter Bedell Smith as Director of Central Intelligence*, 263, 264, 265.

3. DWIGHT D. EISENHOWER AND ALLEN DULLES

1. Leonard Mosley, *Dulles: A Biography of Eleanor, Allen and John Foster Dulles and Their Family Network* (New York: The Dial Press/James Wade, 1978), 224.

2. Ibid., 370.

3. Evan Thomas, *The Very Best Men: Four Who Dared: The Early Years of the CIA* (New York: Simon & Schuster, 1995), 168.

4. NARA, RG 263, entry 35 (HRP 89-2/00443), box 25, folder 12.

5. Interview with Andrew Goodpaster, May 6, 2004.

6. Stephen E. Ambrose, *Eisenhower: Soldier and President* (New York: Simon & Schuster, 1990), 461.

7. Goodpaster interview.

8. National Intelligence Estimate (NIE) 65.

9. Dulles's summary of Special Estimate 46.

10. John P. Burke et al., *How Presidents Test Reality: Decisions on Vietnam, 1954 and 1965* (New York: Russell Sage Foundation, 1989), 105.

11. Goodpaster interview.

12. Richard E. Neustadt, *Presidential Power and the Modern Presidents: The Politics of Leadership from Roosevelt to Reagan* (New York: Free Press; Toronto: Collier Macmillan Canada; New York: Maxwell Macmillan, 1990), 9.

13. Goodpaster interview.

14. John L. Helgerson, *Getting to Know the President: CIA Briefings of Presidential Candidates, 1952–1992* (Washington, D.C.: Center for the Study of Intelligence, Central Intelligence Agency, 1996), 39.

15. U.S. Congress. Senate. Select Committee to Study Governmental Operations with Respect to Intelligence Activities (Church Committee), 1976, 62.

16. Christopher M. Andrew, *For the President's Eyes Only: Secret Intelligence and the American Presidency from Washington to Bush*, 1st ed. (New York: HarperCollins, 1995), 240.

17. Burke et al., *How Presidents Test Reality*, 32.

18. Ibid., 34, 40.

19. Ibid., 49.

20. Goodpaster interview.

21. Daniel P. Moynihan, *Secrecy: The American Experience* (New Haven: Yale University Press, 1998), 187.

22. Mosley, *Dulles*, 457.

23. Goodpaster interview.

4. JOHN F. KENNEDY, DULLES, AND McCONE

1. Rhodri Jeffreys-Jones, *The CIA and American Democracy*, 3rd ed. (New Haven: Yale University Press, 2003), 116.

2. Jeffreys-Jones, *The CIA and American Democracy*, 2nd ed. (New Haven: Yale University Press, 1998), 127.

3. James Srodes, *Allen Dulles: Master of Spies* (Washington, D.C.: Lanham, Md.: Regnery; National Book Network distributor, 1999), 521.

4. Jeffreys-Jones, *The CIA and American Democracy*, 3rd ed., 134.

5. Ralph Edward Weber, *Spymasters: Ten CIA Officers in Their Own Words* (Wilmington, Del.: SR Books, 1999), 163, 164.

6. Lyman Kirkpatrick, Jr., *The Real CIA* (New York: Macmillan, 1968), 245.

7. Ibid., 239.

8. Ibid., 240.

9. Weber, *Spymasters*, 223.

10. Kirkpatrick, *The Real CIA*, 236.

11. Victoria S. Price, *The DCI's Role in Producing Strategic Intelligence Estimates* (Newport, R.I.: Report prepared for the Center for Advanced Research, Naval War College, 1980), 63, fn 11.

12. Ibid., 65.

13. Ibid.

14. Richard M. Pious, *The American Presidency* (New York: Basic Books, 1979), 211.

15. Rhodri Jeffreys-Jones, *Cloak and Dollar: A History of American Secret Intelligence* (New Haven: Yale University Press, 2002), 194.

16. U.S. Congress. Senate. Select Committee to Study Governmental Operations with Respect to Intelligence Activities (Church Committee), "Final Report, Book IV: Supplementary Detailed Staff Reports on Foreign and Military Intelligence" (94th Congress, 2nd session, 1976), 68.

17. Richard Reeves, *President Kennedy: Profile of Power* (New York: Simon & Schuster, 1993), 337.

18. Evan Thomas, *The Very Best Men: Four Who Dared: The Early Years of the CIA* (New York: Simon & Schuster, 1995), 289–90.

5. LYNDON B. JOHNSON, McCONE, RABORN, AND HELMS

1. Ray S. Cline, *The CIA Under Reagan, Bush and Casey: The Evolution of the Agency from Roosevelt to Reagan* (Washington, D.C.: Acropolis Books, 1981), 236.

2. Michael R. Beschloss, *Reaching for Glory: The Secret Johnson White House Tapes, 1964–1965* (New York: Simon & Schuster, 2001), 298–99.

3. Cline, *The CIA Under Reagan, Bush and Casey*, 237.

4. John L. Helgerson, *Getting to Know the President: CIA Briefings of Presidential Candidates, 1952–1992* (Washington, D.C.: Center for the Study of Intelligence, Central Intelligence Agency, 1996), 72.

5. Helgerson, *Getting to Know the President*, 72.

6. Ralph Edward Weber, *Spymasters: Ten CIA Officers in Their Own Words* (Wilmington, Del.: SR Books, 1999), 230.

7. Helgerson, *Getting to Know the President.*

8. John Prados, *Keepers of the Keys: A History of the National Security Council from Truman to Bush*, 1st ed. (New York: Morrow, 1991), 139.

9. Ibid., 150.

10. Weber, *Spymasters*, 257.

11. U.S. Congress, Senate Select Committee to Study Governmental Operations with Respect to Intelligence Activities (Church Committee), "Final Report, Book IV: Supplementary Detailed Staff Reports on Foreign and Military Intelligence" (94th Congress, 2nd session, 1976), 70.

12. Weber, *Spymasters*, 246.

13. Ibid., 257.

14. Beschloss, *Reaching for Glory*, 186.

15. Rhodri Jeffreys-Jones, *The CIA and American Democracy*, 2nd ed. (New Haven: Yale University Press, 1998), 148.

16. Weber, *Spymasters*, 212.

17. Ibid., 247.

18. Ibid., 211.

19. Beschloss, *Reaching for Glory*, 266.

20. Jeffreys-Jones, *The CIA and American Democracy*, 150.

21. Thomas Powers, *The Man Who Kept the Secrets: Richard Helms and the CIA*, 1st ed. (New York: Knopf, 1979), 193.

22. Ibid., 193–94.

23. Jeffreys-Jones, *The CIA and American Democracy*, 151.

24. Powers, *The Man Who Kept the Secrets*, 38.

25. Weber, *Spymasters*, 244.

26. Richard Helms and William Hood, *A Look over My Shoulder: A Life in the Central Intelligence Agency*, 1st ed. (New York: Random House, 2003), 295.

27. Ibid., 297, 298.

28. Weber, *Spymasters*, 248.

29. Helms and Hood, *A Look over My Shoulder*, 246, 376.

30. Weber, *Spymasters*, 251.

31. Ibid., 235.

32. Jeffreys-Jones, *The CIA and American Democracy*, 154.

33. Helms and Hood, *A Look over My Shoulder*, 280.

34. Weber, *Spymasters*, 246; Helms and Hood, *A Look over My Shoulder*, 328.

35. Walter Isaacson and Evan Thomas, *The Wise Men: Six Friends and the World They Made* (New York: Simon and Schuster, 1986). The group included George Kennan, Dean Acheson, Charles "Chip" Bohlen, Robert Lovett, Averell Harriman, and John McCloy.

36. John Prados, *Lost Crusader: The Secret Wars of CIA Director William Colby* (New York: Oxford University Press, 2002), 200.

37. Helms and Hood, *A Look over My Shoulder*, 376.

6. RICHARD NIXON, HELMS, SCHLESINGER, AND COLBY

1. Thomas Powers, *The Man Who Kept the Secrets: Richard Helms and the CIA*, 1st ed. (New York: Knopf, 1979), 230.

2. Richard Reeves, *President Nixon: Alone in the White House* (New York: Simon & Schuster, 2001), 350.

3. Amy B. Zegart, *Flawed by Design: The Evolution of the CIA, JCS, and NSC* (Stanford, Calif.: Stanford University Press, 1999), 46.

4. Interview with Brent Scowcroft, July 6, 2004.

5. Richard Helms and William Hood, *A Look over My Shoulder: A Life in the Central Intelligence Agency*, 1st ed. (New York: Knopf, 1979), 383, 394, 395–96.

6. Ibid., 382–83.

7. Ray S. Cline, *The CIA Under Reagan, Bush and Casey: The Evolution of the Agency from Roosevelt to Reagan* (Washington, D.C.: Acropolis Books, 1981), 240.

8. Powers, *The Man Who Kept the Secrets*, 233.

9. Helms and Hood, *A Look over My Shoulder*, 381–93.

10. Ibid., 309.

11. Interview with James Schlesinger, August 5, 2004.

12. Schlesinger interview.

13. Powers, *The Man Who Kept the Secrets*, 249.

14. Helms and Hood, *A Look over My Shoulder*, 309.

15. Reeves, *President Nixon*, 259.

16. Helms and Hood, *A Look over My Shoulder*, 404.

17. Schlesinger interview.

18. "Central Intelligence—Origin and Evolution," ed. by Michael Warner, Center for the Study of Intelligence, Central Intelligence Agency, 2001, p. 78.

19. Powers, *The Man Who Kept the Secrets*, 237.

20. Schlesinger interview.

21. U.S. Congress, Senate Select Committee to Study Governmental Operations with Respect to Intelligence Activities (Church Committee), Final Report, Book I (94th Congress, 2nd session, 1976), 78.

22. Reeves, *President Nixon*, 483.

23. Helms and Hood, *A Look over My Shoulder*, 410.

24. Ibid., 395.

25. Ibid., 412.

26. Interview with Peter Earnest, June 10, 2004.

27. John Prados, *Lost Crusader: The Secret Wars of CIA Director William Colby* (New York: Oxford University Press, 2002), 276.

28. Schlesinger interview.

29. Schlesinger interview.

30. Nathan Miller, *Spying for America: The Hidden History of U.S. Intelligence* (New York: Marlowe & Co., 1997), 392.

31. Ibid., 394.

32. Prados, *Lost Crusader*, 260.

33. Schlesinger interview.

34. Scowcroft interview.

35. William E. Colby and Peter Forbath, *Honorable Men: My Life in the CIA* (New York: Simon & Schuster, 1978), 54–55.

7. GERALD FORD, COLBY, AND GEORGE H. W. BUSH

1. John Prados, *Lost Crusader: The Secret Wars of CIA Director William Colby* (New York: Oxford University Press, 2002), 294.
2. William Doyle, *Inside the Oval Office: The White House Tapes from FDR to Clinton* (New York: Kodansha, 1999), 202.
3. Ibid., 203.
4. Ibid., 205.
5. Fred I. Greenstein, *The Presidential Difference: Leadership Style from FDR to Clinton* (New York: Martin Kessler Books, 2000), 115.
6. Interview with President Gerald R. Ford, August 7, 2003.
7. Rhodri Jeffreys-Jones, *Cloak and Dollar: A History of American Secret Intelligence* (New Haven: Yale University Press, 2002), 210.
8. Interview with James Schlesinger, August 5, 2004.
9. Prados, *Lost Crusader*, 295.
10. William E. Colby and Peter Forbath, *Honorable Men: My Life in the CIA* (New York: Simon & Schuster, 1978), 310.
11. Ibid., 444.
12. Prados, *Lost Crusader*, 303.
13. Ford interview.
14. Interview with Brent Scowcroft, July 6, 2004.
15. Prados, *Lost Crusader*, 311.
16. Doyle, *Inside the Oval Office*, 213.
17. Prados, *Lost Crusader*, 324.
18. Scowcroft interview.
19. Ford interview.
20. Prados, *Lost Crusader*, 314.
21. Scowcroft interview.
22. Ford interview.
23. Scowcroft interview.
24. Ford interview.
25. Prados, *Lost Crusader*, 305.

8. JIMMY CARTER AND TURNER

1. As per my best recollection.
2. As per my recollection.
3. As per my recollection.
4. As per my recollection.
5. As per my recollection.
6. My recollection of a recounting by participants.
7. Interview with Jimmy Carter, September 23, 2004.
8. Ibid.
9. Interview with Harold Brown, July 20, 2004.
10. I had been to a conference with Frank and was impressed by his sagacity and his overall reputation.

9. RONALD REAGAN, CASEY, AND WEBSTER

1. Interview with Admiral Bobby Ray Inman, April 1, 2004.
2. Joseph E. Persico, *Casey: From the OSS to the CIA* (New York: Viking, 1990), 202.
3. Ibid., 181.
4. Bob Woodward, *Veil: The Secret Wars of the CIA, 1981–1987* (New York: Simon & Schuster, 1987), 239.
5. Rhodri Jeffreys-Jones, *The CIA and American Democracy*, 2nd ed. (New Haven: Yale University Press, 1998), 230.
6. Robert Michael Gates, *From the Shadows: The Ultimate Insider's Story of Five Presidents and How They Won the Cold War* (New York: Simon & Schuster, 1996), 192.
7. Ibid., 286.
8. Jeffreys-Jones, *The CIA and American Democracy*, 231.
9. Persico, *Casey*, 112.
10. James McCullough, "Coping with Iran-Contra: Personal Reflections on Bill Casey's Last Month at CIA," *Studies in Intelligence* 39, no. 5 (1996).

11. Gates, *From the Shadows*, 217.

12. Ibid., 216.

13. Persico, *Casey*, 174.

14. Ibid., 175.

15. Woodward, *Veil*, 42.

16. Ibid., 47.

17. Inman interview.

18. Inman interview.

19. Gates, *From the Shadows*, 286.

20. Woodward, *Veil*, 135.

21. Gates, *From the Shadows*, 218–19.

22. John L. Helgerson, *Getting to Know the President: CIA Briefings of Presidential Candidates, 1952–1992* (Washington, D.C.: Center for the Study of Intelligence, Central Intelligence Agency, 1996), 142.

23. Gates, *From the Shadows*, 207.

24. John A. Gentry, *Lost Promise: How CIA Analysis Misserves the Nation* (Lanham, Md.: University Press of America, 1993), 84.

25. Inman interview.

26. Inman interview.

27. Persico, *Casey*, 228.

28. Ibid., 393; Woodward, *Veil*, 377.

29. Persico, *Casey*, 392.

30. Inman interview.

31. James M. Scott, "Interbranch Rivalry and the Reagan Doctrine in Nicaragua," *Political Science Quarterly* 112, no. 2 (1997).

32. Ibid.

33. Inman interview.

34. Jeffreys-Jones, *The CIA and American Democracy*, 238; Woodward, *Veil*, 333.

35. Woodward, *Veil*, 467.

36. McCullough, "Coping with Iran-Contra."

37. Persico, *Casey*, 550.

38. McCullough, "Coping with Iran-Contra."

39. Persico, *Casey*, 555.

40. Ibid., 557.

41. Kate Doyle, "The End of Secrecy: U.S. National Security and the New Openness Movement," in *National Insecurity, U.S. Intelligence after the Cold War*, Craig R. Eisendrath, ed. (Philadelphia: Temple University Press, 2000), 101.

42. Gates, *From the Shadows*, 420.

43. Ibid., 419.

44. Bill Webster and I had attended Amherst College together as class-mates and became fast friends. We remained in contact over the years, though we saw each other only occasionally, as at Amherst reunions. Then, in 1978, President Carter selected Bill Webster to head the FBI. The next three years Bill and I worked together very closely. Over the years there had been lots of unhealthy rivalry between the FBI and the CIA. Bill and I made a determined effort to curtail that, and we both believe we did. For instance, one of Bill's top assistants said to me at a dinner party, "When our people learned that you and Judge Webster were playing tennis together once a week at 7:00 A.M., we decided our two agencies could not keep fighting each other." From these years of friendship, I can attest to the fact that Bill Webster is a man of the greatest integrity.

10. GEORGE H. W. BUSH, WEBSTER, AND GATES

1. John L. Helgerson, *Getting to Know the President: CIA Briefings of Presidential Candidates, 1952–1992* (Washington, D.C.: Center for the Study of Intelligence, Central Intelligence Agency, 1996), 143.

2. Robert Michael Gates, *From the Shadows: The Ultimate Insider's Story of Five Presidents and How They Won the Cold War* (New York: Simon & Schuster, 1996), 455.

3. Henry R. Appelbaum and John H. Hedley, "U.S. Intelligence and the End of the Cold War," *Studies in Intelligence*, no. 9 (Summer 2000).

4. John L. Helgerson, *Getting to Know the President*, 146.

5. Michael R. Beschloss and Strobe Talbott, *At the Highest Levels: The Inside Story of the End of the Cold War*, 1st ed. (Boston: Little Brown, 1993), 26.

6. Helgerson, *Getting to Know the President*, 146.

7. Gates, *From the Shadows*, 452.

8. Loch K. Johnson, "DCI Webster's Legacy: The Judge's Self-Assessment," *International Journal of Intelligence and Counterintelligence*, 5, no. 3 (1991): 289.

9. Helgerson, *Getting to Know the President*, 144.

10. Eytan Gilboa, "The Panama Invasion Revisited: Lessons for the Use of Force in the Post Cold War Era," *Political Science Quarterly* 110, no. 4 (1995): 552.

11. Bob Woodward, *The Commanders* (New York: Simon & Schuster, 1991), 92.

12. Gilboa, "The Panama Invasion Revisited," 555.

13. Ibid.

14. Woodward, *The Commanders*, 128.

15. Interview with Brent Scowcroft, July 6, 2004.

16. Woodward, *The Commanders*, 351.

17. Rhodri Jeffreys-Jones, *Cloak and Dollar: A History of American Secret Intelligence* (New Haven: Yale University Press, 2002), 261.

18. Scowcroft interview.

19. Beschloss and Talbott, *At the Highest Levels*, 47.

20. Gates, *From the Shadows*, 458.

21. Ibid., 454.

22. Helgerson, *Getting to Know the President*, 155.

23. Gates, *From the Shadows*, 540–41.

24. Senate Select Committee on Intelligence Report, Executive Report 102–19, October 24, 1991.

25. Gates, *From the Shadows*, 540–41.

26. Johnson, "Smart Intelligence," *Foreign Policy* Winter, No. 89 (1992): 53-69.

27. Loch K. Johnson, *Secret Agencies: U.S. Intelligence in a Hostile World* (New Haven: Yale University Press, 1996), 58.

28. Scowcroft interview.

29. Melvin A. Goodman, "Ending the CIA's Cold War Legacy," *Foreign Policy* 106, no. 1 (1997): 128.

30. Stansfield Turner, "Intelligence for a New World Order," *Foreign Affairs* 70 (Fall 1991), p. 161.

31. Beschloss and Talbott, *At the Highest Levels*, 48.

32. NIE 11-18-89.

33. Appelbaum and Hedley, "U.S. Intelligence and the End of the Cold War."

34. Ibid., 147, 99, 66.

35. *Soviet Aerospace & Technology*, December, 16, 1991, 1.

36. NIE 11-18-91.

37. Appelbaum and Hedley, "U.S. Intelligence and the End of the Cold War."

38. Ibid.

39. Peter Gillman, "Return of the Cold Warriors," *The Independent* (London), March 6, 1994.

40. Gates, *From the Shadows*, 510.

41. Scowcroft interview.

42. Scowcroft interview.

11. BILL CLINTON, WOOLSEY, DEUTCH, AND TENET

1. Jim Woolsey and I had an interesting friendship with an amusing twist. When we joined the Carter administration, we were both Rhodes scholars and had known each other through various Rhodes activities. From time to time, Jim and his boss, Secretary of the Navy Graham Claytor, would want to get an opinion on some naval matter from someone with a naval background but no immediate stake in the issue. We would arrange to meet on Saturday mornings. They preferred not to let it be known that they were consulting with me. In addition, I had a borderline legal problem in meeting with them, since military officers serving as DCI are forbidden by law from playing any role in military affairs. Responding to questions did not seem to me to be violating that law. Still, we tried to meet surreptitiously. I would go to an office I maintained in downtown

Washington, rather than to the CIA in Langley. Graham and Jim would ease over on their way home and we'd have some good chats.

2. Bill Clinton, *My Life* (New York: Knopf, 2004), 456.

3. David Halberstam, *War in a Time of Peace: Bush, Clinton, and the Generals* (New York: Scribner, 2001), 192–93.

4. Douglas C. Waller, "Wrong Spy for the Job," *Time*, January 9, 1995, 36.

5. Richard A. Clarke, *Against All Enemies: Inside America's War on Terror* (New York: Free Press, 2004), 243.

6. Loch K. Johnson, *Bombs, Bugs, Drugs, and Thugs: Intelligence and America's Quest for Security* (New York: New York University Press, 2000), 1.

7. Michael M. Gunter, "The Iraqi Opposition and the Failure of U.S. Intelligence," *International Journal of Intelligence and Counterintelligence* 12, no. 2 (1999): 152.

8. Gregory McCarthy, "GOP Oversight of Intelligence in the Clinton Era," *International Journal of Intelligence and Counterintelligence* 15, no. 1 (2002): 48, fn 49.

9. Waller, "Wrong Spy for the Job," 36.

10. Walter Pincus, "Panel Head Presses Clinton, CIA to Close Gap," *Washington Post*, December 3, 1994.

11. Robert E. White, "Too Many Spies, Too Little Intelligence," in *National Insecurity: U.S. Intelligence after the Cold War*, ed. Craig R. Eisendrath (Philadelphia: Temple University Press, 2000), 53.

12. "The CIA and Haiti," *New York Times*, December 8, 1995, A30.

13. Waller, "Wrong Spy for the Job," 37.

14. Interview with R. James Woolsey, January 27, 2005.

15. Pincus, "Panel Head Presses Clinton, CIA to Close Gap."

16. Both had served as undersecretary of the navy.

17. "Central Intelligence, Origin and Evolution," CIA History Staff, Center for the Study of Intelligence, Central Intelligence Agency, Washington, D.C., 2001, 68.

18. Rhodri Jeffreys-Jones, *Cloak and Dollar: A History of American Secret Intelligence* (New Haven: Yale University Press, 2002), 265.

19. Waller, "Wrong Spy for the Job," 36.

20. Woolsey interview.

21. "A Tinkerer Leaves the CIA," *New York Times*, December 30, 1994; A30.

22. Tim Weiner, "Clinton Chooses Retired General to Be CIA Head," *New York Times*, February 8, 1995.

23. In 1963, as a commander in the navy, I was assigned to an office of systems analysis within that of the secretary of defense. I had just completed a tour of duty as commanding officer of a navy destroyer. Captains of ships are important people within their commands, and I was still feeling pretty important when I arrived in Washington. When I reported in, my boss showed me to my office, which was a small cubicle with one desk. Sitting at the desk was a young man. I was told that he was a summer intern from Amherst College (which I had also attended), but that he would be leaving in two weeks. In the interim they would crowd in another desk, but without a telephone. I assumed the young man, John Deutch, would volunteer to vacate the principal desk and deferentially turn it over to this important navy commander. Not so! It was two weeks later that I got command of that desk!

24. Jeffrey R. Smith and Dana Priest, "CIA Aid Halted for Army Unit in Guatemala," *Washington Post*, April 4, 1995.

25. "The CIA in Guatemala," *Washington Post*, July 7, 1996.

26. John M. Broder, "Clinton Offers His Apologies to Guatemala," *New York Times*, March 11, 1999.

27. Charles Lane and Thom Shanker, "Bosnia: What the CIA Didn't Tell Us," *The New York Review of Books*, May 9, 1996, 10–12.

28. McCarthy, "GOP Oversight of Intelligence in the Clinton Era," 33.

29. William J. Daugherty, *Executive Secrets: Covert Action and the Presidency* (Lexington: University Press of Kentucky, 2004), 59.

30. Jeffreys-Jones, *Cloak and Dollar*, 275; White, "Too Many Spies, Too Little Intelligence," 107.

31. To the best of my recollection.

32. CIA press release, March 16, 1998.

33. Clinton, *My Life*, 737.

34. Jeffreys-Jones, *Cloak and Dollar*, 276.

35. Clinton, *My Life*, 749.

36. McCarthy, "GOP Oversight of Intelligence in the Clinton Era," 34.

37. Stephen F. Hayes, "Why Does Tenet Have Tenure? Clinton's CIA Chief Is Alive and Well as a Bushie," *Weekly Standard*, October 29, 2001, 19.

38. Craig R. Eisendrath, ed., *National Insecurity: U.S. Intelligence after the Cold War* (Philadelphia: Temple University Press, 2000), 2.

39. Ibid., 2.

40. Ibid., 39.

41. Johnson, *Bombs, Bugs, Drugs, and Thugs*, 113.

42. Ibid., 165–66.

43. Russ Travers: "A Blueprint for Survival: The Coming Intelligence Failure," *Studies in Intelligence*, no. 1 (1997).

44. McCarthy, "GOP Oversight of Intelligence in the Clinton Era," 41.

12. GEORGE W. BUSH, TENET, 9/11, AND BEYOND

1. Scot J. Paltrow and David S. Cloud, "Reports on 9/11 Say Clinton, Bush Missed Chances in Terrorism," *Wall Street Journal*, March 24, 2004, 1.

2. Clearly Tenet had a change of heart from his days as staff director of the Senate Select Committee on Intelligence. Back then he drafted legislation and held hearings in 1992 to create a director of national intelligence and a separate director of the CIA (S. 2198).

3. Walter Pincus, "Tenet Criticizes Intelligence Bill," *Washington Post*, December 2, 2004.

4. David C. Morrison, "U.S. Intelligence Reform," in *Great Decision*, 2005 ed., Foreign Policy Association, New York, 11.

5. Ibid., p. 16.

6. Bob Woodward, *Plan of Attack* (New York: Simon & Schuster, 2004), 249.

7. Morrison "U.S. Intelligence Reform," 10.

8. *Central Intelligence: Origin and Evolution* (Washington, D.C.: CIA History Staff, Center for the Study of Intelligence, Central Intelligence Agency), 29.

9. Ibid., 50.

10. Ibid., 68.

11. Ibid., 131.

12. Report of the Commission on the Intelligence Capabilities of the United States Regarding Weapons of Mass Destruction, Overview of the Report, 5.

13. Ibid., 17.

14. Ibid., 6.

15. Ibid., 18.

16. Ibid., 6.

17. Ted Shackley with Richard A. Finney, *Spymaster: My Life in the CIA* (Dulles, Va.: Potomac Books, 2005), 284.

18. H.R. 10, The 9/11 Recommendations Implementation Act, Section 1012, 17.

INDEX

301